NONE OF
YOUR BUSINESS

NONE OF YOUR BUSINESS

*World Data Flows,
Electronic Commerce,
and the European Privacy Directive*

PETER P. SWIRE *and* ROBERT E. LITAN

BROOKINGS INSTITUTION PRESS
Washington, D.C.

Library of Congress Cataloging-in-Publication data

Swire, Peter P.
    None of your business : world data flows, electronic commerce,
and the European privacy directive /
Peter P. Swire and Robert E. Litan.
        p.   cm.
    Includes bibliographical references and index.
    ISBN 0-8157-8240-3 (alk. paper)
    ISBN 0-8157-8239-X (pbk. : alk. paper)
    1. Data protection—Law and legislation—European Union
countries. 2. Council of the European Union. Directive on data
protection. I. Litan, Robert E., 1950– II. Title.
    KJE6071.A431998 S93 1998
    341.4'81—ddc21
                                                            98-25515
                                                               CIP

                    9 8 7 6 5 4 3 2 1

The paper used in this publication meets the minimum requirements of the
American National Standard for Information Sciences—Permanence of Paper
for Printed Library Materials, ANSI Z39.48-1984.

Typeset in Adobe Garamond

Composition by Cynthia Stock
Silver Spring, Maryland

Printed by R. R. Donnelley & Sons
Harrisonburg, Virginia

To
Anne, Nathan, and Jesse Swire
and
Avivah, Ari, and Alisa Litan

Foreword

The preservation of privacy has emerged as one of the more contentious issues of the information age. The Internet has made it easier for anyone to collect personal information about others, prompting calls for new regulation to help protect privacy. Not surprisingly, public opinion polls show that many Americans are not using the Internet to purchase goods and services because they fear that the information they would have to supply about themselves could fall into the wrong hands. The question for the United States is whether that fear will be addressed principally through market responses by businesses interested in gaining the trust of consumers or whether regulators or even Congress eventually will step in to set more formal rules.

The European Union has already resolved this question. Three years ago it issued a sweeping Directive on Data Protection, to go into effect October 25, 1998, and designed to improve privacy protection in its member countries. The Directive has threatened to prohibit the transfer of information from Europe to other countries if the European Commission decides that they lack "adequate" protection of privacy. A great deal of the Commission's attention has been focused on the United States, which has no comprehensive privacy statute and instead addresses privacy concerns through sector-specific regulation and market forces.

The Directive has already provoked a vigorous debate on both sides of the Atlantic about how best to approach privacy issues, especially in the age of the Internet. In this book Peter Swire and Robert Litan examine the Directive and the potential effects it could have on various sectors of the U.S. economy as the Commission applies its adequacy test. The authors conclude that the potential impact could be significant and offer policy recommendations on how to avoid what could be a trade war with Europe over this matter.

The authors conducted a significant amount of their research for this project through personal and telephone interviews, in Europe and the United States, with more than one hundred persons knowledgeable about the Directive and the sectors affected by it. The people interviewed included data protection officials from the European Commission, member states, and other countries; government officials from various departments of the U.S. government; persons active in privacy issues from academic and nonprofit organizations; and persons from a wide array of trade groups, corporations, and other organizations who are engaged in data protection compliance or otherwise knowledgeable about the relevant issues . The authors are grateful for the time that these experts devoted to these interviews and for the comments they received from participants at numerous conferences at which portions of this study were presented.

Peter Swire is Professor of Law at Ohio State University College of Law. Robert E. Litan is the Director of Economic Studies and holder of the Cabot Family Chair at the Brookings Institution. The authors are grateful for the support of the Brookings Center for Law, Economics, and Politics, which publishes research on issues involving a mix of these three disciplines. The Center has received funding from sources that include AT&T, Atlantic Richfield Company, Bell Atlantic, Citicorp, Compaq Computer Corporation, Data General, Hewlett-Packard Company, The Markle Foundation, NCR Corporation, Pfizer, PHARMA, Silicon Graphics Computer Systems, The Starr Foundation, Sun Microsystem, Texaco Inc., Unisys Corporation, Visa U.S.A., and Wyeth-Ayerst International. Peter Swire also expresses appreciation for financial support from the Ohio State University College of Law and from an Ameritech Faculty Fellowship.

The authors appreciate the research assistance of Matthew Fields, Jane Higgins, Jay Macke, Timothy McGranor, Thomas Sinclair, and Robert Wells. James Schneider edited the manuscript, Bridget Butkevich verified its factual content, Carlotta Ribar proofread the pages, and Sherry Smith compiled the index. Carol Peirano, Michele Whetzel-Newton, and Anita G. Whitlock provided administrative support.

The views expressed in this book are those of the authors and should not be ascribed to those persons or organizations whose assistance is acknowledged or to the trustees, officers, or other staff members of the Brookings Institution.

Michael H. Armacost
President

September 1998
Washington, D.C.

Contents

1   Introduction   1

2   The Legal Context of the Privacy Directive   22

3   Data Protection and Information Technologies   50

4   Effects of Data Protection Laws on Electronic Commerce   76

5   Privacy Issues Affecting Many Organizations   90

6   The Financial Services Sector   102

7   Other Sectors with Large Transborder Activities   122

8   Policy Recommendations for Privacy Issues   152

9   The Internet, Electronic Commerce, and World Data Flows   197

Appendix A: European Union Directive on Data Protection   213

Appendix B: Summary of Potential Effects of the EU Directive   247

Index   261

1

Introduction

The United States and the rest of the world are in the midst of a revolution in information processing and communication. Much about this revolution is welcome: personal computers more powerful than mainframes of a generation ago, virtually instantaneous communication of voice and data around the world, and a steadily expanding universe of information available over the Internet. Nonetheless, at least one aspect of the computer revolution has generated significant concern: the potential threat to individual privacy. With the dramatic reductions in the cost of processing and access to information, it is easier than ever to track down people and find out what they buy, what sites they visit on the Web, and much more. It is not surprising, therefore, that public opinion polls report that an impediment to further growth of electronic commerce—doing business on the Internet—is the fear on the part of users that the information they communicate will find its way into other, unwelcome hands and be used in ways they do not approve.

These fears have given businesses interested in electronic commerce a strong incentive to address privacy concerns. Various proposals are now circulating for technological means to build privacy protections into Internet transactions. At the same time, mounting concerns about privacy in the information age have also generated an international controversy about the best institutional mechanisms for protecting privacy. A vigorous debate is under way about what mix of approaches to use for protecting privacy—market mechanisms, technology, industry self-regulation, or mandatory government regulation.[1]

1. For an analysis of many of these issues, see Peter P. Swire, "Markets, Self-Regulation, and Government Enforcement in the Protection of Personal Information," in *Privacy and Self-Regulation in the*

1

Of course, the debate about privacy predates and extends beyond the current issues involving electronic commerce and the Internet. For years, people have expressed concern over the information gathered about them by government and private business. In the United States and other countries, legislatures have responded by enacting statutes addressing privacy-related concerns. Nonetheless, the information revolution, symbolized best by the Internet, has raised privacy issues to an entirely new level of public and political scrutiny. Moreover, unlike earlier discussions, which have been largely domestic, the global reach of the Internet has made privacy a much more prominent subject of international concern and debate.

In this book we take up the first major clash in views about privacy as a global matter. The principal parties are the United States and Europe. The precipitating event for the potential conflict is the adoption by the European Union of its Directive on Data Protection, effective on October 25, 1998.[2] (Although the actual title refers to "data protection," we have chosen to use "European Privacy Directive" in the title of this book to communicate the nature of the subject matter to a wider audience.) A crucial provision of the Directive prohibits transfer of personal information to other countries that lack "adequate" protection of privacy. There are a limited number of exceptions, or "derogations," to this prohibition. For transfers that do not fit within the exceptions, it becomes illegal to send the personal data out of Europe to the offending country. Determinations of adequacy made in Europe, therefore, can have significant effects on businesses and other organizations outside Europe.

The requirement of adequacy applies to all countries that are not members of the European Union. At the time of this writing, however, the European Union and the United States in particular are on a collision course over the meaning of "adequate protection."[3] Unlike the nations of western Europe, the United States does not have a single, comprehensive privacy law. Nor does it have an agency charged with administering privacy law. The U.S. approach has been more selective, regulating the private sector fairly strictly in certain areas but not legislating for a wide range of uses. Under the standards established by the Directive, there is a strong possibility that routine information practices in the United States are not adequate

Information Age (U.S. Department of Commerce, 1997); also available at www.osu.edu/units/law/ swire.htm.

2. Directive 95/46/EC of the European Parliament and the Council, October 24, 1995, *Official Journal of the European Community*, L281 (November 23, 1995), p. 31. See Appendix A for the full text.

3. This book describes the situation as of May 1998. Later developments are treated only selectively.

under European law.[4] The amount of commerce affected could be enormous. U.S. exports of goods and services to the European Union totaled $253 billion in 1995, and imports were $270 billion.[5]

"None of Your Business"

It is against this backdrop that we are writing this book. Its title, *None of Your Business: World Data Flows, Electronic Commerce, and the European Privacy Directive,* describes the Directive in three senses. First, the Directive is about privacy, about the fundamental idea that "my" personal information is none of "your" business. As we discuss more fully later, the Directive treats privacy as a basic human right and seeks to protect individuals against violations of that right. On the international level, the Directive says to other countries that it is none of their business to intrude on the privacy rights of persons in the European Union.

A second meaning of "none of your business" invokes the concern of other countries that the European Union is trying to impose its privacy rules in an extraterritorial fashion. The Directive could have far-reaching effects on business practices within the United States and other "third countries" (countries that are not part of the European Union). Mainframes and Web sites in the United States might be cut off from data from Europe. Marketing and management practices that are routine in the United States might be disrupted. In the European view these effects are not extraterritorial because the Directive governs only the personal information of people in Europe. But the view expressed by some Americans is that it is "none of your business" for the European Union to dictate how business operations should be carried out in the United States.[6]

4. For an excellent guide to U.S. privacy law, especially as it applies to electronic commerce, see Fred M. Cate, *Privacy in the Information Age* (Brookings, 1997). Another fine examination of data protection in the United States is Paul M. Schwartz and Joel R. Reidenberg, *Data Privacy Law: A Study of United States Data Protection* (Charlottesville, Va.: Michie, 1996).

5. Bureau of Economic Analysis, *International Accounts Data: Balance of Payments: Transactions by Area* (U.S. Department of Commerce, September 1997), as found at http://www.bea.doc.gov/bea/di/bparea-d.htm.

6. The opposition of the United States to claimed "extraterritorial" effects might be tempered by recalling how Washington itself has acted in recent years to extend the reach of various laws beyond the country's borders. Examples include application of antitrust laws, enactment of the Helms-Burton Law to impose sanctions against countries that do business with Cuba, and limits on the export of strong encryption products even to longtime allies.

A third meaning is closely related to the second. Under the global trade regime administered through the World Trade Organization (WTO), laws that appear to prevent free trade in goods and services are carefully scrutinized. Data protection rules such as the Directive can have the effect of excluding companies in the United States and other third countries from the European market.[7] One way to comply with some of the Directive's requirements would be to move data processing operations, and the accompanying jobs, to Europe. An American concern is thus that the Directive will be protectionist, having the effect of saying "none of your business" to U.S. firms.

The title of our book also invokes world data flows and electronic commerce. Our research on the Directive has led us to conduct a systematic study of the situations in which personal data move from Europe to the United States and other third countries. This systematic study is essential to the central topic of the book, which is to understand the effects of the Directive on countries outside the European Union. More generally, the analysis of world data flows is potentially illuminating for many purposes in what is often called "the information age."

One result of studying data flows is to understand more clearly what is meant by the term "electronic commerce." The world has witnessed a steady increase in the volume of international trade since the end of World War II. With the rise of the Internet, there is a widespread sense that international trade in goods and services will explode. In particular, by using the Internet, people will have an unprecedented opportunity to purchase instantaneously and directly from sellers all over the world. As this trade develops, the world will need to devise new legal and institutional ways to cope with the problems that will inevitably arise. Many of the Directive's effects fall directly on the information technologies that will be at the heart of electronic commerce. As we study the interaction of the Directive and information technologies, we can learn important lessons about the feasibility and desirability of other legal restrictions on emerging areas of electronic commerce. The European Union Data Protection Directive thus provides an early testing ground for the transnational governance of the Internet and related information technologies.

---

7. As discussed in chapter 8, however, the General Agreement on Trade in Services has a specific provision that authorizes many data protection laws as long as they are not applied in a discriminatory manner.

Reasons for Data Protection Laws

Before plunging into a discussion of the Directive and its potential effects, it is useful to set forth the reasons why laws have been passed in recent decades, not only in the United States but throughout the world, to govern uses of personal data. Scholars have written a great deal about why privacy matters, and we will not repeat that extensive discussion here.[8] Instead, we will first look at the threats to individual liberty and democracy that can occur when personal information falls into the hands of powerful institutions. Then, because the Directive primarily affects how private organizations use personal information, we will examine in somewhat more detail the sorts of failures that may exist in the markets for personal information and begin to explore what mix of markets, self-regulation, and government action might prove most desirable.

Threats to Liberty and Democracy

The best, although admittedly overdrawn, way to begin is by imagining a privacy advocate's worst nightmare—the presence of an Orwellian, all-knowing computer or network that contains a complete dossier on every individual in a society. Such a computer or network might pose risks both to individual freedom and the continued functioning of a democracy.

Consider what sorts of harms might occur if such a computer or network existed. If it were controlled by the government, people might feel chilled by constant surveillance. They might fear government would use the information to retaliate against its political enemies. They might be afraid that those who controlled the computer or network would become an unaccountable elite whose command over secret files would allow entrenchment in power.

The fears hardly disappear if the network were operated by corporations in the private sector. In that case, these private forces might gain extraordinary power vis-à-vis the government. Meanwhile, corporate-

---

8. Among the enormous variety of available sources, see Colin J. Bennett, *Regulating Privacy: Data Protection and Public Policy in Europe and the United States* (Cornell University Press, 1992); Priscilla M. Regan, *Legislating Privacy: Technology, Social Values, and Public Policy* (University of North Carolina Press, 1995); Spiros Simitis, "Reviewing Privacy in an Information Society," *University of Pennsylvania Law Review*, vol. 135 (March 1987), p. 707; Janna Malamud Smith, *Private Matters: In Defense of the Personal Life* (Reading, Mass.: Addison-Wesley, 1997); and Alan F. Westin, *Privacy and Freedom* (Atheneum, 1967).

controlled computers, much like government-controlled computers, could be used to invade personal privacy. Detailed dossiers might let corporations manipulate the desires and behaviors of individuals. The presence of embarrassing facts in the dossiers might be used for blackmail. The risk of revealing embarrassing facts might chill the willingness of people to participate in civil society. In addition, the mere fact that computers are operated by the private sector does not prevent the government from having access to the data. Even in the United States, which has relatively strict controls on how government can gather data, a search warrant is generally enough to force any private organization to open its computer files to government investigators.

Of course, all of these harms have been committed without some overwhelming computer. The Gestapo and other secret police organizations used informants to maintain power and control dissent. Franz Kafka's *The Trial* shows the terrifying power that those controlling paper-based dossiers can exercise over the people whose information is contained in them. Even George Orwell's Big Brother, often used today as the symbol for omnipotent computing, ruled in a predigital world.[9] And well-known abuses of power in our political system did not require a computer. Consider President Richard Nixon's use of the Internal Revenue Service to retaliate against his enemies or J. Edgar Hoover's reported use of secret dossiers on political figures, to name just two examples.

Nonetheless, the computer and information revolutions greatly facilitate the ability of those who want to invade others' privacy. Computers are much better than file clerks at gathering, storing, and retrieving information. Computers can handle previously unimaginable volumes of data. They can mine the data in new ways, so that programmers can seek new patterns and put people into new boxes. Computers might also approach omnipresence: remote sensors and dispersed terminals could allow data to be gathered everywhere and sent to headquarters.

In light of these possible abuses, it is important to have ways to prevent an unaccountable concentration of power. In the United States the Fourth Amendment's restriction on searches and seizures is an important limit on the ability of government to invade people's homes and privacy. Laws have been adopted to further limit the ways that government can gather and use

9. See Peter W. Huber, *Orwell's Revenge: The 1984 Palimpsest* (Free Press, 1994), for an insightful argument about why computer technology, properly understood, tends to undermine centralized authority rather than create it. One especially striking image of the Huber book is the possibility of the proles as hackers, taking over the telescreen itself.

information about individual citizens. For example, the Privacy Act of 1974 has the general rule that information gathered for one purpose, such as income tax liability, cannot be used for other purposes or shared with other agencies. The Freedom of Information Act lets the citizen find out what government files say about him or her, thereby reducing the risk of abuse. Wiretap statutes have created stricter procedures for government surveillance than are required by the Fourth Amendment. Analogous laws exist elsewhere. In many European countries, for instance, the same comprehensive privacy law applies to both the government and private sectors. All these laws reinforce democratic rule and seek to limit the abuse of personal information by government officials.

The Directive and Data Protection in the Private Sector

As important as privacy laws may be to preventing the accumulation of government power, the European Directive has only a limited connection to achieving that goal. As discussed in chapter 2, it applies almost entirely to the private sector—the European Union simply does not have jurisdiction over many governmental uses of personal data. In assessing the effects of the Directive, therefore, we must focus more carefully on how personal data is handled in the private sector.

In analyzing the subject of customer privacy, we start by exploring the failures in the market that might justify government intervention. We then proceed to how best to handle those market failures. Begin by considering a customer and a seller. The goal is to understand what privacy agreement the two sides would reach if they were both well informed and it was not expensive to reach an agreement. The touchstone here is individual consent. If the customer understands the uses of information and agrees to those uses, the market approach succeeds and there is no need for government regulation.[10]

In real life customers often will not be very well informed about privacy rights, and it will often be expensive or difficult for them to make their own privacy bargains. Notably, a company usually knows far more than its customers about how it will use the information. The company, for

10. Critics with a more regulatory bent might take issue with the presumption of freedom of contract described in the text. We believe, however, that the analysis would proceed in much the same way, except that the critics would be more likely to conclude that institutions other than the market are appropriate for handling privacy problems. As in the text, such critics would likely identify certain sorts of failures in the market and then seek to find the best institutions for addressing the failures.

instance, might know how information about customers will be generated, combined with other databases, or sold to third parties. It might be hard for customers to learn about and understand a company's privacy policies. It will be even harder for customers to tell whether companies are actually following those policies. If, contrary to its announced policy, a company sells information to another company, the customer will often not discover what has happened.

These problems can lead to overdisclosure of private information ("overdisclosure" means more uses than the customer has agreed to allow). Consider the incentives of a company that acquires private information. The company gains the full benefit of using the information in its own marketing efforts or in the fee it receives when it sells the information to third parties. The company, however, does not suffer losses from the disclosure of private information. Because customers often will not learn of the overdisclosure, they may not be able to discipline the company effectively. In economic terms, the company internalizes the gains from using the information but can externalize some of the losses and so has a systematic incentive to overuse it.

This market failure is made worse by the costs of bargaining for the desired level of privacy. It can be daunting for an individual consumer to bargain with a distant Internet merchant or a telephone company about the desired level of privacy. To be successful, bargaining might take time, effort, and considerable expertise in privacy issues. Even then, the company might not change its practices. Even worse, a bargain once reached might be violated by the company, which knows that violations will be hard for the customer to detect.

This brief discussion shows why customers' true preferences for privacy might not be achieved through bargains with a company. One tempting, but mistaken, reaction would be immediately to demand government action. Experience with a wide range of public policy issues, however, has shown that merely identifying a market failure does not mean that the best solution is government regulation.

In the United States there has been a growing realization in setting policy that market imperfections must be compared with the imperfections of government or other solutions.[11] Sometimes the cure is worse than

---

11. See, for example, Neil K. Komesar, *Imperfect Alternatives: Choosing Institutions in Law, Economics, and Public Policy* (University of Chicago Press, 1994); and Oliver E. Williamson, *The Economic Institutions of Capitalism: Firms, Markets, Relational Contracting* (Free Press, 1985), p. 327.

the disease. Since the mid-1970s many economic regulations have been rolled back in the United States, even when the resulting market was less than perfectly competitive. This renewed appreciation for the market has, of course, not been limited to the United States. Many countries have privatized important sectors of their economies and tried to reduce the burden of regulation. Indeed, an outstanding accomplishment of the European Union has been to reinforce markets by reducing regulatory barriers to trade among the member states. To pick just one well-known example, the European Court of Justice struck down the German beer purity laws, thereby opening the German market to competition from imported beer.[12] Despite the possible market failures in the form of impure or misleadingly-labeled beer, government regulation was ultimately held to be less desirable than market self-regulation. Along the same lines, the Data Protection Directive has the important goal of reinforcing the internal EU market by ensuring the legality of data flows among the member states. The Directive is designed, among other things, to limit the ability of individual countries to use strict data protection laws as a barrier to trade within the union.

Ways of Protecting Privacy

In considering market failures, then, the ultimate task is to compare the full range of institutional choices. Each choice will have advantages and disadvantages, which may change as attention switches from one privacy setting to another. In a very preliminary way, consider some strengths and weaknesses of various approaches for protecting privacy, such as technology, the media, markets, self-regulation, and mandatory government rules.

Technology

Technology offers rich possibilities for protecting people's privacy, even without government regulation. It is already possible to surf the Net anonymously, and anonymous payment systems are both technically feasible and are being offered by vendors. These methods can be extremely powerful in letting people do business without revealing their identity, and privacy ad-

---

12. Purity Requirements for Beer: *EC Commission* v. *Germany* (case 178/84), Court of Justice of the European Communities [1987] ECR 1227, [1988] 1 CMLR 780, [1988] BTLC 133, March 12, 1987.

vocates would like more systems that preserve anonymity. Pure technology, however, offers less protection for named information that is already in databases. If the company already knows your name and address, technology will not stop it from using the data in new ways or selling it.[13] Once the data are already revealed, other mechanisms will be needed if private information is to stay private.

The Media

Recent media stories about privacy have encouraged rapid and decisive changes in the way institutions have used personal information. In each instance, a substantial number of persons believed that important personal information was being given to other parties without proper protection. In 1996 Lexis/Nexis introduced its P-Trak person locater service, which would have made personally identifiable information, such as mother's maiden name, available to a long list of subscribers.[14] In 1997 America On-Line decided to release its customer lists for telephone marketing, in spite of its earlier assurances to customers.[15] Experian created a new system to allow credit histories to be accessed over the Internet, but the system mistakenly routed some people's histories to unauthorized parties.[16] And the U.S. Social Security Administration created an on-line system for checking the benefits due to an individual, again without strong enough protections against unauthorized access.[17] In each instance, press attention to privacy problems (supplemented by e-mail campaigns and other on-line activity) led to an immediate change of policy. These and other developments in the United States and abroad suggest that the media can be important in correcting at least some abuses of privacy. The fear of negative publicity also undoubtedly deters some organizations from having bad

13. This point is explored in more depth in Peter Swire, *The Uses and Limits of Financial Cryptography: A Law Professor's Perspective* (1997), available at www.osu.edu/units/law/swire.htm.

14. Laurie J. Flynn, "Company Stops On-Line Access to Key Social Security Numbers," *New York Times*, June 13, 1996, p. B11.

15. Rajiv Chandrasekaran, "AOL Cancels Plan for Telemarketing: Disclosure of Members' Numbers Protested," *Washington Post*, July 25, 1997, p. G1.

16. Frank James, "Internet Service Goes Haywire With Credit Reports; Users Get Other People's Financial Reports; Company Ends System Within 48 Hours," *Chicago Tribune*, August 19, 1997, p. N3.

17. Robert Pear, "Social Security Closes On-Line Site, Citing Risks to Privacy," *New York Times*, April 10, 1997, p. A15.

privacy practices. But not all media stories are created equal. Media pressure works best for stories that affect many people, have attractive victims, and can be explained vividly in a sound bite. For other privacy problems, the stories may simply not get written.

The Market

When the media are effective watchdogs, markets work better. Fear of bad publicity can help ensure that companies have good privacy practices. Put in a more positive way, companies may advertise their strict privacy practices to attract customers. Swiss banks, and their rules against disclosing customer secrets, are a well-known historical example. In evaluating the effectiveness of the market, significant empirical issues include the extent to which companies compete on privacy grounds, customers are attracted by good privacy practices, and bad privacy practices become known and lead to loss of business.

Mandatory Government Rules

The opposite of an absolute market approach would be a government approach, in which individuals' rights would be protected by law. There would be a public announcement of the rights and responsibilities of individuals and companies so people would know what privacy practices are allowed. Legal enforcement could provide compensation to those whose privacy has been invaded and deter potential wrongdoers. Public agencies could assist people in pressuring companies to change bad practices. But mandatory privacy rules might suffer from all of the concerns expressed about government regulation generally. In our context, these include the difficulty of setting forth rules to cover the enormously diverse ways that personal data are handled and the complications of enforcing those rules in a society in which the number of merchants doing business on the Internet continues to grow rapidly.

Self-Regulation

A great deal of attention has been given to a third way between market- and government-based means of ensuring privacy. Especially in the United States the hope has been that self-regulation might offer some of the advantages of the other approaches while minimizing the disadvantages.[18] In June 1998 a consortium of nearly fifty American companies, the Online Privacy Alliance, announced its intention to develop effective privacy policies for companies doing business over the Internet.

When done well, self-regulation might draw on industry expertise, create and enforce norms for good behavior, and lead to rules that are well adapted to each company's or industry's circumstances. Especially when there is a strong threat of government enforcement, self-regulation might lead industry to make significant efforts to protect privacy without requiring the rigidity of creating and enforcing detailed rules for every circumstance.

But self-regulation may be drafted with little concern for those outside a given industry, those who are not part of the "self." Privacy advocates fear that self-regulation will not be strict enough and may in practice end up resembling an unregulated market. American proponents of self-regulation respond that firms that agree to self-regulation but do not follow through on their commitments open themselves to private suits for misrepresentation and fraud as well as actions by the Federal Trade Commission and the states to redress unfair trade practices. These remedies, proponents argue, may be even more effective enforcement tools than those deployed by any European-style privacy bureau. Skeptics respond that privacy self-regulation in the United States has not been nearly as strict as European laws.

Combined Privacy Mechanisms

In considering the various ways of protecting privacy, it is important to notice how they can sometimes be combined. Consider, for example, the Platform for Privacy Preferences (P3P), a technical standard for creating privacy while browsing on the World Wide Web.[19] Although still under development, P3P would allow users to specify their privacy preferences, such as whether they are willing to have personal information transferred to third parties. If the Web site is not privacy friendly enough for the user, the user might skip away from it and not transact any business there. The P3P standard obviously relies heavily on technology because it builds pri-

---

18. See generally, National Telecommunications and Information Administration, *Privacy and Self-Regulation in the Information Age* (U.S. Department of Commerce, 1997), and http//www.ntia.doc.gov/reports/privacy/privacy-rpt.htm.

19. For background on the P3P project, see http://www.w3.org/Privacy.

vacy rules into the software code of the user and the Web site. To a large extent P3P is self-regulatory because industry groups are taking the lead in drafting the standard. P3P is also market based; a principal goal is to encourage Web sites to adopt good privacy practices to attract more users. Finally, P3P at least potentially has a government component. The rules are being drafted in part to let users choose to have the level of protection offered by the EU Data Protection Directive. In the future the European countries might make the government component more prominent, perhaps by requiring users to set their software to the Directive's specifications.[20]

The Platform for Privacy Preferences illustrates the interconnections among the mechanisms for protecting privacy. In these preliminary descriptions of technology, the media, markets, government rules, and self-regulation, we can only begin to sketch the issues that will be discussed in detail in this book. Economists sometimes warn against the "Nirvana fallacy," the idea that some perfect institutional arrangement can solve all problems. Each of the approaches described here has characteristic strengths and weaknesses. The goal ultimately is to deploy each in ways that promote privacy values while respecting important other goals, including the significant costs that might arise from specific rules.

Overview of the Book

This chapter has introduced the European Union Data Protection Directive and the international debate about privacy that it has generated. We have seen the threats to liberty and democracy that can arise if powerful public and private institutions abuse their citizens' personal information. We have also begun to explore some privacy problems that can arise in the private sector and the various institutional means available for trying to solve those problems.

20. For one such privacy protocol for merging filtering technology and legal rules, see Joel R. Reidenberg, "The Use of Technology to Assure Internet Privacy: Adapting Labels and Filters for Data Protection," *LEX ELECTRONICA*, vol. 3 (Fall 1997), available at http://www.lex-electronica.org/reidenbe.html.

In June 1998 the Working Party of European data protection officials released a report critical of the P3P rules. The report found that the P3P effort "has not been developed with reference to the highest known standards of data protection and privacy, but has instead sought to formalise lower common standards." "Draft Opinion of the Working Party," *Platform for Privacy Preferences (P3P) and the Open Profiling Standard (OPS)*, June 16, 1998.

With these subjects in mind, we can now give an overview of the book. We begin in the next chapter by examining the provisions of the Directive. The chapter explains the logic underlying the European data protection laws while also showing some difficulties that these laws might create in practice. Once the basic legal regime is explained, we begin the task of assessing the Directive's effects. By examining different baselines for compliance, we show why it is possible to describe the qualitative, but not quantitative, effects of the Directive. The chapter continues with a careful look at why it is important to understand what the Directive provides. The sector-by-sector analysis in the rest of the book is based on the view that we should take the Directive seriously and seek to determine how various practices will be regulated under the emerging data protection regime. Even though in practice many organizations might get away with less than full compliance with these laws, at fairly low risk of an actual enforcement action, there are strong reasons why organizations should and will pay attention to the Directive as written.

Chapter 3 explores in some detail the tension between data protection and modern information technologies. We explain how the Directive is more understandable and more likely to be enforceable in the context of mainframe computers. As information technology has shifted to distributed processing, however, the Directive appears to be less well suited to solving privacy problems. One important observation is the apparent overbreadth of the Directive. Its terms appear to forbid a wide range of routine and desirable transfers of data outside the European Union. For corporate intranets, laptop computers, and in other settings, modern information technology accomodates flows of information that are difficult to fit within the European legal regime. For the Internet, it is not yet clear how much the Europeans expect to apply the Directive as written and how much it instead acts as a first step toward a fuller response to the problems of the information society.

Chapter 4 examines the controversial question of how privacy rules will affect electronic commerce. Roughly speaking, there is a tension between the loss caused by burdensome regulation and the gain caused by heightened consumer confidence; we show situations in which each effect is most likely to be significant.

Chapter 5 examines issues that affect many businesses and other organizations. For instance, any transnational company or nonprofit organization maintains employee records and performs audits. Many organizations use business consultants or offer transnational customer service. These functions are affected by the Directive, with potentially significant efforts required for compliance, and in some situations it is not clear what an organization can do to comply.

Chapter 6 focuses on financial services, which are involved in any international transaction. Important issues arise in credit card processing, reinsurance, dealing with credit histories, and selling financial services to individuals and businesses. Particular problems may arise in investment banking, where the Directive seems to make it difficult for market analysts to report on European firms, and creates special problems for the involvement of U.S. firms in takeovers of companies with European operations.

Chapter 7 investigates other sectors that have large transborder operations. Although examining them does not exhaust the likely effects of the Directive, the analyses should provide a good guide to the sorts of issues that would arise for other sectors. The operations of the press raise complex issues. Issues also arise for nonprofit organizations generally, international educational institutions, international conferences, and for non-EU governments that have personnel in Europe. The remainder of the chapter analyzes effects on significant economic sectors, such as pharmaceuticals and medical devices, business and leisure travel, and Internet service providers. There is an extended discussion of direct marketing under the Directive, both in traditional forms and on the Internet. The chapter concludes with a survey of the effect on European individuals, organizations, and governments of restrictions of transfers of personal information to non-EU countries.

The primary focus of chapters 2 through 7 is descriptive, which helps the reader understand the sector-by-sector effects of the Directive. Equipped with this analysis, policymakers and the organizations and individuals affected will be in a better position, we hope, to resolve the significant tensions that will occur with implementation of the Directive. In some instances our analysis suggests that there are fairly simple ways for those processing data to comply with the new laws. The debate about implementation can then proceed without undue worry about these easy cases. In other instances, we identify areas of legal uncertainty, where persons in good faith might differ about whether practices comply with the Directive. By identifying the areas of uncertainty, perhaps this study can assist in clarifying the rules. In yet other instances, however, it appears that routine and desirable categories of transfers will not be legal under the Directive. By identifying these troublesome situations, we hope to focus decisionmakers on finding solutions.

Chapter 8 sets forth our recommendations for how to proceed. It begins by examining what we call the dilemmas of enforcement. On the one hand, the regime is designed to be strict so as to protect important human rights. On the other hand, no European official wishes to create a major trade war or prohibit practices that are important to both the European and other economies. A similar dilemma faces organizations that are subject to the Directive. If it is enforced as written, these organizations must take immediate and substantial measures to comply. If, however, it is primarily hortatory, crash efforts to comply will seem expensive and unnecessary to many organizations.

Amidst this uncertainty, the major actors have, perhaps understandably, been reluctant to soften their positions. There is a temptation on the European side to say that there will be no compromise on human rights. There is a temptation on the American side to praise the U.S. approach to ensuring privacy and to say that foreign privacy laws should not bind U.S. organizations acting on U.S. soil even if they transport EU citizens' data. Finally, there is a temptation for businesses and other organizations not to make serious efforts to comply until forced to do so.

Our goal is to seek a way out of this impasse, with a package of proposals based on the clear self-interest of the affected organizations, the United States, and the European Union. In brief, we propose that the regulated organizations consider adopting self-regulatory measures (SRMs), such as model contracts, when they transfer personal data out of Europe, not just to satisfy the European Union but also to meet legitimate desires of American consumers. For the United States, we propose the creation of an Office of Electronic Commerce and Privacy Policy in the Department of Commerce to provide an ongoing institutional mechanism for handling the privacy and electronic commerce issues that will develop in the Internet age. For the Europeans, we propose a willingness to approve SRMs, even where not every detail of European law is included. We also point out a number of places where the Directive is open to varying interpretations and suggest ways to proceed that protect privacy values while controlling compliance burdens.

For the regulated organizations, the crucial insight is that the Directive applies predominantly to European activities. The affected companies, for instance, generally do extensive business within the European Union. They then sometimes, perhaps often, transfer that information to the United States or other countries. When doing business in Europe, these companies expect to comply with local environmental, minimum-wage, and other laws. The position of the European regulators is that data protection laws should apply in the same way. If companies wish to send personal data out of Europe, they get to do so, but only if there is some reasonable level of protection. In the European view, companies should not be able ship data to places where the information will be used in ways contrary to European law and the expectations of European citizens.

For organizations doing business in Europe, self-interest demands a way to meet the requirements of European law while still achieving reasonable business goals. These organizations may be based in the United States and other countries that do not have comprehensive privacy statutes and national privacy agencies. The non-EU countries may not be found generally to have "adequate" protection. If not, common sense suggests that these organizations should have a way to share information between their European and other operations when good privacy protections are in place. The opposite approach, a ban on transfers, would create economic harm in Europe and elsewhere and would lend credence to fears that the privacy laws are being used in a protectionist way to keep out non-European businesses.

Article 26 of the Directive indeed allows transfers out of the European Union, even to those countries that generally lack adequate protection, when there are other "adequate safeguards" in place. Notably, European regulators can approve self-regulatory measures for organizations that transfer personal information out of Europe. If European regulators are willing to approve SRMs, companies with European operations will have strong reasons to consider adopting them. Such measures would give companies with European operations a way to comply with European law, a result that may be of considerable importance to European managers, employees, customers, and governments. The discussion in this book also develops a number of other reasons why organizations would rather comply than be in systematic violation of data protection laws.

For the U.S. government we emphatically do *not* recommend a comprehensive regulatory approach to data protection. Carefully devised new laws may be appropriate, such as those covering health records and children's privacy. At this time, moreover, there may be an important role for our proposed Office of Electronic Commerce and Privacy Policy (OECPP). Such an office could help respond to American political and popular concerns about privacy, which are closely linked to the Internet and people's new ability to participate in global electronic commerce. An international regime must allow electronic commerce to flourish while meeting legitimate public policy goals such as preventing fraud, guaranteeing accurate payments, protecting intellectual property, and assuring privacy. International discussions about these issues should not be handled solely by privacy commissioners. Instead, international meetings should be broadened to reflect the range of issues that are inextricably linked with how electronic commerce will process personal information.

Creation of the OECPP can serve American interests by becoming an institutional home for expertise on privacy and related issues. The office could coordinate interagency efforts and staff-related White House initiatives, such as those conducted by President Clinton's Internet policy advisor Ira Magaziner. It could also be a useful contact point for the private sector and state governments as SRMs and other privacy initiatives are developed. As an additional benefit, creation of such an office would respond to a concern often voiced by European officials that the U.S. government has not provided an institutional mechanism for ongoing discussions among governments. Although the OECPP would not be a supervisory authority on the European model, it could take a sustained and effective part in international discussions about privacy issues, receiving comments from other countries and articulating American interests.

Concerning actions by European authorities, as Americans we certainly wish to be cautious about recommending how they should proceed. Nonetheless, as a result of our research, we have come to certain conclusions about desirable ways to move forward and avoid an impasse on data protection issues. In the course of our detailed examination of the Directive, we identify a lengthy list of matters that will require clarification as European data protection laws are implemented. We believe it is in the interest of Europe and of the rest of the world for data protection authorities to approve SRMs that will allow data to be transferred out of Europe while remaining subject to adequate protection.

Throughout the book, we point out particular texts in the Directive that are susceptible to multiple interpretations. To take just one example, transfers are permitted wherever there is "unambiguous consent" in advance by an individual. Unambiguous consent, however, can be interpreted in many ways, depending on the setting. In interpreting this and similar terms, we make recommendations about how to achieve privacy goals while keeping implementation workable.

Similarly, we analyze context as well as text. The sector-by-sector chart in appendix B provides one handy way to encapsulate the special issues that arise for certain sectors. In the course of our analysis, we point out some especially difficult areas. For example, in chapter 3 we discuss how intranets are becoming a pervasive technology for medium and large-sized enterprises. Unfortunately, it also appears to be difficult to operate company intranets consistently with the Directive as written. By pointing out such implementation issues and making suggestions for solutions, we hope to contribute to the unfolding of a workable data protection regime.

Such problems of text and context are normal and understandable in the early stages of broad new legislation. For some EU member states, the drafting of the Directive has led to the creation of entirely new supervisory authorities and data protection rules. For all other member states, there are significant modifications of existing regimes. As we raise issues of text and context, and suggest possible solutions to European authorities, it would be wrong to think that we are somehow seeking to weaken a Directive that was created to protect human rights. Instead, we believe that our extensive research provides a basis for identifying what questions will need to be answered as the laws are implemented. Put another way, we are seeking to add to the transparency of the Directive so that national officials, the organizations affected, and concerned individuals can better understand what steps are expected to protect privacy and what steps would be an unnecessary burden.

Beyond the analysis of text and context, our principal recommendation to European authorities is that they be open to well-drafted SRMs. It is not realistic for the European Union to expect that all other countries will duplicate its government-led comprehensive enforcement regime. A central question for European and American organizations will be the legal basis for handling vast amounts of data that flow across the Atlantic. Europeans have a legitimate interest in making sure that other countries are not used as havens to deliberately circumvent the effect of European laws on European individuals. At the same time, simple fairness, world trade laws, and economic self-interest all dictate that many data flows should proceed without interruption.

In particular, the coming collision over privacy can be averted if the European Union gains sufficient guarantees that companies doing business in its member states will use personal data of EU citizens in ways that are consistent with the protections set forth in the Directive. We believe that much progress toward this goal can be accomplished through well-drafted self-regulatory measures.

After making the policy recommendations about privacy, we conclude in chapter 9 with some implications of our study for the future of the

Internet, electronic commerce, and world data flows. In many ways the most significant legal effect of the Internet will be that individuals, far more than before, will gain information and buy goods from other countries. Legal conflicts will arise concerning not only the misuse of private information but also the availability of pornography or gambling, consumer protection issues in international commerce, and many other areas where citizens of one country can suffer harm because of Web sites in other countries.

As we explore ways to resolve these legal conflicts, we introduce the metaphor of "elephants" and "mice" to help understand where countries will be most successful in regulating perceived social harms. As we explain in more detail later, elephants are large and powerful corporations. Because they are subject to local jurisdiction and cannot hide from enforcement, they generally can be regulated in each country where they operate. An example would be mainframe processors, who keep large and readily identifiable databases. By contrast, mice are small and nimble enterprises that breed very quickly. An example on the Internet might be pornography sites, which can reopen under a new name as soon as they are shut down. Drastic measures, such as shutting down the Internet entirely, might get rid of the mice but would also kill off the good things the Internet can provide.

Where the perceived social harms come from mice, which often hide in other jurisdictions, countries have few choices for legal controls. They can punish the Internet users, regulate the Internet service providers, or try to clamp down on the financial system that transmits money to the mice. Because each of these approaches has significant limitations, an intriguing challenge will be to discover whether new models of Internet commerce and communication can be developed that address the needs of the affected parties: the individuals using the Internet, those selling or providing content on it, and the societies concerned about potential harm to their citizens. We explore some of the emerging models, and conclude that they are now in only the early stages of development. As a result, we recommend that countries remain extremely hesitant to impose binding rules on electronic commerce, at least and until the commerce becomes substantial enough that harms are documented and not simply hypothetical.

One final comment is in order. This book focuses on the effects of the EU's Directive on the United States. We are very aware that it will have similar effects on many other countries. Outside western Europe, an enormous diversity of laws and practices now exist for protecting privacy. Few countries in the third world, for instance, have privacy laws as extensive as those in the United States. Few countries globally have security practices that compare with those used in the United States. If sectors of the U.S. economy are found to lack adequate protection, transfers of information to these other countries would presumably be subject to similar objections.

Recognizing the truly global implications of the Directive, we nonetheless concentrate much of our attention on effects on the United States and on Europe itself. In part, this is because we understand the American terrain best and could most easily conduct research into actual information flows and privacy practices. In part, too, we believe that the analysis here can be generalized readily to the conditions in other countries. In addition, the United States has taken the lead in presenting an alternative vision of global information flows, one based more on technology, market forces, and self-regulation than on a comprehensive regulatory regime. To assess the competing visions, we will need to say more about world data flows, electronic commerce, and the likely prospects for privacy under the Directive.

2

The Legal Context
of the Privacy Directive

This chapter introduces the reader to the European Union Directive on Data Protection and to European data protection laws more generally. The goal is to explain the logic underlying the laws and show some of the difficulties they might create. Once the basic legal regime is explained, we begin considering the Directive's effects. By examining different baselines for compliance, we show why it is possible to describe the qualitative, but not quantitative, effects of the Directive.

We conclude the chapter with a careful look at why it is important to understand what the Directive provides. The analysis in the rest of the book is premised on the view that we should take the Directive seriously and seek to determine how various practices will be regulated under the emerging data protection regime. Even though in practice many organizations might get away with less than full compliance with these laws, and at fairly low risk of an actual enforcement action, there are strong reasons why organizations should and will pay attention to the Directive as written.

European Data Protection Laws

Europe has seen the gradual spread of privacy legislation since the German state of Hesse enacted the first data protection statute in 1970. As Fred Cate has commented, European data protection laws generally have four features:

typically they apply to both public and private sectors; they apply to a wide range of activities, including data collection, storage, use, and dissemination; they impose affirmative obligations (often including registration with national authorities) of anyone wishing to engage in any of these activities; and they have few, if any, sectoral limitations—they apply without regard to the subject of the data.[1]

By the early 1990s, many European Union members had adopted national legislation containing these features. However, the national laws showed some notable differences. For instance, the French National Commission on Informatics and Freedoms (CNIL) has powers that at least in theory are as sweeping as its title. Companies processing personal information are expected to register their proposed data processing with the CNIL, and the agency has significant powers to deny the proposed processing. The CNIL not only has broad powers over data protection but has separate subcommissions on freedom to work, research and statistics, local government, and technology and security.[2] On a much different model, German data protection law assigns responsibility for data protection to both state (*Land*) and national officials. The data protection commissioners at both levels are expected to mobilize public support and urge private and public entities to be cautious in their uses of personal information. Other European national laws exist somewhere between the French regulatory system and the German advisory system. When the drafting of the Directive began in the early 1990s, Italy, Greece, Spain, and other European nations had not enacted national data protection statutes.

Along with the development of these binding national laws, there have been multinational data protection efforts. In 1980 the Committee of Ministers of the Organization for Economic Cooperation and Development (OECD) issued *Guidelines on the Protection of Privacy and Transborder Flows of Personal Data*.[3] The guidelines provide basic principles for data protec-

1. Fred H. Cate, *Privacy in the Information Age* (Brookings, 1997), pp. 32–33.
2. Cate, *Privacy*; and David H. Flaherty, *Protecting Privacy in Surveillance Societies: The Federal Republic of Germany, Sweden, France, Canada, and the United States* (University of North Carolina Press, 1989).
3. O.E.C.D. Doc. © 58 final (September 23, 1980), available at http://www.oecd.org/dsti/sti/it/secur/prod/priv_en.htm. According to its Web page, "The Organisation for Economic Co-operation and Development, based in Paris, France, is a unique forum permitting governments of the industrialised democracies to study and formulate the best policies possible in all economic and social spheres." See http://www.oecd.org. As of August 1997 the OECD had twenty-nine member countries including Australia, Canada, Japan, Mexico, New Zealand, the United States, and many European countries.

tion that are broadly similar to the principles embodied in the EU Data Protection Directive. The United States has signed the guidelines, but they do not create binding law. In 1981 the Council of Europe promulgated a convention *For the Protection of Individuals with Regard to Automatic Processing of Personal Data.*[4] The convention, which again announces broadly similar principles, has been ratified by some, but not all, of the twenty-nine member countries.[5]

The EU Directive represents a dramatic increase in the reach and importance of data protection laws. Once it goes into effect in October 1998, a unified and comprehensive data protection regime will apply to all fifteen countries and 370 million people in the European Union. Important for this book and for the international trade regime are the effects of the Directive on flows of personal information from Europe to the rest of the world. Article 25 of the Directive, with limited exceptions, forbids the transfer of personal information out of Europe unless the other countries meet Europe's standards for "adequate" protection of privacy.

Those outside Europe that are concerned with the effects of Article 25 can easily miss the compelling logic of the Directive within the context of the development of the European Union. The history is now familiar of how European nations since World War II have gradually moved toward economic and political union. The European Coal and Steel Community, created in 1951, formed an important basis for the Treaty of Rome in 1958.[6] The treaty created what was then called the European Economic Community among Germany, France, and four other countries. Over time the EEC expanded to include Great Britain and most other noncommunist European countries. The depth of economic and political integration also increased, culminating with the political union embodied in the Treaty on European Union signed in 1992 in Maastricht and with plans to introduce the Euro as a transnational currency.[7]

---

4. Eur. T.S. no. 108 (January 28, 1981), available at http://www.cor.fr/eng/legaltxt/108e.htm.

5. See Joel R. Reidenberg, "The Privacy Obstacle Course: Hurdling Barriers to Transnational Financial Services," *Fordham Law Review,* vol. 60 (March 1992), pp. S137, S143–48.

6. Treaty Establishing the European Economic Community, March 25, 1957, 28 U.N.T.S. 3, art. 2 (1958), as amended by the Single European Act, O.J. L 169/1 (1987), [1987]2 C.M.L.R. 741, and the Treaty on European Union, February 7, 1992, O.J. C 224/01 (1992), [1992] C.M.L.R. 719, reprinted in I.L.M., vol. 31 (March 1992), p. 247.

7. Treaty on European Union, February 7, 1992, O.J. C224/01 (1992), [1992] C.M.L.R. 719, reprinted in I.L.M., vol. 31 (March 1992), p. 247.

For the past forty years the chief engine of European integration has been the desire to develop a common market, now usually referred to as a unified internal market.[8] The Data Protection Directive, in many respects, is simply a next logical step in creating that internal market. Because member states have had varying data protection laws, and some countries have had no such laws at all, businesses operating in multiple countries have been forced to deal with differing and sometimes inconsistent national rules, precisely the sort of obstacle to the free movement of goods and services that the internal market is supposed to avoid.

The Data Protection Directive is designed to further the creation of a unified market in Europe.[9] It requires all member states to devise national laws that meet minimum standards for protecting the privacy of personal information. Once these laws are in place, the general effect of the Directive will be to allow personal data to be sent or processed within the entire European Union on the same terms as within a member state.[10] In important respects, therefore, the Directive increases the free flow of information within the European Union. Under the Directive member states will no longer be allowed to ban flows of personal information to other member states, as France threatened in the late 1980s with respect to transfers of certain personal information to Italy, which then had no data protection statute.[11] Indeed, member states with relatively strict data protection laws have been concerned that by allowing transfers throughout the European Union the Directive will actually weaken their citizens' privacy protections.

Although the Directive supports the flow of information within Europe, Article 25 can cut off the flow from Europe to other countries. The logic of Article 25 is clear enough. There would be little gained by promulgating the Directive if privacy rights are systematically violated by those

---

8. Data protection issues are handled by Directorate Generale XV of the European Union Commission, responsible for Internal Market and Financial Services. The relevant office within DG XV is the Directorate for "free movement of information and data protection, including international aspects." See http://europa.eu.int/comm/dg15/en.

9. Directive, findings (1) to (9).

10. As with any complex piece of legislation, there are certain exceptions to this sweeping statement. The Directive allows national legislation to vary to some extent. In addition, the choice-of-law provisions of Article 4 may permit member states, in certain instances, to prohibit processing of their citizens' personal data in other member states.

11. See Paul M. Schwartz, "European Data Protection Law and Restrictions on International Data Flows," *Iowa Law Review*, vol. 80 (March, 1995), 491–92. In the particular dispute, Fiat-France eventually entered into a contract with Fiat-Italy, which required Fiat-Italy to offer the protection of French law to the information once it was transferred to Italy.

handling EU citizens' personal data outside Europe. One fear is that other countries may become "data havens," allowing the very practices the Europeans have prohibited. For instance, businesses in the data havens might compile secret dossiers or conduct intrusive marketing practices by mail, telephone, or e-mail. Transborder data restrictions are thus a necessary component of an effective data protection regime.

A primary challenge for this book is how to reconcile Article 25 and its possible restrictions on transborder data flows with public interest concerns expressed in other countries. At the extreme the requirements of Article 25 could lead to a massive disruption of data flows between Europe and its major trading partners. No one desires this sort of disruption, and there are numerous legal and policy routes open to avoid it. Our recommendations for some of the best are set forth in chapter 8.

Before the effects of the Directive can be assessed, one must understand what the Directive provides. We begin by outlining provisions that apply within Europe and then turn to the rules applying to transfers of personal information out of Europe. The discussion here necessarily involves a certain level of detail. The Directive is a complex document, subject to multiple amendments during its drafting. Attention to some of its legal intricacies will be necessary to understand, in later chapters, what particular effects it is likely to have on the practices of business and other entities. No effort is made here, however, to provide an encyclopedic discussion of legal issues arising under the Directive.

Application within the European Union

The Directive is sweeping. With few exceptions it applies to all "processing" of "personal data" (Article 3(1)). "Processing" is a broad term that means "any operation or set of operations which is performed upon personal data, whether or not by automatic means" (Article 2(b)). Processing includes any collection, recording, use, or storage of personal information. Personal data is a similarly broad term, meaning "any information relating to an identified or identifiable natural person ('data subject')" (Article 2(a)). The inclusion of "identifiable" means that the Directive applies even when a person's name is not listed, but when the person can be identified by reference to an identification number or by other means.

The Directive exempts two categories of personal data from its scope. First, it does not apply to government activities over which member states have retained substantial sovereignty. Article 3 states that the Directive applies only where the European Union, rather than the individual member states, has power to set law.[12] Nor does the Directive apply in any case to processing operations concerning public security, defense, state security, and the activities of the state concerning criminal law (Article 3(2)). Article 13 provides additional exceptions for a range of governmental operations.[13] The result of these exceptions is to focus the Directive primarily on the private sector, in contrast to earlier national laws that, by their terms, applied more equivalently to both government and private processing of personal data.

The second exemption from the scope of the Directive concerns personal use of data. The Directive does not apply to processing of personal data "by a natural person in the course of a purely personal or household activity" (Article 3(2)). This exemption presumably would allow a person or household to keep an address list for sending out family announcements without needing to comply with the Directive. However, the text of the Directive apparently applies in a pervasive fashion to many sorts of processing. For instance, any list of addresses on someone's personal computer, containing both personal and business names, would seem to be regulated by it.[14]

---

12. Article 3 exempts activities that fall "outside the scope of Community law, such as those provided for by Titles V and VI of the Treaty on European Union." Title V of the Maastricht Treaty governs common rules on competition, taxation, and approximation of laws. Title VI governs economic and monetary policy. Each title reserves certain powers for the member states.

Read in context, the "outside the scope of Community law" exception should not be understood as a blanket exemption for data processing activities that take place outside the European Union. Articles 25 and 26 give detailed provisions that affect such activities.

13. Under Article 13, member states can pass legislation that exempts certain governmental operations from some of the Directive's key requirements, including the principles relating to data quality (Article 6), the information to be given to the data subject (Articles 10 and 11), the data subject's right of access to data (Article 12), and the publicizing of processing operations (Article 21). The government operations that qualify for such exemptions include a necessary measure to safeguard national security, defense, public security, and criminal enforcement, as in the blanket exemption of Article 3. Article 13 also allows exemptions for "an important economic or financial interest" of a government and for many regulatory functions (Article 13 (1)(e)-(f)).

14. Article 3(1) also provides that the Directive shall apply "to the processing otherwise than by automatic means of personal data which form part of a filing system or are intended to form part of a filing system." As discussed in chapter 6, important categories of named information might be excluded from the Directive because they are not "part of a filing system or . . . intended to form part of a filing system." Notably, this exclusion could apply for information processed about individuals in their business capacity, rather than about them in their personal capacity.

Data Protection Requirements

The Directive sets forth a number of legal requirements with which the controller must comply. "Controller" in this setting means whoever "determines the purposes and means of the processing of personal data" (Article 2(d)). The controller must comply with rules governing the principles relating to data quality, the information to be given to the data subject, the data subject's right of access to data, and the data subject's right to object. Controllers are subject to enforcement actions for violations of these obligations and to other requirements. Special rules govern the use of sensitive data such as information on racial or ethnic origin.

Data Uses and Quality

Article 6 sets forth a number of principles relating to data quality. Perhaps the strictest and most surprising principle in American eyes is the limitation on "secondary use" of data. In particular, the data collected must be "adequate, relevant and not excessive in relation to the purposes for which they are collected and/or further processed" (Article 6(1)(c)). At the same time, although data may be collected "for specified, explicit and legitimate purposes," they may not be "further processed in a way incompatible with those purposes" (Article 6(1)(b)). The other principles in Article 6 state that data must be processed "fairly and lawfully," must be "accurate and, where necessary, kept up to date," and must be kept in an identifiable form no longer than necessary.

Mandatory Disclosure to the Data Subject

Article 10 provides that when collecting information from the data subject, controllers and their representatives must disclose their identities as well as the purposes for the processing (Article 10(a)-(b)).[15] The controller must also disclose, in appropriate cases, certain further information: the recipients or categories of recipients of the data, whether replies to the questions are obligatory or voluntary, and the existence of the data subject's right to access and rectify the data concerning him. This further information must be disclosed where it is "necessary, having regard to the specific

15. The disclosure here, and elsewhere under Articles 10 and 11, is not required when the data subject already has the information.

circumstances in which the data are collected, to guarantee fair processing" (Article 10(c)).

Similar rules apply where the information has not been obtained from the data subject. Disclosure by the controller or his representative is triggered either by further disclosure to a third party or "at the time of undertaking the recording of personal data" (Article 11(1)). The necessary disclosures are essentially the same as those made when the controller obtains the information directly from the data subject. An exception exists, however, where information is not obtained directly from the data subject and disclosure would be impossible or involve a disproportionate effort.[16]

The nature of required disclosure will raise intricate compliance issues. Some countries, such as France, have already had broadly similar disclosure requirements. Companies operating in these countries have experience in how to draft disclosures to customers. Other companies, however, will for the first time need to define the purposes for which they collect data and determine how to word the required disclosures. Organizations subject to the Directive will also need to learn what is meant by the vague requirement of disclosure that is "necessary . . . to guarantee fair processing" (Article 10(c)). In the face of this complexity, some persons familiar with the Directive have suggested that a new consulting industry may emerge to advise on which disclosures are required and how to make disclosures while meeting a company's marketing and other goals. The chief advantage of having such a consulting industry would presumably be better compliance with data protection law and principles. Disadvantages would include cost to those hiring the consultants and the loss of flexibility for the many organizations that regularly change either their data processing routines or the information they provide the public.

Other Rights of the Data Subject

Data subjects are granted extensive rights to discover how data about them are used, correct inaccurate data, and object to some categories of data processing. Under Article 12, the data subject can require the controller to divulge the following: whether data relating to him are being processed, the purposes of the processing, the categories of data concerned, and the recipients or categories of recipients to whom the data are dis-

---

16. Article 11(2). This exception applies in particular "for processing for statistical purposes or for the purposes of historical or scientific research."

closed. The data subject has the right to receive this information "in an intelligible form" and to learn any available information as to the source of the data. These rights apply "without constraint at reasonable intervals" and "without delay or excessive expense" (Article 12(a)).

Where data about an individual are incomplete or inaccurate, the person has the right to correct the information. For processing that fails to comply with the Directive, the data subject has the right to rectify, erase, or block processing (Article 12(b)). Individuals can also object to the lawful processing, notably when the controller anticipates using the data for direct marketing. Individuals have the right to be informed by the controller before personal data are disclosed for the first time to third parties or used on their behalf for direct marketing (Article 14(b)). When processing is for direct marketing, the individual has the right to object free of charge to such uses.

The Directive creates the general rule that a person shall not be subject to a decision based solely on automated processing of data for the purpose of evaluating certain personal matters, such as performance at work, creditworthiness, reliability, and conduct (Article 15(1)). Exceptions are set forth, such as when a law lays down measures to "safeguard the data subject's legitimate interests" (Article 15(2)(b)).

Sensitive Data and Free Expression

Additional rules apply to processing sensitive data "revealing racial or ethnic origin, political opinions, religious or philosophical beliefs, trade-union membership, and the processing of data concerning health or sex life" (Article 8(1)).[17] Processing of sensitive data is generally prohibited, although a number of complicated exceptions exist. For instance, processing is permitted if the data subject gives his explicit consent, but member states can prohibit processing even in such cases. Certain nonprofit organizations can process sensitive information relating to members or persons who have regular contact with the organization. Processing medical information is permitted under a somewhat wider set of circumstances, but only when the data are processed by a health professional subject, by national law or otherwise, to the "obligation of professional secrecy" (Article 8(3))—a term that is not further defined. When the obligation is absent,

---

17. Beyond these categories of sensitive data, processing of data relating to offenses, criminal convictions, or security measures is carried out under the special rules of Article 8(5).

such as may occur outside the European Union, there may be very strict limits on processing medical data.[18] In short, great care must be used in processing any data defined as sensitive by the Directive.

The Directive groups its treatment of sensitive data with Article 9, concerning processing personal data and freedom of expression. Article 9 instructs member states to make exemptions for processing personal data carried out solely for journalistic purposes or the purpose of artistic or literary expression. Exemptions are permitted, however, "only if they are necessary to reconcile the right to privacy with the rules governing freedom of expression." The use of "only" and "necessary" suggest that free expression will prevail over privacy rights less often than would be true under the First Amendment to the U.S. Constitution.

Transfer of Personal Data to Third Countries

The discussion so far has referred to the flow of personal data within the European Union, either within one country or between two member states. Now we turn to Articles 25 and 26, the provisions that in many ways are central to this book because they govern the transfer of personal data out of the European Union. The Directive refers to these transborder data flows as transfers to "third countries," such as the United States or any other non-Union member.

The basic structure of Articles 25 and 26 is simple enough. Article 25 states that transfers of personal data are permitted only if the third country ensures an "adequate" level of protection. Article 26 lists the derogations, or exceptions, to this adequacy requirement. Hidden beneath this surface simplicity, however, are the possibilities for intricate legal and political arguments about transfers to third countries.

Article 25 and "Adequacy"

We have already discussed the rationale supporting Article 25: that the purpose of the Directive could be frustrated by non-European countries that house data banks. These havens could compile the individual dossiers that the Directive is designed to prevent. Even worse, the data havens might

---

18. When the obligation is absent, medical data may still qualify for the other exceptions, such as explicit consent from the data subject.

attract cutting-edge service industries that feed on data about European consumers. The result could be the loss for Europe of both individual privacy and desirable jobs.

In light of this concern, Article 25 requires member states to allow transfers of personal data to a third country only if the country "ensures an adequate level of protection" (Article 25(1)). The definition of "adequate" is potentially very flexible. The assessment of adequacy shall be made "in the light of all the circumstances" (Article 25(2)) surrounding the data transfer. Particular consideration should be given to "the nature of the data" and "the purpose and duration" of the processing. This language appears to contemplate the possibility that less-sensitive data might be transferable to a country even when protections are not strict enough to permit transfer of highly sensitive data. Next, the adequacy determination should look to both general and sectoral rules of law in force in the third country. The reference to sectoral laws highlights the possibility that transfers of data may be permissible for certain industries. To take one example, the detailed provisions of the Fair Credit Reporting Act in the United States might allow transfers of credit information for credit, insurance, or employment purposes, even if transfers for other sectors were prohibited.[19] Finally, the definition of adequacy refers to the "professional rules and security measures which are complied with in that country" (Article 25(2)). This language recognizes that some kinds of privacy protections can come from good practices as well as good laws. For instance, encryption use is often greater and other security practices tighter in the United States than in Europe, and the Directive's language permits such practices to be considered in assessing adequacy.[20]

The Article 31 process for determining adequacy is discussed later. When the European Union finds, pursuant to that process, that a third country does not ensure adequate protection, member states are required to "take the measures necessary to prevent any transfer of data of the same type to the third country in question" (Article 25(4)). The Directive's lim-

19. 15 U.S.C. 1681 et seq. as amended by Pub. L. 104-208 (September 30, 1996).

20. The greater use of encryption, and consequent higher security, is especially easy to see when comparing the United States, where "strong" (unbreakable) encryption is currently available for domestic use, with France, where private sector use of encryption has generally been prohibited. See Lawrence J. Speer, "French Internet Plan Calls for Crypto Debate, Transition from Minitel to Internet Services," *Electronic Information, Policy & Law Report*, vol. 3 (January 28, 1998), pp. 101–02; and "French Government Publishes Encryption Decrees," *Electronic Information, Policy & Law Report*, vol. 3 (March 4, 1998), p. 286.

its on transfers to third countries build on existing law in many member states, which have already authorized data embargoes.[21]

Although Article 25 is designed to be strict enough to prevent the use of data havens, Europeans familiar with the Directive have repeatedly emphasized how carefully it was drafted to avoid arbitrary or parochial bans on transfers to third countries. The long definition of "adequacy" in Article 25 creates a means of finding adequacy in a variety of situations. Moreover, the final Directive amended earlier drafts, which would have required that third countries have "equivalent" data protection regimes. Equivalence is indeed required among the previously disparate regimes of the member states, and the Directive imposes significant new requirements on the member states. But third countries, in order to receive data from Europe, must meet only the lesser standard of adequate protection of data.[22]

Despite these indications of flexibility, governments and businesses in third countries have expressed a great deal of concern about possible restrictions on data flows. A central task of this book is to evaluate the extent to which these concerns are justified. Later chapters examine the effects of the Directive on various sectors. Our analysis shows that there is legitimate reason for concern about whether transfers will be permitted under the Directive as it is currently drafted and being interpreted by data protection officials.

Article 26 and Derogations from the Requirement of Adequacy

In certain limited circumstances, transfers of personal information are permitted to third countries even when that country lacks adequate protection. Attention to the effects of these derogations (exceptions) will occupy much of our attention in later chapters. At this point we introduce the seven categories of exceptions in Article 26, and give a general sense of why the exceptions matter.

For the first six exceptions, transfer is permitted under the Directive "save where otherwise provided by domestic law governing particular cases" (Article 26(1)). Here is one notable deviation from harmonization under the Directive: for transfers to third countries, member states can write stricter rules. For the seventh exception, concerning self-regulatory mea-

21. Paul M. Schwartz, "European Data Protection Law and Restrictions on International Data Flows," *Iowa Law Review*, vol 80 (March 1995), p. 471.

22. Schwarz, "European Data Protection," p. 471.

sures (SRMs), a separate mechanism exists for harmonization, as discussed later.

UNAMBIGUOUS CONSENT. Transfers to third countries are permitted when the data subject "has given his consent unambiguously" to the proposed transfer (Article 26(1)(a)). This exception, although potentially very broad, contains some strict limitations. The breadth exists because consent might be granted in an enormously wide range of settings. If consent has been properly given, the transfer can go forward. But there are three important limitations. First, the past tense of "has given" suggests that the consent must be given before the transfer. Second, the consent must be given "unambiguously," an apparently strict standard that as of summer 1998 has not been further defined. Third, discussions with European officials suggest an understanding of the provision that would not be apparent to most American readers. In their view, consent to the proposed transfer requires consent to the *particular uses* to which the data will be put. This European position comports with the Directive's overall view of data protection rules: notice must be given to the data subject of the purpose of the data collection, and consent only exists as to uses for which the data subject is on notice.

NECESSARY FOR THE PERFORMANCE OF A CONTRACT. Transfers are permitted when they are "necessary for the performance of a contract between the data subject and the controller" (Article 26(1)(b)). For a significant range of transactions, personal information must be sent from Europe to the United States for the transaction to take place. A simple example is someone in Europe who provides his or her name and address when ordering merchandise from the United States. The name and address are necessary for the merchandise to be shipped. If the merchandise is purchased on credit, it may be necessary for the seller to receive additional information about the purchaser's credit history. The seller might also wish to learn the purchaser's annual income, marital status, age, and other information. It would be difficult to argue that this additional information is "necessary for the performance of a contract." To gather this latter sort of information and transfer it to a third country, the seller might need to get unambiguous consent from the individual.

CONTRACT IN THE INTEREST OF THE DATA SUBJECT. A related exception permits transfers in some contracts between the controller and a third party.

Transfers are allowed that are "necessary for the conclusion or performance of a contract concluded in the interest of the data subject between the controller and a third party" (Article 26(1)(c)). Suppose, for instance, that a payor in Europe wishes to send a wire transfer to a payee in the United States. To make the payment work, the name and account number of the payor needs to be transferred from Europe. Along the way, various banks and other entities may handle the payments information containing personal information. This exception allows such transfers because they are necessary for performance of the payments contract concluded in the interest of the payor.

The language of this exception does contain ambiguities. Transfer is permitted with respect to a "contract concluded in the interest of the data subject between the controller and a third party." Many types of transfers are arguably in the interest of the data subject. For instance, direct marketers can claim that they benefit a data subject by making him or her aware of purchasing opportunities. If this view of the direct marketers is accepted, many transfers would be permitted under the following argument: direct marketers enter into contracts with controllers to receive personal information; those contracts are "in the interest of the data subject" (Article 26(1)(c)); and transfer of the information is "necessary for the conclusion or performance of a contract" (Article 26(1)(b)) between the direct marketer and the controller. In response, European authorities likely believe that a much narrower range of transfers are truly "in the interest of the data subject." They would consider many forms of direct marketing an invasion of privacy rather than a potential benefit to the consumer.

Those critical of transfers to third countries with inadequate protection would also highlight the word "necessary" in both this and the previous exception. To be permitted, transfers must be necessary for the performance of a contract, not merely helpful. Those supporting broader transfers will contend that a wider range of information is necessary to the performance of the contract, once the purpose of the contract is properly understood. To provide good customer service, for instance, one can argue that it is necessary for a business to know a customer very well.

LEGAL CLAIMS AND PUBLIC INTEREST GROUNDS. The next exception seeks to reconcile the Directive with competing laws and public policies. Transfers are permitted where "necessary or legally required on important public interest grounds" (Article 26(1)(d)). This public policy exception appears to apply to important public interests as defined by either Europe or third countries. Once again, the term "necessary" provides possible room for argument about the scope of an exception. The exception also applies "for the establishment, exercise or defense of legal claims" (Article 26(1)(d)).

VITAL INTERESTS OF THE DATA SUBJECT. The Directive permits transfer to third countries "to protect the vital interests of the data subject" (Article 26(1)(e)). An example given by European officials is transfer of a patient's medical records if the patient is unconscious or otherwise not able to give unambiguous consent. This exception is limited by the requirement that the interest at stake be "vital."

TRANSFER FROM PUBLIC REGISTERS. Personal data can be sent to third countries when the transfer is made from a register "intended to provide information to the public" (Article 26(1)(f)). To qualify, the register can be open to consultation by the public in general. It can also be open to a person who can "demonstrate legitimate interest, to the extent that the conditions laid down in law for consultation are fulfilled in the particular case."

American readers should be warned that the scope of public records in Europe is often considerably narrower than in the United States. American law shows strong support for openness in government, exemplified by the Freedom of Information Act and the guarantees of free speech and free press under the First Amendment. Although national laws in Europe vary considerably, Americans should not assume that information in the public domain in the United States will also be contained in public registers in Europe.

ADEQUATE SAFEGUARDS AND SELF-REGULATORY MEASURES. As a separate category of exception, a member state may authorize transfer to third countries lacking adequate protection "where the controller adduces adequate safeguards with respect to the protection of privacy" (Article 26(2)).[23] In particular, such safeguards may result "from appropriate contractual clauses." The possibility of self-regulatory measures, including contracts and codes of conduct, has attracted a good deal of attention from industries involved in transborder data flows. For an individual company that transfers personal data out of Europe, a contract approved by a member state could

---

23. The full language may be more restrictive: "where the controller adduces adequate safeguards with respect to the protection of privacy and fundamental rights and freedoms of individuals and as regards the exercise of the corresponding rights" (Article 26(2)).

solve the problems caused by lack of adequate protection in third countries. The company would merely have to comply with the contract. It
could then transfer data out of the European Union without the need to fit
within the previous six exceptions. Citicorp has reached a much publicized
agreement with a data protection authority in Germany that might serve as
a model for future contracts.

European officials have taken steps to discourage companies from ex-
pecting widespread use of the contractual approach. In speeches and meetings they have warned that the use of contracts will be very limited. In the
summer of 1997 the Working Party on the Protection of Individuals with
Regard to the Processing of Personal Data, known as the Working Party,
which has an important advisory role under the Directive, released its first
report.[24] It stated, "such contractual solutions have inherent problems, such
as the difficulty of a data subject enforcing his rights under a contract to
which he is not himself a party, and that they are therefore appropriate only
in certain specific, and *probably relatively rare*, circumstances" (emphasis
added).[25] As discussed in chapter 8, however, European officials' statements
in the spring of 1998 were more supportive of an important role for self-
regulatory measures.

A closely related approach would use codes of conduct as a way to
assure European authorities that fair information practices are being complied with in third countries or some sectors in countries that have otherwise not been found to have adequate protection. Article 27 provides that
member states and the European Commission "shall encourage the drawing up of codes of conduct . . . taking account of the specific features of the
various sectors." Under a code of conduct, a company might bind itself to
follow certain privacy practices. The code might state how to verify compliance and might specify consequences for violations. The Working Party
released its views on self-regulation and codes of conduct in early 1998.[26]

---

24. The Working Party is established in Article 29 of the Directive. Its operation is discussed later
in this chapter.

25. Working Party on the Protection of Individuals with Regard to the Processing of Personal Data,
"First Orientations on Transfers of Personal Data to Third Countries—Possible Ways Forward in
Assuring Adequacy," discussion document adopted by the Working Party on June 26, 1997, p. 1. In
addition, the "Working Party will seek to examine separately the circumstances in which *ad hoc* contractual solutions may be appropriate, and set out some principles as to the possible form and content
of such solutions in future work."

26. Working Party, "Working Document: Judging Industry Self-Regulation: When Does It Make a
Meaningful Contribution to the Level of Data Protection in a Third Country?" DG XV D/5057/97,
January 14, 1998.

As with the contracts approach, the Working Party document expects codes of conduct to enable transfers to third countries only when strict conditions are satisfied.

Our analysis finds much that is promising in self-regulatory measures. Both contracts and codes of conduct allow compliance with the Directive and transfers to third countries by organizations that wish to comply in good faith. Without the measures, it is difficult to see how many routine and desirable sorts of transfers will be permitted to countries or sectors that do not meet the EU adequacy requirements. For the many third countries where comprehensive new privacy statutes cannot reasonably be expected, contracts and codes of conduct may provide the only workable way to allow transfers to go forward while offering legal assurances to the European Union that privacy rights will be protected. We return later to an analysis of self-regulatory measures, especially in chapters 3 and 8.

Implementing Institutions

The Directive requires each EU country to create one or more privacy agencies. It also establishes new institutional structures for coordinating the enforcement authorities of the fifteen nations.

SUPERVISORY AUTHORITIES. Article 28 provides that each member state shall have one or more public authorities responsible for monitoring the provisions adopted pursuant to the Directive. These "supervisory authorities" are a prominent feature of European data protection law. Most member states have a national authority for data protection, although Germany assigns significant responsibilities to each state (*Land*). The basic idea is that data subjects should have a public agency on their side. In many European countries the agency is significantly independent from the rest of the government in the sense that agency leadership does not necessarily change with a change in the party controlling the government.

The Directive states that supervisory authorities should have investigative powers, such as access to data forming the subject matter of processing operations. They must have effective powers of intervention. Article 28 lists examples of effective powers, such as delivering opinions before processing operations are carried out; ordering the blocking, erasure or destruction of data; and imposing a temporary or definitive ban on processing. The authorities must also have the power to engage in legal proceedings for violations of national data protection laws or to bring these violations to the attention of judicial authorities. Decisions by the authorities may then be appealed through the courts.

Under existing law the most common practice has been for data protection authorities to work informally with controllers when complaints are filed. In many instances the controller explains why the practice in fact complies with applicable standards or else agrees to modify it. Discussions with European officials suggest that this nonlitigious method is likely to predominate under the Directive as well. Nonetheless, if an organization does flout data protection rules, supervisory authorities will have the power to engage in legal proceedings that could culminate ultimately in various penalties, including criminal penalties, under national law.

PROCEDURES FOR DETERMINING ADEQUACY AND HARMONIZING MEMBER STATE LAWS. Before the Directive was passed the member states had widely varying legal regimes for data protection. Germany and France had strict rules. Italy and Greece, among others, had no data protection laws at all. As part of the long-term effort to create a unified internal market, the European Union decided in the Directive to take a major step toward harmonizing these laws. That harmonization is incomplete, but there are detailed provisions for resolving differences among the national laws.

We can identify three major sources of differences among national laws. First, the European Union decided to use the legal form of a Directive, which simply directs the member states to pass data protection laws. Each country thus enacts its own statutes, which inevitably differ. Second, several provisions in the Directive allow each member state to adopt different rules on particular subjects. For instance, Article 8 allows countries to prevent a data subject from consenting to the processing of sensitive data. The derogations in Article 26(1), permitting transfers to third countries, can be narrowed by national law. Approvals for contracts under Article 26(2), for transfers to third countries, are also given at the national level. Third, actual enforcement decisions are made at the national or subnational level. Because of the discretion given regulators, even countries with identical statutes might have very different enforcement policies.

The Directive provides both a binding and a nonbinding process to address the lack of harmonization. The binding, or "comitology," process is described in Article 31. Suppose that, in an enforcement proceeding in one country, there is a determination that the United States, or a sector in the United States, lacks adequate protection. This finding of inadequacy could then be appealed to the Article 31 Committee. The committee would be chaired by a representative of the European Commission, who would submit to the committee a draft of measures to be taken. The member states would then vote on the proposal in committee, according to a weighted system in which larger countries have a greater vote. The national representatives to this committee would be political appointees, and not necessarily data protection officials. After the vote, the European Commission would adopt measures that would apply immediately.[27]

A slightly different procedure applies for situations coming under the jurisdiction of Article 26(2), in which a member state authorizes a contract or other safeguard as adequate for transfer to a country that otherwise lacks adequate protection. Member states are required to inform the European Commission and the other member states of authorizations they grant under Article 26(2). If a member state or the commission objects on justified grounds, the commission shall take appropriate measures under the comitology process.

This binding process, with its formal votes in committee, is supplemented in Article 29 by the Working Party. The Working Party is composed of a representative of the supervisory authority or authorities for each member state, along with a representative of the European Commission and one for any authority or authorities established for EC institutions. The principal task of the Working Party is to render expert advice on matters arising under the Directive. To contribute to harmonization, the Working Party will examine the national laws implementing the Directive. It shall give the European Commission an opinion on the level of protection in the European Community and in third countries, give an opinion on codes of conduct drawn up at the EC level, and advise the commission on any proposed amendment to the Directive. Its opinions and recommendations on specific matters are also forwarded to the European Commission and the Article 31 Committee.[28]

The Working Party is entirely advisory, but is nonetheless likely to be influential in data protection issues. Composed of representatives from each country's data protection authorities, it will be better informed about privacy issues than a national government. When it comes time to amend

27. If the Commission's measures are not in accordance with the opinion of the Committee, the Commission shall defer application of the measures for three months. During that time the Council of the European Union, acting by qualified majority, may take a different decision.

28. Many actions of the Working Party are posted at the web site of Directorate General XV, at http://europa.eu.int/comm/dg15/.

national law, recommendations of the Working Party may be the only EU-wide effort to address the detailed issues that arise in data protection. National legislators might thus find it easy to adopt the position of the Working Party, both out of deference for the members' expertise and because of the convenience of following recommendations agreed upon at the EU level.

Just as there is reason to applaud the Working Party's potential to mobilize expertise and examine data protection issues, so too there is some basis for concern about ceding too much authority to the advisory opinions of the group. At various points in this book, we will discuss some of the group's early reports. On the whole, they seem to take a strict approach to data protection. For example, a 1997 report stated that contracts to transfer data should only "rarely" be permitted under Article 26(2).[29] One possible reason for this strictness would be if data protection officials, when meeting together, insist on strong rules rather than risk appearing uncommitted to the protection of privacy. A more fundamental concern is that the members of the Working Party, drawn from among specialized data protection authorities, do not have direct responsibility for other relevant public policy goals such as developing electronic commerce, seeking macroeconomic growth, maintaining good relations with allied countries, and ensuring the rights of free expression. In the course of resolving formal disputes, these other goals might be considered in decisions of the Article 31 Committee. On many issues, however, there will be no such formal decision. In such situations, there is some possibility that the Working Party may tend toward an overly strict interpretation of the Directive.

Defining the Baselines: What Are the Transborder Effects of the Directive?

Now that we have canvassed the rules, we can begin our assessment of the Directive's transborder effects. A concern of American officials and corporate leaders is that the Directive will create large and unreasonable compliance costs. To assess this concern, we must define baselines for measuring the effects of the Directive, especially with respect to transfers of personal information from Europe to the United States. As we shall ex-

---

29. The working paper, Directorate General XV, European Commission, "First Orientations on Transfers of Personal Data to Third Countries—Possible Ways Forward in Assessing Adequacy," XVD/5020/97-EN final, June 26, 1997, is discussed in detail in chapter 8.

plain, these effects can be presented in qualitative but not quantitative form.

One baseline is the cost of compliance for entirely European firms operating entirely within Europe. The effects of the Directive will vary considerably by country. Some, including France and Germany, have long had binding data protection regimes. Businesses operating in these countries are likely to face only incremental changes in the applicable laws. Other member states, including Italy and Greece, have passed their first general data protection laws in response to the Directive. Firms operating in these countries will face the full set of data protection laws for the first time. Within Europe, moreover, the costs of complying with the Directive will be offset by the benefits resulting from the assurance that data flows that are legal in one country can now be sent anywhere in the European Union.

In measuring the effects of the Directive on American and other non-European companies, we first observe that foreign firms ordinarily expect to comply with local laws. U.S. companies that have chosen to operate in Europe, for example, expect to comply with the local minimum wage or antipollution laws. These local regulations are not an attack on U.S. interests, except where there is evidence that they are discriminatory or otherwise have international repercussions. Put another way, European firms will have a baseline level of compliance costs after the Directive goes into effect. Where U.S.-based firms face the same compliance costs, we would not usually speak of the transborder effects of the Directive.

That said, the Directive's limits on transborder data flows will have especially significant effects on U.S. and other non-European organizations. Although some member states have long had legal restrictions on these data flows, the Directive begins a new era. It has made the rules far more visible and has applied those rules to all member states. Some of its provisions are stricter than any current national rules.[30] Perhaps most important, the process of agreeing on the Directive has given a new urgency and legitimacy within Europe to the enforcement of data protection rules. The rules are now in place for the entire internal market, and data processors are on much fuller notice about what is expected of them.

In this new era of restrictions on transborder data flows, there are predictable, differential effects on non-EU organizations. For one thing, a

---

30. For instance, Article 23 provides that any person who has suffered damage as a result of an unlawful processing operation or of any act incompatible with national provisions is entitled to receive compensation from the controller for the damage suffered. Our research as of the spring of 1998 indicates that no member state currently has an express provision in law approving this sort of compensatory remedy for the individual.

limit on transborder flows will obviously affect international companies more than entirely domestic ones: only international actions involve the rules on transfers. More subtly, limits on transborder flows are likely to have a more profound effect on companies based in a third country than on those based in Europe. Companies based in Europe will typically design their data processing operations for local conditions and thus more routinely take the Directive into account. Companies based elsewhere often will not establish their internal processing procedures with European regulations clearly in mind. An additional difference is that the central processing operations of companies based in third countries will typically take place in those countries. Management decisions will be made there, and managers expect to have access to the underlying information needed for decisions. The flow of named information from Europe to third countries is thus likely to be greater for companies based in the United States and other third countries.

On the European side, then, the costs of complying with the Directive are likely to increase from purely European firms to transnational firms to transnational firms headquartered in the United States and other third countries. On the American side, the cost of compliance will depend on the privacy practices that are in effect in the United States. To see this point, consider two extreme examples. In the first, the United States has no privacy protections at all, either in law or practice. As the Directive goes into effect, U.S. firms that wished to enter the European market would face compliance costs that would rise from zero to the full cost of complying with the Directive. In the second example the United States would already have the same privacy protections as the Directive, so U.S. firms would face no extra compliance costs in deciding to enter European markets.

The reality in the United States, of course, differs from both examples. As Paul Schwartz and Joel Reidenberg have documented, there is an extremely complex web of privacy laws and practices in the United States.[31] Sometimes the net effect is greater privacy protection than in Europe. For instance, wiretaps are more strictly regulated than in many European countries, and specialized pockets of strict regulation exist for such diverse areas as video rentals, student records, and home telephone records. But sometimes, probably often, the net effect is less strict privacy protection in the United States, especially in the private sector. In assessing the effect of the Directive, therefore,

31. Paul M. Schwartz and Joel R. Reidenberg, *Data Privacy Law: A Study of United States Data Protection* (Charlottesville, Va.: Michie, 1996).

one would need to measure the difference between the European standard and the rules and practices applying in each sector in the United States, a complex task with many areas of legal and practical uncertainty.

Measuring the effects of the Directive becomes even more complicated when one takes account of the ongoing changes in law and practice on both sides of the Atlantic. The European Commission has made clear that it intends to continue to develop privacy protections, especially for the on-line world. The United States may itself find law and practice changing significantly in response both to domestic politics and to the Directive itself.

In summary, there is no single baseline against which to measure the effects of the Directive. The precise meaning of European and American law is uncertain at many crucial points, and the relevant laws and practices are likely to change. Accurate data to gauge costs of compliance are also very difficult to gather. Making a quantitative estimate of the value of flows of information from Europe to the United States, and then quantifying how those flows would be affected by the Directive, is a task well beyond the data we have been able to gather. Nonetheless, we know that U.S. exports of goods and services to the European Union totalled $253.6 billion in 1997, and imports were $270.5 billion.[32] The costs of the Directive could clearly be substantial if compliance costs constitute even a small percentage of the value of the trade or if a small percentage of the trade were disrupted. Strict enforcement of Article 25 could undoubtedly have a severe economic effect.

Finally, measuring the effects of the Directive will depend on how broadly or narrowly any findings of inadequacy are made. In a conclusion based on interviews with responsible EU officials, it seems highly unlikely as of spring 1998 that the European Union will make a general finding in October 1998 that the United States lacks adequate privacy protection in all areas. Such a blunt finding would lead to serious political difficulties and perhaps spark a trade war. But U.S. privacy law is not nearly as strict as the Directive for many sectors. A close examination of U.S. practices in some sectors might support a conclusion of inadequacy under European standards.[33] We have yet to learn much in practice about how findings of

32. Bureau of Economic Analysis, *International Accounts Data: Balance of Payments: Transactions by Area* (U.S. Department of Commerce, September 1997), as found at http://www.bea.doc.gov/bea/di/bparea-d.htm.

33. Schwartz and Reidenberg, *Data Privacy Law,* while appropriately cautious about making generalizations, offers a good deal of evidence questioning the "adequacy" of U.S. practices, especially in some large sectors such as direct marketing and medical data.

inadequacy will be made. Until and unless there are assurances of adequacy for particular sectors, a great many transfers of data to the United States and other third countries will be subject to credible challenge under Article 25, if not immediately after the Directive becomes effective in October 1998, then sometime thereafter. Data protection officials in each member state will be able to claim inadequacy. Individual data subjects, perhaps spurred on by European competitors of U.S. firms, might also seek enforcement and a finding of U.S. inadequacy. Any such enforcement actions would then likely become the subject of political controversy, be a topic of discussion in the Working Party under Article 30, and be subject to the comitology process of Article 31. As this process works out, the *threat* of an inadequacy finding will be ever present, long before particular findings are made.

Why What Is Legal under the Directive Matters

This book carefully analyzes the Directive as written. Each section follows a three-step approach: describe the categories of data flows in a given sector, analyze possible means of compliance and the applicability of exceptions to the Directive, and discuss the categories of data that apparently would not be permitted under the Directive. In the course of this analysis we highlight a number of important sectors of the economy that may face difficulties complying. We also identify some surprising situations in which the Directive would appear to forbid certain transfers to third countries where there is no finding of adequate protection. For example, the Directive may disrupt standard practices for accounting, investment banking, and pharmaceuticals research. It also appears to regulate the press, charities, and the U.S. government in their transfers of data out of Europe.

Our attention to the Directive as written, including the use of examples from different sectors, has drawn criticisms in our conversations with data protection officials and others. A first objection has been to point out that no enforcement will take place under the Directive itself; instead, enforcement will occur under the laws of each member state. In response, we note that the important provisions in the Directive are written in mandatory form, with the expectation that member states will comply and with elaborate procedures to harmonize the national laws. It is indeed a slight simplification to write that "the Directive forbids . . . ," but the simplification accurately conveys the Directive's intent to create binding rules. Moreover, in many respects the Directive sets the *minimum* requirements for national law, while member states are free to regulate even more strictly. Notably, they can be stricter in the treatment of sensitive data (Article 8) and in defining the derogations in Article 26 that allow transfers to third countries.

A second objection is that a literal reading of the Directive is at odds with the historical enforcement of data protection laws. According to this objection, our examples unfairly portray the Directive as draconian, while the experience under existing laws has been modest and reasonable. In response, we note that the Directive is indeed a major step in the development of European data protection law. Ulf Brühann, a senior official in the European Commission responsible for implementing the Directive, said in September 1997, "Nobody should underestimate the problem by doubting the political will of the European Union to protect the fundamental human rights of citizens."[34] He specifically noted that the exceptions in Article 26 are "tightly worded and unlikely to be applicable to the majority of situations." In the face of such statements by responsible European officials, it is understandable why organizations may wish to understand what is permitted and forbidden under the Directive.

A related objection to a literal reading is that data protection officials can be trusted to exercise sound discretion in enforcement. Officials are likely to concentrate their limited resources on the most important cases, and will not risk undermining their own legitimacy by enforcing where it is not appropriate. In response, we of course share the hope that data protection officials will use their enforcement discretion wisely. That hope, however, is not entirely reassuring to organizations that must comply with the Directive. After the effective date, data protection officials in all fifteen member states will be able to initiate enforcement proceedings. Officials in any one country can assert that a third country, such as the United States, does not have adequate protection, and that transfers to that country are therefore illegal.[35] In addition, the Directive contemplates that individuals

---

34. Ulf Brühann, "Data Protection in Europe: Looking Ahead," speech before the Nineteenth International Conference of Privacy Data Protection Commissioners, September, 1997.

35. Any such enforcement action can eventually be appealed to the European Commission under the complex procedures in Article 31. These procedures only imperfectly protect the controller, however, because of the expense of defending against enforcement and the bad publicity and other negative consequences arising from the enforcement action. In addition, because of the weakness of U.S. privacy laws compared with European laws in some areas, the claim of inadequacy in a given situation may be plausible.

will have the right to a remedy for breaches of national laws, including payment of damages (Articles 22 and 23). Faced with this variety of possible enforcement actions, organizations will wish to understand their obligations under the Directive rather than simply rely on the sound discretion of agency officials.

Clarifying the legal rules instead of relying on the sound discretion of enforcement officials is especially important for organizations that undertake expensive, long-term investments in Europe. The need for understandable laws can be seen, for instance, for companies that are investing in their next generation of information systems. Such systems can be enormously complex, expensive, and difficult to change once put into operation. The best architecture for a system will depend on the data protection rules governing how customer, employee, and other information can flow within the company, including its transnational operations. It may be risky for a company to create the system in a way that seems forbidden by the language of the law but is allowed under the discretion of the current officials. Over time the views of officials may change, and the text of the law can become the basis for enforcement action, bad publicity, or other adverse consequences.

A final objection has come from an experienced data protection official, who stated that reading the Directive literally and picking out a few vivid examples "trivializes" data protection law, thereby distracting attention from more important issues.[36] In response, we find it helpful to contrast the perspectives of the regulators and the regulated. For the data protection agencies, the Directive is designed to protect fundamental human rights to privacy. These rights will not be protected if there are too many loopholes. The logic of protecting rights thus leads to provisions such as Article 25, which protects against data havens, and Article 3, which ensures that regulation applies except for purely personal activity. From this perspective the Directive must be strict to approach its lofty goals.[37] For organizations regulated by the Directive, the perspective can appear far different. If its language forbids routine transfers of data out of Europe, each organization must decide whether it will knowingly violate the law. It is no trivial decision to adopt a deliberate corporate policy of noncompliance.

---

36. The comment was directed specifically at the attention paid in the interim report of this book to the treatment of laptop computers under the Directive. Laptop computers are discussed in chapter 3.

37. In defense of the data protection regime, the draft Directive was modified in a number of pragmatic ways to take account of the concerns of various parties. A notable example of such change was to allow transfers to third countries with "adequate" protection, rather than requiring stricter "equivalent" protection.

The analysis in this book focuses carefully on what the Directive says, and it is useful to consider some reasons why organizations should and do care about the letter of the law. At the most basic level, many people feel a moral obligation to obey the law. These moral obligations are reinforced by institutional reasons why many will attempt to comply. The data protection manager in a company may find it personally uncomfortable, not to mention legally risky, to have the corporation follow a policy of violating the Directive. A European manager in a transnational company may wish to report to senior management that the company is in compliance—failure to comply may be a source of risk to the company and an indication that the manager is not doing a proper job. Lawyers giving counsel to a company are under ethical and legal obligations; they may face penalties if they knowingly assist in the violation of a law. For all of these persons there are moral and legal objections to participating in systematic noncompliance.

Violations of the law can have other consequences. Many violations of data protection rules are actually criminal in the member states (although criminal enforcement has historically been exceedingly rare). Individuals and organizations may be especially wary about breaking criminal laws, and organizations may face heightened penalties in other settings if they are shown to have routinely violated criminal laws.[38] Failure to follow the law also exposes the organization to risks beyond whatever fines are levied by the state: noncompliance can lead to public criticism and other sanctions, creating embarrassment for the lawbreakers and an advantage for competitors.

One additional reason for paying careful attention to the text of the Directive is that paying close attention to the letter of the law can assist in the resolution of disputes between Europe and other countries on privacy issues. An important goal of this project is to provide an accurate description sector by sector of what is permitted and forbidden under the Directive. Some alleged problems will turn out to have ready solutions—exceptions to the Directive will apply or compliance will be easy to achieve. Other problems will be properly seen as serious and placed on the agenda for resolution by the various countries. Some of these problems may call for clarification or amendment of the Directive, even without weakening its effect, such as when new technologies outdistance specific provisions now

---

38. For instance, a violation of non-U.S. criminal laws may be considered as a factor in establishing a criminal history, resulting in a harsher penalty under U.S. law. *Federal Sentencing Guidelines Manual*, 1994–95 edition (St. Paul: West Publishing, 1994), p. 257.

being implemented. As these problems are addressed, we can hope for precedents for the way other situations will fit within the data protection regime. In short, this study may contribute to the transparency of the Directive. Just as the Europeans stress that transparency is important for the data subject when dealing with a controller, so too is transparency important for organizations required to comply with the Directive. By understanding what it provides, we can hope for a smoother and more just process for resolving the international issues that its implementation creates.

3

Data Protection and Information Technologies

In examining the effects of the Directive, we begin with information technologies. We are in the midst of an information explosion. Data protection rules seek to block flows of information. What will happen as the (perhaps) irresistible force of data flows confronts the (perhaps) immovable object of privacy rules?

Seen another way, the rise of computers and computer networks is a major reason countries have promulgated data protection rules in recent decades. In both the United States and Europe, debates are being driven by fears that computers pose a threat to privacy. That is, computers are *the key reason* for data protection rules. But changing computer technology also makes the Directive's rules seem badly matched to the reality of information flows.

The Directive's approach is designed for the regulation of mainframe computers, in which one expects a relatively small number of hierarchical systems. Information technology, however, has shifted radically to new configurations such as client-server systems and the Internet. Today there is a much larger number of systems organized into distributed networks rather than simple hierarchies. The data protection regime designed for mainframes performs much less well when applied to the many and the distributed.

The language of the Directive evokes its mainframe, top-down assumptions. Consider the terms "controller" and "data subject." A controller is at the top of a hierarchy, the person in command of a unified computer system. One expects a "controller" to have many minions, who carry out com-

50

mands. A data subject is clearly much less powerful—acted upon and subject to manipulation by the one who controls.

This language is far less apt in a world of personal computers and the Internet. The entity running a Web site is often an individual or a small company—hardly worthy of the term "controller." The persons browsing may be equipped with a large variety of tools for protecting their privacy. For instance, they might be able to browse anonymously, use software to disable a site's "cookies," or submit false information on any forms that the site employs.[1] Such people are no longer passive and powerless. They instead may be more sophisticated than the operators of the Web site and will often be employed by major corporations.

Beyond language the link between data protection and mainframe computers tracks the historical experience. Early data protection efforts primarily applied to major government computers such as those used by the tax and census systems. Only gradually were the laws extended to private databases, and the focus of enforcement has remained processing by governments and the largest enterprises.[2]

Although the history and the philosophy of the Directive are strongly influenced by its mainframe roots, its terms do not distinguish among different sorts of information technologies. As a legal matter, the broad definition of "processing" in Article 2 applies to mainframes, personal computers, the Internet, and all other forms of computerized transmission or storage of information.[3]

Notwithstanding the legal equivalence, the practical application of the Directive varies widely for different sorts of information technology. In this chapter we examine how the Directive creates distinct issues with respect to such technologies, including mainframes, client-server systems, intranets, extranets, and the Internet, including the Web, e-mail, computerized facsimiles, and laptops.

---

1. Anonymous Web browsing is available through experimental programs at various places on the Web. See, for example, http://infotrek.simplenet.com/anonymous.html; www.anonymizer.com. Cookie cutter software allows the person browsing to prevent a Web site from setting cookies, that is, the software protects a user's hard drive against intrusion by the site. See http://www.junkbusters.com/links.html#measures. Recent polling reported a high percentage of users who admitted to having submitted false information to Web sites when personal information has been requested of them. Available at http://www.cc.gatech.edu/gvu/user_surveys/survey-10-1996/.

2. In interviews, a senior data protection official for one country estimated that about half of the databases had registered, although the official stated that almost all the major databases had registered. An official in another EU country reported that most small- and moderate-sized enterprises in that country do not register.

3. Less strict rules, however, apply against manual filing systems (Article 32(2)).

Surveying these information technologies is inherently interesting. It gives us insights into world data flows as we begin an era of greatly expanded electronic commerce. The survey also is crucial to understanding the effects of the Directive, especially on transborder data flows. In reading the discussion of information technologies, it will be useful to keep in mind the following subjects:

—*International flows of data.* International flows of information are increasing rapidly within companies, as they create global intranets, and between companies, as they use extranets with their strategic partners. The continued growth in world trade, especially the rise of electronic commerce at the retail and company-to-company levels, will similarly increase international data flows.

—*Number and power of processors.* The world has shifted decisively from a relatively small number of mainframes to an enormous number of personal computers and other distributed processing power. The number of computer operators has increased correspondingly.

—*Lack of data protection expertise.* A mainframe computer center has security specialists and a staff available for complying with data protection rules. Similar expertise is challenging to develop as routine users gain the power to assemble databases on tens of millions of desktop computers.

—*Shifting advantages and disadvantages of data protection.* The costs and benefits of data protection rules change with the information technology. Historically, the costs of regulating mainframes were relatively low because of their small number, the relative expertise of the personnel, and the location of processing inside one country. The benefits were potentially significant because of the large amount of sensitive data in each mainframe. In an Internet world, however, there are many computers, inexpert personnel, and pervasively international transfers. Moreover, the benefits of regulation are reduced because of the difficulty of international enforcement. Under the Directive, the law applying to mainframes and the Internet may be the same, but the practical costs and effectiveness of the laws may be quite different.

Mainframes

Mainframe computers are involved in transfers of enormous quantities of data from Europe to the United States. Such transfers can present major difficulties under the Directive if the United States or sectors in the

United States are found not to have adequate protection. But mainframe computers may be easier to fit within the data protection regime than other forms of modern information technology for two principal reasons. First, mainframes generally exist within major organizations, which are easily identified by regulators and have staff to devote to compliance efforts. Second, mainframe operations are a natural setting for self-regulatory measures such as contracts that can be approved by European authorities. The discussion in this section shows the potential problems that mainframes may pose, and ways within the Directive to address those problems.

Transborder Data Flows

Mainframes are typically used where there are huge volumes of a certain sort of record—telephone call records, credit card transaction records, or the billing records kept by an Internet service provider (ISP). For these and similar categories of transactions, one would expect millions of transactions each year from Europe to the United States. In later discussions, we analyze the effects of the Directive on the credit card, ISP, and other industries. For now, it is enough to recognize the volume of transaction information that flows across borders.

The modern economics of mainframe operations also creates reasons to transfer data across borders. In some instances a company may have mainframe computers in both Europe and the United States. A wide range of company needs may dictate sharing information between the mainframes. For example, accounting and other departments may need to create unified reports, or the computer in the United States may serve as a vital backup for operations usually done in Europe. There may also be economies of scale that favor having a single mainframe center, which may be located in the United States. In such cases, data from around the world can only be processed at the central mainframe site.

Compliance by Mainframes

For many uses of mainframes, it would be impossible or very costly to cut off flows of personal information from Europe to the United States and other third countries. Some of these flows would fit within various exceptions to the Directive, such as when there is unambiguous consent by the data subject or the transfer is necessary for the performance of a contract. The rest of our analysis will examine these sorts of issues sector by sector.

The general conclusion is that, even under fairly generous readings of the exceptions, there are many flows of data involving mainframes that do not appear to be legal under the Directive if the European Union finds privacy protection in the United States inadequate.

Even where no exception applies for current practices, in some situations controllers can change their practices so as to process the data and still comply with the Directive. For instance, if backup by a U.S. mainframe is not legal under the Directive, an organization might find ways to archive records in Europe. If it is not legal to send all records to a U.S. mainframe, some organizations may find it worth the millions of dollars that it can cost to establish a new mainframe center in Europe.[4] As with the use of Article 26 exceptions, our general finding is that compliance of this sort is sometimes possible with mainframes but will not provide a satisfactory solution to many important categories of data transfers.

If this analysis is correct, we would expect large flows of data to third countries that do not fit within exceptions to the Directive and that are not amenable to easy compliance. Despite this conclusion, there are reasons to be optimistic about the possibility that mainframe centers can comply with the EU data protection rules, even in third countries or sectors where there is not otherwise adequate protection. Just as there are economies of scale in processing data, so too there are often economies of scale in compliance. A mainframe system will typically employ numerous programmers, including one or more professionals devoted to security. The compliance burden of data protection laws can be spread across this professional staff with particular individuals assigned responsibility for the organization's compliance. It is of course an expense to the organization to write specialized software or otherwise respond to the Directive. For mainframes, that expense can be amortized across the very large volume of records that are regularly processed. And compliance is relatively manageable when the controller has the personnel and organizational structure to respond to data processing problems.

Beyond having a structure in place for compliance, mainframe centers also offer data protection officials an especially ready target for enforcement activities. Mainframe computer centers tend to be big, expensive,

---

4. In a Harvard Business School study about the economics of Internet service providers, the cost of a data center increased with the number of users, but ranged between $15 million "to build a small center" to $50 million a year in hardware and maintenance for a large center. David B. Yoffie and Tarun Khanna, *Microsoft Goes Online: MSN 1996*, Harvard Business School reprint N9-797-088 (as revised 1997).

and hard to operate secretly.[5] For credit card operations, telephone billing, and other purposes they routinely receive data from other established companies. Enforcement officials can thus generally find mainframes operating in Europe. In addition, mainframes are usually operated by large companies that have other substantial assets in Europe. Enforcement officials thus generally have jurisdiction over the company and a ready way to ensure payment of judgments. To some significant degree these large companies become European companies staffed with European employees and wish to avoid problems with public or employee relations. Such companies would often rather comply with the Directive than risk an embarrassing enforcement action.

Self-Regulatory Measures for Mainframes

A central concern of European officials has been to ensure the enforceability of data protection rules. Such officials have often voiced concern about purely self-regulatory approaches because they believe that industry bodies will not dependably take enforcement actions against companies that improperly use personal information. With respect to mainframe computer centers, our considered view is that the European Union has it largely within its power to ensure enforcement of data protection rules. At least for the large companies that typically establish mainframe centers, enforcement should be manageable through self-regulatory measures (SRMs) such as contracts and codes of conduct.

Article 26(2) of the Directive allows a member state to authorize transfers of personal data to countries that lack adequate protection when the controller adduces adequate safeguards. Such safeguards "may in particular result from appropriate contractual clauses." Article 26(4) furthermore permits the European Commission, in accordance with the procedures contained in Article 31, to determine that certain standard contractual clauses offer sufficient safeguards. These contracts would be written between two organizations involved in a data transfer, subject to approval by the member states.[6]

---

5. In the terminology we develop in chapter 9, mainframe centers are "elephants," powerful and thick skinned but also extremely difficult to hide.

6. For many businesses it is standard procedure to have separate, affiliated corporations operating in the United States and Europe. In such instances, the contracts would be between the affiliates. It is less clear from the text of the Directive how the "contract" would be formed when the same organization was involved in sending the data out of Europe and receiving the data in the third country. For

Although industry groups have stressed the potential of Article 26(2) to facilitate compliance with the Directive, European authorities have played down the role of SRMs. In public statements and an early report of the Working Party on the Protection of Individuals with Regard to the Processing of Personal Data, data protection officials have said that the contracts approach will only "rarely" be applied. Four reasons have been suggested. First, the supervision of a large number of contracts, which may vary widely from industry to industry and even among companies in an industry, would strain the limited resources of data protection authorities. Second, it would be difficult and unwise to apply the contracts approach to small- and medium-sized enterprises, both because of the number of contracts and the burden negotiations would impose on the companies. Third, there are concerns about how readily data subjects and data protection authorities would be able to ensure enforcement of the contracts, especially when the breach occurs outside of Europe. Fourth, European officials have frankly hoped to encourage the United States and other third countries to adopt comprehensive privacy legislation. By deemphasizing the use of contracts and other SRMs, the Europeans can try to apply more pressure on other countries to adopt privacy-protective legislation.

None of these arguments is very persuasive with respect to large mainframe computer centers. For one thing, it is unlikely that the United States will adopt comprehensive privacy legislation in the immediate future. Once this is accepted, there seems to be little point in refusing to use SRMs, which are clearly permitted by the Directive, to authorize major and necessary flows of personal information. Second, supervising the contracts of the limited numbers of large mainframe centers should not place undue burdens on data protection authorities. Indeed, for these major centers, some tailoring of the rules for the different industries may be desirable. It seems possible, for instance, that procedures for handling data will differ somewhat for the credit card, telephone, and ISP industries. Third, although it may well be difficult for small- and medium-sized enterprises to draft and enforce contracts approved by data protection authorities, the experience within Europe, according to our interviews with data protection commissioners, is that a great many European small- and medium-sized enterprises do not currently comply with data protection laws. If

---

example, salespeople in Europe would need to send information back to the home office in the United States. In such circumstances, perhaps the organization would request authorization from the member state about whether its internal procedures ensure adequate safeguards.

European companies do not comply, it is unrealistic to expect compliance by these enterprises in third countries. At least during the initial stages of implementing the Directive, it probably makes sense to use available tools such as contracts to bring the largest data processors within the regime.

Perhaps the strongest argument for applying the contracts approach to large mainframe centers is that they are ready subjects of enforcement. As already mentioned, mainframe centers are typically operated by large companies that have substantial assets and business operations in Europe. Some data protection officials have suggested that there are legal impediments under European law to enforcement by data subjects and supervisory authorities for breach of data protection contracts. If such impediments indeed exist, it is entirely within the power of European countries to remove them and to have effective enforcement against companies that enter into such contracts. Furthermore, the concern about the need for enforcement by the individuals, as an objection specifically to the use of contracts, may be somewhat overstated. To date, it appears that member states have not provided compensatory remedies to individuals even for violations occurring within the European Union. Thus the lack of the remedy in third countries seems a weak basis for prohibiting transfers. In addition, some legal impediments to enforcement might be addressed by the contract that authorizes transfer of information. For instance, the organization receiving the data can consent to be treated, say, as a British or German organization for purposes of data protection enforcement. The relevant supervisory authority would then have the same ability to take action against the organization as would be available against a British or German organization.

Under a similar analysis it is easy to see how industry codes of conduct may provide a feasible and sensible way to supplement the contract approach, especially for major organizations, in which enforcement within Europe is clearly possible. Article 27 encourages the use of codes of conduct to contribute to the proper implementation of the national provisions adopted pursuant to the Directive. Within the language of Article 27 there appears to be room for these codes of conduct to describe how transfers of personal data, consistent with the laws of each member state, may be made to third countries. Major organizations with substantial assets and business operations in Europe might decide to adhere to one of these codes with respect to transfers to the United States and other third countries. As one potentially promising example, the Center for Social and Legal Research, headed by privacy expert Alan Westin, is now seeking to develop model contracts and codes of conduct, addressing the goals of the Directive to provide substantive protections and assurances of verifiability of compliance. European law could then be used to bring enforcement actions against any organization that violates the SRM to which the organization has promised to adhere (in addition to any enforcement actions that aggrieved U.S. citizens, the Federal Trade Commission, or the states may lodge in the United States).

Client-Server Systems, Intranets, and Extranets

During the past two decades traditional mainframes have lost their dominant position in the world of computing. Corporations and other organizations have shifted to client-server systems, developed organizational intranets, and begun to create multiorganization extranets. At each of these steps there is less hierarchical governance of processing by a company's controller. The shift is to a model of distributed processing. Other computers in the network do much of the processing, and the centralized computer operators have less and less control over how data are gathered and processed at remote locations. The adoption of distributed processing makes it harder to implement a data protection regime that presumes the existence of a centralized controller. Far more people in the organization gain the power to process and transfer data, and thus potentially violate data protection rules.

Client-Server Architecture

We begin with client-server architecture, which has become the standard business practice for a vast array of industries and applications.[7] The basic idea in client-server systems is that a large number of client computers routinely exchange data with a server that performs specialized tasks. The clients here are often powerful computers in their own right, in contrast to the dumb terminals that were classically linked to a mainframe and under strong centralized controls. The managers of the modern server may have little or no ability to monitor what data are gathered and processed within the client computers. Indeed, a principal advantage of this architec-

---

7. The shift to the client-server model is so pervasive that IBM, for instance, has renamed its mainframes as "enterprise servers." Nick Turner, "Computers & Technology No More Black and White: PC Industry Lines Graying," *Investor's Business Daily*, May 13, 1998, p. A8.

ture is that it keeps data closer to where it is needed, and reduces the need for all of an organization's data to flow through a single chokepoint.[8]

If the Directive bans transfers to the United States or sectors in the United States, there could be harsh results for organizations using a client-server architecture. If the server is outside Europe, routine transfers from client to server would be prohibited. Examples would include any European sales office that needs to send data to the United States for bookkeeping and other purposes. The burden may fall disproportionately on small- and medium-sized enterprises, which may have too few employees in Europe to justify establishing and maintaining a server in Europe for all of the company applications. Business practice would thus tend to require these businesses to transfer employee and customer information to a server in a third country.

Similar problems would arise when the server is in Europe, but the client computers are in the United States. The Directive would allow cli-

8. At the time of this writing, in the spring of 1998, there was considerable ferment in the computer industry about whether and in what way control will shift back to companies' information system managers. Such a centralization of power may seem contrary to our theme of increased decentralization of computer processing. As we shall explain, however, these developments do not alter our analysis about the increasing challenges that modern information technology poses to data protection laws.

The computer industry debate pits the "network computer" model supported by Oracle, Sun, and other companies against the personal computer-based model supported notably by Microsoft and Intel. Both approaches are seeking to reduce the total cost to organizations of running their computer networks. Under the network computer approach, software applications used at a person's desktop would be housed elsewhere in the network. The advantages claimed are lower hardware costs (network computers cost less than personal computers) and centralized software management.

Under the personal computer approach, there are also new initiatives to reduce what is called the "total cost of ownership." Under this approach, systems managers would use new tools to manage and service the desktop computer. Remote servicing of the computer would become more effective, and it would be harder for individuals to load their computers with unauthorized software, which can lead them to crash. Adam Bisby, "Thin-Client Advocates Split into Two Camps," *Computer Dealer News*, vol. 14 (January 19, 1998), p. 19; and Bernard McAleer, "2 Camps Divide Network Computing," *Electronic News*, vol. 43 (September 29, 1997), p. 52.

Although both models would return some power to centralized computer management, these recent developments do not alter the basic analysis about data protection. Under either model, individual users would still retain the power to gather, process, and transfer enormous amounts of personal information. Even if management of the computer system becomes more centralized, there is no similar idea to centralize decisions about how the data are used. Under the personal computer model, individuals would continue to gain processing power at the desktop. Under the network computer model, according to our discussions with persons involved in developing them, the individual user would also continue to have enormous power to process data as he or she desired. People throughout the organization would have access to the processing power needed to gather, process, and transfer personal information.

ents to send data into Europe, but any flows from the server to the client computer could be cut off. Examples would include the European manager's ability to send instructions about actions with respect to individual employees or customers. These would be personally identifiable transfers, which would be permissible only under the exceptions in Article 26.

Sometimes an exception would apply, permitting the transfer between client and server. Some transfers would be based on unambiguous consent and others would be necessary to the performance of a contract. A ban on transfers from Europe to the United States would nonetheless pose significant problems for many client-server systems. Under guidance from attorneys inside or outside their companies, computer professionals would need to scrutinize the typical flows of data and prohibit all the transfers that did not fit within one of the exceptions. Many systems would not have any mechanisms in place for this sort of scrutiny, and establishing them could be costly. For companies with servers only on one side of the Atlantic, data that did not fit within an exception would presumably be illegal to transfer. The disruption of business operations, perhaps especially for small enterprises, could be extensive.

Intranets

The next step toward a less hierarchical system is an organizational intranet. An intranet is defined as a mechanism for sending data within an organization, using Internet protocols. The intranet may be the mechanism for implementing a client-server architecture, where computer professionals are typically required to maintain each server. More generally, however, the intranet may involve other ways to share data among an organization's computers. Using e-mail and Web browsers, a company may accumulate and transfer important information among ordinary personal computers. For instance, one employee may be designated to gather information about all employees who are interested in working on a new project or all customers who seem likely candidates for a new product. People from around the company may send e-mail to that employee, who may create a Web page with information about the initiative. Significantly, this data gathering, transfer, and communication can all take place on personal computers without any intervention or control by centralized computer management.

Companies are investing heavily in intranets based in part on the development of "fire wall" technology. Fire walls are designed to permit authorized people to enter the organization's intranet but to exclude all other users. Fire walls typically also place restrictions on the flow of certain kinds of programs and other information into and out of the system. Companies have strong incentives to implement good security for their intranets to avoid loss of commercially valuable information.

Intranets are significant today and their use is growing rapidly.[9] They are quickly becoming a vital way that companies manage information. One high-technology company, for instance, said, "We run the company off an intranet." Every department has its own files, which they maintain and post. There is no phone list, except on the intranet. "Our goal is to have it all up on the net, or on e-mail. That's how we publish data." Personnel lists, organization charts, information about benefits, company policies— all are kept in electronic form. In discussing the possible effects of the Directive, a knowledgeable person in the company said, "Without the intranet, you can't run your European sales offices or subsidiaries as part of the company."

We will say more later about the sectoral effects of the Directive and the extent to which exceptions can apply to important categories of data. For now it is sufficient to point out the variety of personally identifiable data that is likely to be included in organizational intranets. It seems likely that much of the data would be difficult to fit within the listed exceptions in Article 26.

For data that do not fit, a company would face unpalatable choices. The first would be compliance through new technology. Current intranet software, however, generally does not tag the country of origin of each piece of data, much less accompany the data with a judgment about the applicability of Article 26 exceptions. In discussions with intranet producers, it has been hard even to conceive of a technical fix.[10] The second choice would be compliance by training people throughout the organization in how to comply with European data protection rules. In the example discussed above, "every department has its own files," and every department

9. A February, 1997 report by Delphi Consulting and Xplor found "intranet use, virtually nonexistent in 1994, is now truly pervasive and accelerating. Thirty-seven percent of the organizations surveyed already have over 75 percent of their desktops connected to an intranet. Three years from now, over 82 percent of firms expect this . . . which essentially marks full deployment." "Companies Discovering the Value of Intranets," *Electronic Commerce News,* vol. 2 (February 10, 1997).

10. An exception may exist for specialized software that already includes a country code for each individual's data. Notably, software exists for human resources records that already tracks the individual's place of employment in order to comply with taxation, benefits, and other regulations. When personal data are tightly linked to a country of origin, technical fixes may be more feasible.

would therefore need to learn what is permitted. Such a continuing program in education would require a major effort for companies that may
have tens of thousands of employees worldwide. Smaller companies, which
lack the same level of in-house legal resources, would need to develop data
protection expertise and spread it widely among employees. Furthermore,
even after training, there are no guarantees that employees will necessarily
follow the rules.

Privacy advocates would favor this level of education about data protection rules. Organizations running intranets may decide that this level of
compliance effort outside of Europe is not worthwhile. This conclusion is
especially likely if European authorities do not consider training and related compliance efforts to be good enough to establish adequate protection by a company. (For instance, it is not yet clear how a training-based
program would be evaluated by officials if it were included in a self-
regulatory measure.) In such instances, the third choice is simply to exclude European operations from the organizational intranet. If transfers of
personal information from Europe to the United States are indeed prohibited, this last choice may be the only one for many organizations in the
affected sectors.

Extranets

Even further toward decentralized processing are corporate extranets.
We use the term "extranet" to refer to situations in which data move across
two fire walls from the sending organization to the receiving organization.[11]
Encryption and other security measures guard against unauthorized access.
Such an extranet is even more decentralized than an intranet because data
now flow among more than one organization.

The usefulness of an extranet can be seen in the case of a manufacturer
that shares data with its suppliers and customers. With its suppliers, the
manufacturer may insist on just-in-time delivery. The extranet helps make
this possible by allowing secure and rapid ways for manufacturers' computers to alert the suppliers' computers about precisely what parts will be

11. "Extranet" is also sometimes used to refer to situations in which an outside party, who does not
have a fire wall, is able to access data hidden behind a fire wall. An example is home banking, where
the individual consumers are able to cross the bank's fire wall and do transactions involving their
accounts. We chose the definition of extranet in the text, which highlights the use of two fire walls, to
emphasize the routine ways in which personal data are increasingly being shared among business
partners.

needed. On the customer side the manufacturer may link its computers with those of wholesalers and retailers, permitting more rapid and precise responses to consumers' needs.

Extranets are an important tool for coping with a global economy characterized by rapid changes, joint ventures, and flexible contracting. Companies in many industries have refocused their resources on their core competencies and decided to contract out tasks for which they are not specialized. Using an extranet, a company can contract out for needed services while retaining the ability to share data as if the task were still handled within the company. Examples could be as prosaic as having an outside company handle the payroll or as exotic as tailoring a database of proprietary technology that can be shared only among certain researchers in the two companies. In a global economy, it is increasingly likely that some parts of an extranet will be both in Europe and the United States.

The Directive poses obvious hurdles to the development of extranets. In essence, extranets create all of the compliance problems of intranets, only more so. An example was reported to us by a major company that was doing manufacturing for a project in the United States. The design work was being done by a company in Europe, which was partly owned by the U.S. firm. The design work was kept behind a fire wall on a secure Web site in Europe. The site contained personal information connected to the design, such as the names of the people who worked on various aspects of the project. To comply with the European country's existing data protection rules, the companies eventually decided that they could not permit the Web site to be accessed from the United States. Individual documents could be airmailed or faxed, but those working on the project were not permitted to use extranet technology to ship information from Europe to the United States.[12]

In this example, there might have been other ways to let the extranet link go forward. For instance, consent might have been obtained in advance from each person whose personal information was available on the European Web site. The example nonetheless suggests the variety of customer and employee information that may be available through extranets. Transfer of much of that information will not fit neatly within the Article 26 exceptions. Extranets, moreover, also face the additional restrictions

---

12. Under Article 3 (1) the Directive applies "to the processing otherwise than by automatic means of personal data which form part of a filing system or are intended to form part of a filing system." Mail or noncomputerized telecopies, which fit within this definition, are covered by the Directive. Article 32, however, allows member states to extend the time period until 2007 before most of the Directive's requirements apply to data already held in manual filing systems.

that apply to transfers to third parties, such as requirements of notice to the data subject and opportunity to object wherever the transfer is "for purposes of direct marketing" (Article 14(b)). The scope of these additional restrictions is discussed in chapter 7 in the section on direct marketing. In summary, though, the Directive could create substantial hurdles to the use of extranets between Europe and countries that do not have adequate protection.

The Internet: E-mail, Facsimiles, and the Web

The volume of business currently transacted on the Internet is less than on organizational intranets.[13] Privacy on the Internet, however, is of great long-term significance to the overall success of data protection efforts. First, about 100 million people are already connected to the Internet worldwide, and the number will undoubtedly continue to rise rapidly.[14] Second, most observers expect Internet business to climb steeply once a better infrastructure for electronic commerce is developed. Third, especially in the United States, polling data and news reporting show that concerns about privacy are strongly focused on Internet issues. The U.S. political response to the overall data protection debate is thus likely to be significantly shaped by Internet privacy concerns. Fourth, and most deeply worrying to privacy advocates, it is far from clear that there is any workable way to implement data protection laws on the Internet. Unless there is some satisfactory solution, some combination of law and technology, data protection efforts in general may become futile. At a minimum, data protection regulations will be harder to maintain when the same personal data are readily available elsewhere on the Internet.

The discussion here examines Internet privacy issues in connection with electronic mail, faxes sent or received by computer, and World Wide Web sites. In each setting the trend continues toward decentralized processing. Other trends identified at the beginning of the discussion of information technologies also continue: increased international flows of data,

---

13. Visa estimates that only $500 million to $600 million in goods and services were bought and paid for over the Internet in 1996. See "Questions Surround SET Pilots," *Electronic Commerce News*, August 18, 1997. This figure is expected to reach at least $7 billion by 2000. U.S. Department of Commerce, "The Emerging Digital Economy," available at http://www.ecommerce.gov/emerging.htm.

14. U.S. Department of Commerce, "The Emerging Digital Economy."

increased number and power of processors, lack of data protection expertise, and shifting advantages and disadvantages of data protection rules.

Electronic Mail

In just the past few years tens of millions of people have come to rely on electronic mail for many personal and business communications. A notable feature of e-mail is the ease and low cost of sending information across national borders. With a personal computer and an e-mail account, an ordinary user can now easily send personal information between Europe and the United States. The user can also attach large files packed with personal information. As Internet observer Tim May commented, "National borders aren't even speed bumps on the information superhighway."[15]

By its terms the Directive would appear to apply to a great deal of e-mail sent from Europe to third countries. As an initial matter it seems likely that sending an e-mail (or attaching a file to an e-mail) would come within the definition of "processing of personal data" in Article 2.[16] Purely personal e-mail would be exempted, but that exemption would be strictly limited by Article 3(2). Only e-mail "by a natural person in the course of a purely personal or household activity" would fall outside of the scope of the Directive. Other e-mail, such as for business, academic, or associational purposes, would apparently be governed by the data protection rules.[17] This conclusion, strict as it may seem, fits within the overall logic of the Directive—protection of fundamental privacy rights regardless of the technology by which the information is processed.

---

15. Timothy C. May, signature file end quote for numerous listserv postings.

16. In examining the definition of "processing of personal data" sending an e-mail that contained personal data would seem to involve "any operation or set of operations which is performed upon personal data." More specifically, sending the e-mail would likely qualify as "disclosure by transmission" or "dissemination." Attaching a file would likely involve "retrieval."

17. As with other areas where the Directive applies, transfers may be permitted under the exceptions in Article 26. For e-mail, an important exception may be the "unambiguous consent of the data subject." A person in Europe who sends an e-mail to an address in the United States may be considered to have consented to that transfer of personal information. Even under this fairly generous view of consent, however, many transfers would be difficult to fit under Article 26. The person in Europe, for instance, might send personal information about other people in the body of the e-mail or might attach files containing personal information. Often there would not have been consent to the transfer by the people named. In addition, e-mail addresses do not always reveal the country of the recipient, or the e-mail might be forwarded from one country to another, so the data subject may not realize that information is being transferred to a country lacking adequate protection of privacy.

At this point it is helpful to review how far we have come from the discussion of mainframes, for which the controller employed an entire staff of computer professionals. The Directive defines the controller as the person who "determines the purposes and means of the processing of personal data" (Article 2(d)). For e-mail, the controller may be an ordinary individual at home or at work with a personal computer. This typical user may "process personal data" by having an in box for mail, saving e-mails in various places on a hard drive, and forwarding messages occasionally. Touching on our themes for information processing, we see routine use of international transfers, a vastly increased number of computer operators, and processing by many people who are inexpert in data protection rules. Whatever the merits of data protection rules in the context of mainframe computing, compliance will be far more difficult to achieve in the case of these e-mail "controllers." Indeed, perhaps the data protection rules should not be extended to ordinary users who receive e-mails.

Application of the Directive to this ordinary user seems overly broad. Still, one can sympathize with the reasoning that led the Europeans to use broad definitions in setting the scope of the Directive. Instead of this "ordinary user," the controller may be a large corporation that harvests information from the many e-mails it receives, generates mailing lists and other business data, and markets the information to third parties. A blanket exemption for e-mail would allow systematic evasion of the Directive.[18] Companies that systematically gather e-mail to use in direct marketing may be risking punishment. Also e-mail is routinely used in organizational intranets and extranets, raising the compliance issues already examined.

Although the eventual treatment of e-mail under the Directive is far from clear, other areas are more likely to be the early focus for enforcement. Jurisdictional obstacles exist to enforcement against persons who simply receive an e-mail outside of Europe and fail to follow EU data protection law. More generally, the Directive was drafted before e-mail became anything like the phenomenon that it has so recently become. European officials are fully aware that additional work will need to be done to define a data protection approach to the Internet. The English Data Protection Registrar, for instance, has stated explicitly that it will not address Internet

18. Another concern, raised by one European official, goes to the practices of the Internet service providers or other entities that route e-mails to individual users. Such entities may accumulate a substantial database of information about the sources and destinations of messages. Furthermore, the messages themselves may be stored on backup tapes. Issues concerning the applicability of the Directive to ISPs are discussed in chapter 7.

privacy issues in its proposal for national legislation to comply with the Directive.[19]

Facsimiles

A fax sent or received by computer is a close relative of e-mail. Most personal computers today are equipped with fax software. If both the sender and receiver use such software, a computer file is sent from one machine over the telephone lines directly to the other. The result is identical to e-mail except that the fax is routed through the telephone network and not through the largely separate network used for Internet communications. When only one side is using a computer, the software can send a computer file to a fax machine, or receive a fax and save it as a computer file. To transfer personal information by fax in the form of computer files is as simple as making an international phone call.

Article 3(1) may be important to determining the extent to which faxes fall within the scope of the Directive. It states: "The Directive shall apply to the processing of personal data wholly or partly by automatic means, and to the processing otherwise than by automatic means of personal data which form part of a filing system or are intended to form part of a filing system." Our understanding is that processing of data by a computer, such as including it within a computer file, constitutes processing "by automatic means." Computer files can typically be searched and sorted in various ways, so we would expect that faxes retained as computer files would indeed fall within the scope of the Directive. By contrast, a traditional fax printed out would fall within the Directive only if it forms part of a filing system or is intended to form part of a filing system. If this analysis is correct, faxes received by a computer in a third country would seem to be subject to the same treatment under the Directive as e-mail. Once again, we might suspect that ordinary users would not need to fear an enforcement action in the near future. But once again, a company that systematically receives faxes and uses that data for direct marketing might be held responsible for illegal transfers to third countries. Here as elsewhere, the broad scope of the Directive may make it difficult for organizations to comply fully with the data protection rules as they are written.

19. "Data Protection and the Internet," available at http://www.open.gov.uk/dpr/internet.htm.

The Web

Privacy on the World Wide Web is likely to be a more hotly contested issue than it is for e-mail and computer faxes. These latter two do create problems under the Directive because they seem to fit within its broad scope and because they routinely assist the transfer of personal data across national borders. A large portion of international e-mails and faxes, however, are similar to telephone calls in that the person providing information from Europe knows the person receiving the information and consents to the transfer. Moreover, many e-mails and faxes that might raise issues under the Directive will be sent by entities in Europe that already are required to comply with data protection laws. Jurisdiction in Europe is typically available, for instance, with respect to a European office that transfers personal information by e-mail to the company's American office, such as through the company intranet.

Consent and jurisdiction, however, may be much bigger problems on the Web. Concerning consent, an ordinary user often will not know the identity of the person or organization that is hosting a Web site. The user often will not know about the site's privacy practices. Does it keep track of personal information and perhaps sell that information to third parties? Is a "cookie" being placed on the user's hard drive to track his or her movements in cyberspace? Even if a site claims to have privacy protections in place, how can the user verify that the policies are followed? In addition, the user also has no ready way to determine whether the site is within Europe, and thus clearly subject to the Directive, or else in a third country that may lack privacy standards. In light of all of these uncertainties, there may be little basis for assuming that an individual has consented to a site's uses of personal information.

There would usually be no difficulty in applying the Directive when the company operating a Web site has operations within Europe. The general choice-of-law rule is that a member state can apply its law where the processing is carried out through an establishment of the controller (Article 4(1)(a)).[20] The trickier issue arises where the controller is not established on EC territory. When the controller "makes use of equipment, automated or otherwise, situated on the territory" of a member state, that

---

20. For more detailed discussion of Article 4 and its choice-of-law rules, see Peter P. Swire, "Of Elephants, Mice, and Privacy: International Choice of Law and the Internet, *International Lawyer* (forthcoming).

nation can apply its law (Article 4(1)(c)).[21] One experienced data protection official stated in an interview that the "makes use of equipment" language would apply to Web browsing. On this view, a U.S. Web site "makes use of equipment" in France or Germany when a user accesses the site from one of those countries. This broad view would, for instance, apply the Directive to any Web site, operating in the United States or other third country, that is open to European visitors.

Our sense is that European data protection officials have not reached consensus on the applicability of the Directive to non-European Web sites. Even if the officials do pursue the broad understanding of Article 4, however, it is far from settled whether the international legal regime will conclude that creating a Web site makes the site operator subject to jurisdiction in every country of the world. We are likely to witness an extended period during which Web site operators located outside of Europe will hotly contest the applicability of the Directive to their operations. When an organization also has European operations, however, jurisdiction will be available against at least the assets in Europe.

With the consent and jurisdiction issues in mind, we are now in a better position to understand both the importance of the Web to the development of privacy and the difficulty of applying enforceable rules to it. The Web is important to privacy because of the huge numbers of users, the expectation that commerce increasingly will occur electronically, the detailed electronic records that can be created for each user and each transaction, the routinely international nature of transactions, the ease of transferring personal data from one controller to the next, and the possibility that information will be gathered without the consent of the data subject. From the European perspective all of these factors pose a threat to data protection because data processors in third countries might be able systematically to evade the Directive's goals.

Despite these compelling reasons to regulate data flows on the Web, the challenges to the data protection regimes are immense. Web operations continue the trend toward decentralized processing that has been a theme of our discussion. New personal computers, for instance, now typically come equipped with the software for building personal Web sites. The "controllers" of these sites are both incredibly numerous and untutored in data protection laws. Even within Europe, it is far from clear that a data

---

21. The member state cannot apply its law when "the equipment is used only for purposes of transit through the territory of the Community" (Article 4(1)(c)).

protection regime conceived for a limited number of mainframes can assure compliance in a world of pervasive personal computers. Outside of Europe, U.S. and other Web site operators are even less likely to comply with the Directive, and many of these operators may remain beyond the jurisdiction of European law. Web sites will also likely be established outside of Europe to process data in ways that are forbidden by the Directive, and it is far from clear that technical methods exist to prevent data from flowing to such sites.

We will return to the difficult questions of Internet privacy both in the discussion of direct marketing in chapter 7 and in the policy discussion in chapter 8. Certain conclusions do emerge, however, from the analysis here. For organizations that operate both inside and outside of Europe, there is a strong legal argument that Web operations are governed by the Directive. Data about named individuals cannot legally be sent to third countries that lack adequate protection unless one of the exceptions in Article 26 applies. This legal enforceability will only provide effective protection of data, however, if there is actual compliance by the many controllers in Europe and some legal and practical way to gain compliance from Web site operators elsewhere.

Laptops or Personal Organizers

Another category of information technology, laptop computers, creates additional problems in complying with the Directive because laptops carried by business travelers are likely to contain personal data. Accordingly, carrying such laptops from Europe to countries that lack adequate protection would appear to violate the Directive. The interim report of this book, released in October 1997, discussed the treatment of laptop computers in some detail. A disproportionate share of the comments on the report focused on laptops. This attention to the issue of laptops is understandable enough. Limits on the transfer of laptops from Europe to the United States would directly affect a great many travelers. Such limits would cause a considerable uproar, and they are correspondingly unlikely to occur in practice. Considerable uncertainly, however, clouds the legal treatment of laptops under the Directive. After analyzing their legal status, we advance a proposal that would address the concerns expressed by data protection officials while exempting laptops from restrictions on transfer out of Europe.

A modern laptop used by a business traveler has megabytes or gigabytes of storage on its hard drive. Personal data will almost invariably be stored in some of the files. For instance, a business traveler might compile information about business meetings taking place in Europe, perhaps including the names of persons at the meetings and things they said. The traveler would likely have computer files listing names, addresses, and other personal information about business contacts. The same sort of information might also be stored in a business traveler's "personal organizer," a typically smaller computerized device that is becoming increasingly popular.[22]

The text of the Directive seems to apply to transfer of these data out of Europe. We have already discussed the broad definition of "processing of personal data" (Article 2) and the narrowness of the exception for processing "by a natural person in the course of a purely personal or household activity" (Article 3(2)). A computer file of "purely personal" friends could be transferred out of Europe. Any business use, however, would bring the data within the scope of the Directive. For any sector that lacked adequate protection, the prohibition on transfer would apply both to a European businessperson traveling to the United States and to an American traveler returning home.

In a late 1997 meeting attended by U.S. and EU officials in which one of the authors of this study participated, there was a mixed reaction to the idea that laptops would be covered by the Directive. One senior EU official flatly stated that business use of laptops would not be covered by the Directive, but the official did not explain the legal basis for that conclusion.[23] A second EU official, in line with previous conversations with national data protection officials, said that laptops would be covered. This official stressed that a laptop might contain highly sensitive databases of personal information. In addition, the official emphasized the principle

22. Much of the information in these examples concerns persons who are identified in their business capacity rather than as private individuals. Although the two sorts of information are treated the same under the text of the Directive, there is substantial doubt whether information concerning a person's business activities warrants the same strict level of protection as more clearly personal information. The application of the Directive to persons in their business capacity is a recurring theme of our study, and is discussed especially in chapter 6 in connection with the rules applying to investment banking and commercial credit reports.

23. A similar conclusion was stated by John B. Richardson, deputy head of the European Union's delegation to the United States, at an October 21, 1997 speech at the Brookings Institution commenting on the interim report of this book. See "EU Delegate Optimistic over Prospect of U.S. Meeting European Privacy Standards," *Electronic Information Policy & Law Report*, vol. 2 (October 24, 1997), p. 1095.

that the Directive does not distinguish among technologies for transferring files to countries that lack adequate protection; transfers are treated under the same rules whether they are sent between mainframes, communicated within a company intranet, or carried in a laptop.

The second official's view, that laptops are covered by the Directive, is consistent with some experience under current national laws. That official reported that a laptop containing sensitive medical information was seized at an airport under Sweden's data protection law. A multinational company reports that, for employees regularly working at home with laptops, the company has been specifically directed to register under the German data protection law. Furthermore, the EU official pointed out that exempting laptops would create an easy way to evade privacy laws. Companies that could not otherwise transfer data could simply send the data out of Europe on laptops.

With the applicability of the Directive to laptops thus in some dispute, we turn to the derogations in Article 26. Business travelers might try to use the unambiguous consent exception. After all, a person who gives another person a business card would not generally object to having that information kept in that person's laptop. Persons attending a meeting with a business traveler can see the laptop, observe the traveler entering notes into it, and deduce that the laptop might be transferred to the United States or another third country. At a commonsense level the data subjects in such circumstances have likely consented to the data processing. The difficulty with this commonsense answer, however, is that it is contrary to the interpretation of "unambiguous consent" as stated in interviews with senior data protection officials. The clear message from these interviews is that notice to the data subject should state that the transfer will be made to a country that lacks adequate protection of privacy. The mere exchange of business cards, or the typing of notes during a meeting, would not give the data subject this sort of notice.

In responding to this EU position, one might hope that implicit consent in the examples used here would be enough to qualify under Article 26. Here and elsewhere the potential harm from the transfer would not seem large enough to require formal notice that the transfer will be made to a country that lacks adequate protection. Even if a broader interpretation of unambiguous consent is adopted, however, many laptops will still contain personal data that do not fit within any of the Article 26 exceptions. For instance, consider a U.S. salesperson who goes to meetings in Europe trying to build up a list of people to contact. Those contacts have not consented to having their names taken out of Europe. More generally, business travelers may pick up a wide range of information about individuals in the course of their business in Europe.

As a practical matter it is certain that European officials are not going to set up new customs stations in airports, scrutinizing laptops as people leave Europe. The unlikeliness of this picture, though, shows yet again the tension between the European data protection regime and modern information technologies. The Directive is set forth in a highly abstract way, equipped with definitions that sweep almost all data processing into the regulatory regime. Much of that data processing, such as the routine use of laptops and personal organizers, is widely accepted as desirable. A problem arises because of the gap between the apparent prohibition in law and the apparent permissibility in practice.

One approach to the laptop problem is essentially to rely on the discretion of enforcement officials. The vast majority of laptop users would know that they were unlikely to be subject to enforcement under data protection laws. Business travelers could thus board their airplanes with something approaching a practical immunity from enforcement. We suggest, however, that this discretionary approach is not desirable for governing the behavior of vast numbers of laptop users whose behavior may well be criminal under the plain meaning of the Directive and the applicable national laws. Our discussion in the previous chapter highlighted a number of difficulties with the purely discretionary approach, including the possibility, contemplated by the Directive, that individuals as well as officials can initiate enforcement actions.

As an alternative we put forward the suggestion that transfer of laptops and personal organizers out of Europe be expressly permitted even to third countries that lack adequate protection. This permission might be subject to two exceptions that address the concerns expressed by data protection officials. The first would concern sensitive data about ethnicity, religion, and the other categories listed in Article 8. In drafting this exception, perhaps the limits on transferring laptops would apply only to "substantial" transfers of sensitive data and to any transfer where there is intent to disadvantage the individual based on the information. Truly harmful transfers of sensitive data would thus be prohibited. Meanwhile, drafting the exception in this way would permit "incidental" transfers of sensitive data, such as where a laptop user lists the religion of a business contact to avoid violating that person's dietary restrictions.

A second exception could forbid the transfer of laptops and personal organizers where there is specific intent by the user to circumvent data protection rules about transfers to third countries. This exception addresses the concern that laptops and other portable computing devices (diskettes, personal organizers, and so forth) would be used systematically to evade the data protection regime. Suppose, for instance, that a company knew from a previous enforcement action that certain transfers are not permitted via the company intranet or other routes. That company should not be able to get around the restrictions simply by loading the data in a laptop. Enforcement would be appropriate against any such effort to evade the laws.

In putting forward this proposal, we are not committed to the details of the exceptions we propose. Data protection officials and the affected community can undoubtedly suggest improvements. We do believe, however, that it is important to gain further guidance about the treatment of laptops and other portable computing devices under the Directive. Portable computing devices will become more powerful and pervasive and will often contain significant amounts of personally identifiable information. It is not hard to foresee a time when most business travelers leaving Europe will carry some such device. If inadequate protection of privacy is found in some countries, or sectors of countries, there must be greater transparency about the legal rules governing laptops. The actions of routine users should not be illegal yet tolerated at the discretion of enforcement officials.[24]

Summary of Effects on Information Technologies

This chapter has traced the movement from mainframes to distributed processing. The trends are toward growing international flows of data, growing numbers and power of processors, and declining availability of data protection expertise (due to the much wider range of people who have the power to transfer personal data). One important theme is the great breadth of the Directive. It appears to forbid a wide range of routine and desirable transfers of data to third countries. Unless there is a finding of adequate

---

24. The means of promulgating such exceptions could range from the formal to the informal. Formal solutions would include amendment of the Directive itself or writing the exceptions into national law. Less formally, Directorate General XV or the Working Party might support such exceptions through official documents or in speeches.

protection in third countries such as the United States, a large portion of current transfers by intranet, extranet, and laptop computer could seem unlawful. The regulation of electronic mail, computer-based faxes, and Web transactions is even less clear under the Directive. For large organizations using mainframes, self-regulatory measures seem to be an especially promising approach.

4

Effects of Data Protection Laws on Electronic Commerce

This chapter examines the effect that data protection laws may have on the development of electronic commerce. By "electronic commerce" we mean the OECD definition of "commercial transactions occurring over open networks, such as the Internet. Both business-to-business and business-to-consumer transactions are included."[1] Assessing the effect of data protection laws on electronic commerce is important to an overall assessment of the desirability of the laws. Proponents have often claimed that good privacy laws will increase consumer confidence in doing business online and thus increase the amount of electronic commerce. To the extent that this claim is true the case becomes stronger for data protection laws. But those skeptical of regulation claim that it will tend to interfere with the operation of the free market, reducing electronic sales. To the extent that this claim is true, the adverse effects on electronic commerce become an argument against adopting data protection rules.

In this chapter, we develop the argument that data protection laws are impediments to free markets. Mandatory rules are especially likely to reduce electronic commerce in situations characterized by new business models, rapid innovation, products dependent on intensive use of personal

1. Organization for Economic Cooperation and Development, Committee for Information, Computer and Communications Policy, *Measuring Electronic Commerce* 3 (1997), available at www.oecd.org/dsti/sti/it/ec/prod/E_97-185.htm.

information, and an important role for new companies. These factors often exist for new businesses on the Internet, suggesting reason for caution about imposing strict regulation.

We then develop the argument that data protection laws may increase the level of electronic commerce. This argument has generally been expressed in terms of how privacy rules can improve consumer confidence. Polling data show that many consumers believe their privacy is at risk when they do business on the Internet, leading to less commerce than would otherwise exist. Although this argument is powerful in certain respects, we note important caveats. We conclude the chapter with an analysis, based on law and economics, of the key determinants of how data protection laws will affect electronic commerce.

Data Protection Laws as Impediments to the Free Market

In assessing the costs of regulation we assume that those subject to privacy rules are expected to learn what the rules require. Simply learning the meaning of data protection rules is no small feat. This book, with its focus on transfers to third countries, can address only some of the complexities arising under the Directive. Persons in each organization governed by the law will have to spend costly time understanding how the law applies to their organization.

Next, an organization must alter its behavior to meet the requirements of the legal regime. There could be large transition costs as the organization adapts its information processing to new requirements. Established practices must be changed, and employees must spend time adjusting old data and systems to the new rules. Experts may need to be hired to draft privacy disclosures or structure information systems to comply with the law. For a number of European countries, organizations must register their databases with a supervisory authority. Part of the transition, moreover, may include abandoning existing lines of business. Products and services that depend on processing personal information may need to be discontinued or reduced in scope. In chapter 7, when we examine the effects of the Directive on direct marketing, we explore specific ways that data protection rules might reduce Internet marketing.

Uncertainty about the meaning of the Directive would create additional costs, especially during the transition to new national laws. Consider the effect of new laws on companies planning to invest in the next generation of information systems. It is often difficult to determine the meaning of data protection laws both within Europe and as applied to transfers to third countries. Companies wishing to comply with the laws would probably want to delay purchase of new systems until uncertainty is cleared up. If they do implement a new system, but some practices are later ruled illegal, they would have to bear the expense of adapting to the unanticipated rulings. Similar incentives to delay introducing new products would exist for software designers, who could find it difficult to know in advance what privacy practices should be included in their programs.

Under standard economic theory, these compliance burdens would tend to reduce the overall amount sold in the affected industries.[2] Perhaps even more important, mandatory rules could prevent new products and services from being developed. This dampening effect is possible with any regulation, but the effect would be more dramatic with electronic commerce because of the rapid pace of change and the prominence of start-up companies. We know very little today about what business models will ultimately succeed in electronic commerce. Companies are experimenting with widely varying approaches for making money. The conventional wisdom shifts in "Internet time," where a year's worth of changes seem to happen in a month. As for start-up companies, many of the most prominent Internet companies—for instance, Netscape for browsers and related products, Yahoo! for search engines, and Firefly for the use of intelligent agents—have become internationally known very shortly after beginning operations.

Under conditions of rapid change, mandatory rules could have an especially strong effect in reducing innovation. A major concern is that regulation would be drafted with existing practices in mind, without taking account of as-yet-undiscovered ways to do business. Promising experiments may have to be abandoned because they conflict with one or another of the rules. In addition, even if regulators in good faith seek to create exceptions or adapt the rules, the change could come too late to get the innovation to market, especially in markets in which product cycles are often measured in months.

The dampening effect on innovation is especially acute for smaller and start-up companies. These companies typically are focused on their new

2. More precisely, the supply curve would be shifted inward due to the costs of learning the new rules, making the transition to required new practices, discontinuing products and services that conflict with data protection rules, and facing uncertainty about the lawfulness of products and services. The demand curve would be shifted inward because of the uncertainty buyers would face about the legal treatment of new information systems.

products, and do not have much regulatory expertise in-house. They may be physically distant from those who make regulatory decisions. In contrast to major companies, small companies usually have no representatives who can work closely with regulators. For all of these reasons, regulatory barriers that can be hurdled by major corporations may prove insurmountable to new or smaller companies.

The need to minimize regulation has been strongly recognized in major governmental studies on electronic commerce undertaken by the United States and the European Union.[3] These studies appreciate the advantages of market-driven, self-regulatory practices, especially during this early stage of the development of electronic commerce. Although the European Union white paper expressly states that privacy rules are appropriate for electronic commerce, it does not provide any detailed explanation of how to reconcile its general approval of market-driven approaches with required rules for data protection.

Thus there are strong reasons to suspect that mandatory rules will reduce electronic commerce. They are especially likely to have an adverse effect in a market featuring new business models, rapid innovation, products dependent on intensive use of personal information, and new companies.

The Consumer Confidence Argument

Supporters of government data protection rules have two significant arguments in response: that privacy laws will actually increase electronic commerce, primarily by increasing consumer confidence in how data will be handled, and that any reductions in electronic commerce are more than offset by the benefits of protecting privacy.

The consumer confidence argument builds on the intuition, often stated in conferences on privacy, that people will feel more confident doing business on line if they know that their personal information will be carefully protected.[4] After all, goes this argument, wouldn't you be more willing to buy on line if you knew your own information would not be released else-

3. "A Framework for Global Electronic Commerce," available at http://www.ecommerce.gov/framework; and "A European Initiative in Electronic Commerce," available at http://www.cordis.lu/esprit/src/ecomcom.htm.

4. For a thoughtful academic version of the argument, see Joel R. Reidenberg and Francoise Gamet-Pol, "The Fundamental Role of Privacy and Confidence in the Network," *Wake Forest Law Review*, vol. 30 (1995), p. 105.

where? Haven't you hesitated about doing certain transactions because you did not trust how the Web site would handle your data?

Assessing the consumer confidence argument is difficult, in part because both proponents and critics may have incentives to overstate their position. Those supporting the argument might be unrepresentative: privacy advocates might care unusually deeply about privacy. Some privacy advocates and data protection officials, furthermore, might not care whether electronic commerce is increased, but might find it politically useful to claim that it will be. On the other side, those who critique the argument could represent companies that engage in electronic commerce. Some companies may wish to conduct business in ways that would violate data protection laws. Others may act out of a general skepticism of regulation.

There are important reasons for believing the intuition that strong privacy laws would bolster electronic commerce. Polls show that 80 percent of U.S. consumers believe they have "lost all control over how personal information about them is circulated and used by companies."[5] A 1998 *Business Week* poll showed that 61 percent of non-Internet users cited privacy as a key reason for nonuse. This figure exceeds those for whom price was the reason by 10 points.[6] In a poll conducted by Alan Westin and Danielle Maurici, for those who said they were not likely to access the Internet in the next year, greater privacy protection was the factor that would *most* likely convince them to do so, outranking other factors such as reduced cost, ease of use, security of financial transactions, or more control over unwanted marketing messages.[7] One 1997 study, conducted by the Boston Consulting Group for TRUSTe, estimated that electronic commerce would double to over $12 billion in 2000 if privacy programs were widely adopted by commercial Web sites.[8]

5. Louis Harris and Associates and Alan F. Westin, "Equifax-Harris Consumer Privacy Survey 1995" (1995). This and other English-language surveys on privacy issues are available at http://www.privacyexchange.org. The percentage climbed from 71 percent in 1990.

6. "Online Insecurity," *Business Week*, March 16, 1998, p. 102.

7. Of five factors presented, nonusers rated their positive likely effect on using the Net as follows: privacy of personal information and communications would be protected, 44 percent; security of financial transactions was assured, 40 percent; use became less complicated, 40 percent; more control over businesses sending unwanted marketing messages, 36 percent; and cost was reduced, 35 percent. Alan F. Westin and Danielle Maurici, "E-Commerce & Privacy: What Net Users Want," Privacy and American Business and Price Waterhouse (June 1998), p. viii.

8. eTRUST Internet Privacy Study, "Summary of Market Survey Results" (1997), p. 20. The name of the sponsoring organization has since been changed to TRUSTe. See http://www.truste.org.

Such polling data and estimates are evidence of widespread concern about privacy. In addition, fair credit should be given to the statements of privacy advocates and data protection officials concerning the importance of consumer confidence. After all, these experts know far more than the average citizen about the uses actually made of personal information, some of which are surprising and upsetting to those who learn about them. The well-informed persons may represent how many people would feel if they discovered how the information is used. The experts may also foreshadow a reluctance to participate in electronic commerce until the uses of personal information are more widely appreciated.[9]

In light of the polling data and the statements of experts, it seems likely that reassurance on privacy would indeed lead some persons to engage in electronic commerce that they would otherwise avoid. We are not aware, however, of any empirical evidence that would allow us to compare this increase in electronic commerce with the possible decreases in electronic commerce that were discussed earlier. We can, however, identify two important caveats on the consumer confidence argument: the distinction between security and privacy and the leading role of business-to-business, rather than business-to-consumer, electronic commerce.

The Distinction between Security and Privacy

There is an important distinction to be made between security and privacy.[10] Security in this context refers to the problems that arise when a hacker or other unauthorized person gets information about a transaction. For example, there is a security breach if a hacker learns a customer's credit card number as the number is transmitted to the merchant. There is also a security breach when someone masquerades as a legitimate merchant to get the credit card number or other information. By contrast, privacy in this context refers to data protection: once a seller or other organization legiti-

---

9. Concerning the possible coming reluctance of customers to reveal their personal information, and possible business responses to this problem, see John Hagel III and Jeffrey F. Rayport, "The Coming Battle for Customer Information," *Harvard Business Review* (January-February 1997) available at http//www.hbsp.harvard.edu/graps/hbr/index.html.

10. For further discussion of the distinction between security and privacy, see Peter P. Swire, *The Uses and Limits of Financial Cryptography: A Law Professor's Perspective*, available at www.osu.edu/units/law/swire.htm (arguing that strong cryptography is extremely useful for security, but much less useful for protecting privacy).

mately receives personal data, who may have access to the information and what other uses of it are permitted?

Few would doubt that greater security would increase consumer confidence and lead to an increase in electronic commerce. The fear of stolen credit card (or debit card) numbers has been a frequently expressed worry about doing business on line.[11] More generally, customers are less likely to do business in any setting where they believe their money is likely to get stolen or the merchants are not likely to deliver the goods.

A combination of technological and legal solutions is in the process of increasing consumers' sense of security in cyberspace. On the technological side cryptography reduces the risk that credit card and other information will be stolen. Even cryptography that can be broken by experts, such as that built into widely used browsers today, likely promotes a significant sense of security in many consumers. Consumers probably know, in other words, that locks and other security measures are useful even when expert safecrackers would not be stopped. Another technological enhancement of security will come when credit card companies implement the SET (secure electronic transfer) or other new protocols.[12] Under these protocols, cryptography will protect the credit card number so that it cannot be seen by the merchant, by the merchant's bank, or in transit. Only the consumer and the consumer's bank will be able to link the transaction to a credit card number. Such protections would provide significantly more security in cyberspace than is true of current transactions, in which any waiter or telephone operator has access to the customers' numbers.

These technological protections are complemented by laws. For instance, breaking into a computer system is now a criminal offense in the United States.[13] This sort of rule is the cyberspace equivalent of no-trespassing and antitheft laws. Such laws do not, of course, eliminate trespassing or theft, but they undoubtedly help deter illegal entry. The legal system also limits the customers' security risks in other ways. For instance, U.S. law typically limits a customer's loss to $50 in the event of theft or other unauthorized use of a credit card.[14] In large part because of these techno-

---

11. See, for example, Scott Mendintz, "Are Your Theft Fears Overblown?" *Money* (June 1998), pp. 137–39; and Saul Hansell, "Internet Merchants Try to Fight Fraud in Software Purchases," *New York Times,* November 17, 1997, pp. D1, D8.

12. "SET Secure Electronic Transaction at Visa," available at http://www.visa.com/cgi-bin/vee/nt/ ecomm/set/main.html.

13. 18 U.S.C. §1030.

14. 15 U.S.C. §1643.

logical and legal protections, credit card transactions have established themselves as the dominant form of payment on the Internet.

This increased confidence in security sharpens the issue of the extent to which the growth of electronic commerce depends on government regulation of privacy. Consumers have considered on-line commerce generally risky. A 1997 survey by eTrust (now TRUSTe) and the Boston Consulting Group found that up to 40 percent of respondents do not make a clear distinction between privacy and security.[15] Now one can separate the analysis into the security risk to consumers, which is apparently becoming small, and the privacy risk. For proponents of the consumer confidence theory, the argument must become more nuanced: even where security risks are low, will consumers gain enough confidence from data protection laws to increase their use of electronic commerce? Privacy laws are likely to be significantly less important for bolstering consumer confidence if the security risk, and the accompanying risk of direct financial loss, is understood to be small.

Business-to-Consumer Electronic Commerce

A different critique of the consumer confidence theory is that consumer transactions constitute only a small part of electronic commerce. Even if privacy laws greatly affect consumer confidence, they may have a much smaller effect on overall electronic commerce.

Although the definition of electronic commerce is itself open to debate, we follow a study by the Organization for Economic Cooperation and Development in referring to "commercial transactions occurring over open networks, such as the Internet. Both business-to-business and business-to-consumer transactions are included." After surveying estimates of electronic commerce, the study concluded that "electronic commerce infrastructure and business-to-business electronic commerce represent the bulk of all electronic commerce."[16] The numerical estimates are inevitably based on less than perfect data, but it is clear that business-to-consumer sales are relatively small.

Electronic commerce infrastructure includes hardware (such as personal computers, routers, and servers), software to run this hardware and

---

15. eTRUST Internet Privacy Study, "Summary of Market Survey Results" (March 12, 1997), p. 12.

16. Organization for Economic Cooperation and Development, Committee for Information, Computer and Communications Policy, *Measuring Electronic Commerce* 3 (1997), p. 12, available at www.oecd.org/dsti/sti/it/ec/prod/E_97-185.htm.

electronic commerce packages, Internet service providers, and enabling services (such as electronic payments, authentication and certification services,
and advertising). Hardware sales are currently $10 billion to $30 billion,
although these estimates are for all Internet-related hardware, not just the
portion of Internet use dedicated to electronic commerce. The software to
run the personal computers, servers, routers, and support networks was
estimated at $300 million to $900 million in 1996, growing to over $4
billion by 2000. A growing software segment will be packages that allow
merchants to set up storefronts on-line, with estimates of over $3 billion by
2000. The OECD reported current estimates for Internet service providers
of $125 million in revenues; in the near future, however, this figure would
rise to $12 billion annually if 50 million people pay an annual fee of $240
for Internet access. Additional services, including directories, advertising,
authentication, and certification, will also develop. Advertising revenues
were more than $300 million in 1996 but are climbing rapidly toward a
possible $4.8 billion in 2000.[17]

The OECD report also gave estimates showing the dominance of business-to-business electronic commerce. For instance, General Electric alone
reported about $1 billion in this commerce in 1996, higher than estimates
of *total* business-to-consumer commerce. General Electric has announced
plans to move all of its procurement, over $5 billion, to the Internet by
2000, and other companies are moving in the same direction. Hardware,
software, and travel services are particularly prominent sectors for on-line
purchasing by businesses, although the range of purchases is expanding
rapidly. In addition, this leadership of business-to-business commerce is
not surprising, since it constitutes roughly two-thirds of all gross output in
traditional commerce.[18]

In business-to-consumer sales, the transactions usually contemplated
in popular discussions of Internet commerce, total sales for 1996 were estimated at $500 million, although obviously growing rapidly. The largest
categories of tangible goods have been computers, clothing, and food and
drink. The OECD estimated electronic sales in these sectors at $120 mil-
lion, $90 million, and $40 million in 1996. The Internet may prove par-

17. OECD, *Measuring Electronic Commerce*, pp. 10, 12. Advertising targeted at consumers was
treated by the OECD as part of the infrastructure of electronic commerce, presumably because the
money is paid by someone other than a purchaser, namely, the advertiser. Advertising might also be
considered part of business-to-consumer electronic commerce, on the theory that the advertising
revenues exist due to consumer use of electronic commerce sites.

18. OECD, *Measuring Electronic Commerce*, pp. 11, 12, 24.

ticularly attractive, though, for intangible products, including software, financial services, and entertainment because these can be received directly through the network. Estimates for entertainment are especially imprecise, considering that the largest categories are likely pornography and gambling, for which accurate sales figures are elusive at best.

The OECD statistics on electronic commerce infrastructure, business-to-business sales, and business-to-consumer sales help place in better context the claim that privacy laws will increase consumer confidence and thus overall electronic commerce. Data protection laws apply to many transfers of information in the business setting. Procurement by companies, for instance, often will include named information concerning the persons involved in ordering, servicing, and administering the sale of goods and services. In this electronic procurement, companies will care a great deal about the security of the transaction. They will wish to protect against financial loss and loss of valuable property such as trade secrets. By contrast, it seems unlikely that the level of company purchases will depend heavily on data protection laws. Procurement decisions, including the decision to use the Internet, are not likely to turn on legal rules about how employees' names are circulated in the buying and selling companies.

More generally, many of the transfers analyzed in this book involve nonconsumer information, often flowing within and between companies through intranets, extranets, and other modern networks. These transfers include a great deal of named information. The consumer confidence argument, by its own terms, applies only to business-to-consumer transfers. These transfers are important and interesting, and chapter 9 addresses some of the distinctive legal issues that arise as individuals enter cyberspace in ever larger numbers. But the bulk of electronic commerce occurs and will occur outside of the consumer realm. To the extent data protection rules affect consumer confidence, they may help increase the level of business-to-consumer commerce. For the other, larger sorts of electronic commerce discussed here, data protection regulations seem more likely to be restraints on growth, which can be justified, if at all, by the benefits of protecting privacy rather than because they contribute to the growth of electronic commerce.

Law and Economics as Justification for Data Protection Rules

Debates about privacy laws have too often been fought between those supporting more regulation (because this will increase consumer confidence

and protect privacy) and those supporting less regulation (because regulation will interfere with the workings of the free market). A more useful
path is to consider more generally *when* legal rules increase commerce.
This more general inquiry has been a central concern of the law and economics school of scholarship. The general conclusion is that commerce
will be promoted by clear assignment of property rights and efficient rules
for making and enforcing contracts.[19] Commerce will also be increased by
good criminal and tort laws that reduce the costly efforts people must otherwise make for self-protection.[20] Recast in this way, the claim of privacy
advocates could be that strong privacy laws will contribute to a regime of
good property, contract, tort, and criminal laws for electronic commerce.
In this context, greater consumer confidence in privacy protection is one
possible result of a well-crafted legal regime. The actual level of electronic
commerce, however, will depend on many legal and market considerations
in addition to the level of confidence in privacy.

There is a growing number of studies that draw on law and economics
insights to analyze privacy rules. Initial articles by Richard Epstein and
Richard Posner were skeptical of the efficiency of privacy rules and emphasized their interference with agreements that would otherwise be reached
between buyers and sellers.[21] Subsequent studies by Peter Huang, Jerry Kang,
Richard McAdams, Richard Murphy, Paul Schwartz, and Peter Swire have
all discussed situations in which this skepticism may be misplaced.[22] The
later articles have focused on ways that property and contract rules, which
are closely related, might improve the market for personal information. In
property terms the data subject might be allocated certain rights, so that

19. See, for example, Richard A. Posner, *Economic Analysis of Law*, 4th ed. (Little, Brown, 1992),
pp. 32–35, 89–96.

20. Richard A. Posner, "An Economic Theory of the Criminal Law," *Columbia Law Review*, vol. 85
(October 1985), p. 1193.

21. Richard A. Epstein, "Privacy, Property Rights, and Misrepresentations," *Georgia Law Review*,
vol.12 (Spring 1978), pp. 463–65; and Richard A. Posner, "The Right of Privacy," *Georgia Law
Review*, vol. 12 (Spring 1978), p. 422.

22. Peter H. Huang, "The Law and Economics of Consumer Privacy versus Data Mining," avail-
able at http://papers.ssrn.com/paper; Jerry Kang, "Information Privacy in Cyberspace Transactions,"
Stanford Law Review, vol. 50 (1998), p. 1193; Richard H. McAdams, "The Origin, Development,
and Regulation of Norms," *Michigan Law Review*, vol. 96 (November 1997), pp. 425–27; Richard S.
Murphy, "Property Rights in Personal Information: An Economic Defense of Privacy," *Georgetown
Law Journal*, vol. 84 (1996), p. 2381; Paul M. Schwartz, "Privacy and the Economics of Personal
Health Care Information," *Texas Law Review*, vol. 76 (November 1997), p. 1; and Peter P. Swire,
"Cyberbanking and Privacy: The Contracts Model," abstract of talk for Computers, Freedom, &
Privacy '97, San Francisco (March 1997), available at http://www.osu.edu/units/law/swire.htm.

data could not be used without permission of the property holder. In contract terms the consumer contract between the individual and the seller (or other parties) might be established in ways that correct for market failures. Some of these market failures—high transaction costs to consumers in bargaining for privacy or the incentives for organizations to overuse personal information when consumers cannot easily monitor their behavior—were discussed in chapter 1. More analytic and empirical work will need to be done to clarify the situations in which the market failures are significant enough, and mandatory rules efficient enough, so that the rules would actually increase electronic commerce. For now, however, we can note that debate has been joined on the efficiency of rules for data protection.

Some additional lessons from the law and economics method are reasonably straightforward. First, the effects of data protection laws on the level of electronic commerce will clearly depend on the type of law. A draconian law, such as a ban on all transfers of personal information to third parties, would certainly reduce electronic commerce. Instead of saying that data protection laws will foster or reduce commerce, it is important to analyze particular rules or sets of rules. Throughout the book, we consider the possible efficiency or inefficiency of various aspects of the Directive.

Second, some sorts of laws will indeed increase electronic commerce. Examples come from our discussion of how to promote security in Web commerce. Criminal laws against theft are likely to increase security and commerce. (Such laws may be ineffective, but they would not ordinarily reduce commerce unless written in ways that criminalize desirable behavior.) Contract laws that limit customers' financial loss may also increase security and promote commerce.

Third, we would expect data protection rules to have the greatest effect on promoting commerce in certain transactions in which individuals fear that sensitive personal data will be revealed. One definition of sensitive data is contained in Article 8 of the Directive, which includes "revealing racial or ethnic origin, political opinions, religious or philosophical beliefs, trade union membership, and the processing of data concerning health or sex life." Some commercial transactions would expose this sort of data. Some people might refuse to get health care because of fears about privacy. For instance, if transcripts of sessions with a psychiatrist (whether in person or in virtual space) are made available to insurers and third parties, some people will stop talking to psychiatrists. Strong data protection laws seem most likely to contribute to the growth of commerce for these and other transactions involving sensitive material.

Fourth, both for sensitive and less sensitive data, the influence of data protection laws will depend on the laws' effectiveness compared with alternative methods of protection, including technological fixes, market discipline, and self-regulation. The matter of comparative institutional competence arises repeatedly in this book. If laws or self-regulatory measures are universally violated, they will do little to increase commerce. The same is true for technological protections of privacy if they are routinely evaded by countermeasures. In each instance, the impact on electronic commerce depends on the extent of compliance and the perceived extent of compliance. In considering the results, we cannot avoid analyzing the extent to which data protection laws will be followed and the ways these laws work together with other ways to promote privacy.

Conclusion

This chapter has attempted to assess the ability of data protection laws to increase electronic commerce. Despite the broad claims by proponents and opponents of the laws, there can be no general conclusion about their effects. The analysis here has shown ways to assess whether particular privacy rules or sets of privacy rules are likely to increase commerce.

Polling data and personal intuition support the argument that people will engage in more electronic commerce if they believe their privacy will be protected. Any such increases may be offset by the decreases in commerce that can occur because of interference with the free market. Progress on maintaining security may reduce the overall perceived riskiness of electronic transactions; if so, privacy alone may not be as important to consumer confidence. Also, business-to-business transactions often dwarf the scale of business-to-consumer transactions, but privacy laws are especially unlikely to significantly increase business-to-business electronic transactions. The adverse effects of privacy laws are thus more likely to predominate in business-to-business settings.[23]

Legal rules can increase electronic commerce. In discussions of law and the Internet, there has been a romantic hope that cyberspace could

---

23. In Chapter 6 and elsewhere, we argue that the net beneficial effects of data protection rules are especially unlikely to exist for many business-to-business transactions, where the risk to privacy is relatively low and the costs of compliance can be substantial.

somehow avoid the legal regulation that exists in real space.[24] Our discussion of law and economics showed, by contrast, that commerce can actually be encouraged by rules that are part of an efficient regime of contract, property, tort, and criminal law. Some contractual or property rights to data protection, for instance, might foster commerce, although very expansive rights can be drafted that would undoubtedly constrain it. A beneficial effect on electronic commerce may be especially likely for transactions involving sensitive data. Benefits are also more likely where there is a regime that takes advantage of markets, technology, self-regulation, and mandatory rules as appropriate in context.

Finally, even if particular data protection laws do reduce commerce, they may still be desirable when the harm is outweighed by gains from increased privacy protection. Valuing any such trade-off will be extremely difficult and will vary with the beholder. Rather than attempt to assess that trade-off here for the entire range of possible data protection laws, we have sought to clarify the situations in which privacy laws are most likely to increase or decrease electronic commerce.

24. For a persuasive critique of this notion see Jack Goldsmith and Lawrence Lessig, *Grounding the Virtual Magistrate*, available at http://www.law.vill.edu/ncair/disres/groundvm.htm.

5

Privacy Issues Affecting Many Organizations

This chapter examines issues under the Directive that will affect a wide range of businesses and other organizations. It explores issues arising with respect to employee records, auditing and accounting, business consulting, and call centers and other worldwide customer service. It also examines the general effects of the Directive in terms of the differences in language between Article 7, which authorizes data processing within the European Community, and Article 26, which authorizes transfers to countries that lack adequate protection. Later chapters will look at effects in particular sectors and settings, such as financial services and other industries with large transborder components.

In considering the effects of the Directive, one should keep in mind its applicability not just to corporations but to other organizations that process personal data. It applies to nonprofit organizations and governments, although with some special provisions in both instances. With respect to employee records and other personal data, however, the usual rule is that the Directive governs processing of personal data by all organizations.

Human Resources Records

Every organization keeps personally identifiable records about its employees. It likely keeps employee directories, containing phone numbers, e-mail addresses, job titles, and so forth. It also keeps information about the experience of employees, including their resumes, job skills, and evaluations of their performance. It keeps detailed records about benefits, often including salary, pension, dependents and beneficiaries, and medical information. Other categories of personal information might easily be added.

For organizations that operate in more than one country, there are many circumstances where these records may be transferred across borders. Employees throughout the world may use an e-mail or telephone directory. Persons putting together a new project might need to learn about the job skills of many people in order to gather the needed expertise. Managers involved in setting salary and other benefits may compare how similar employees are compensated elsewhere in the company.

The likelihood of transborder transfer of employee information is increasing rapidly, in part because of the continued growth of world trade and the number of transnational enterprises. Transborder data flows are increasing especially quickly, however, due to the continued spread of information technologies such as client-server systems and corporate intranets. The Directive's limits on transborder data flows directly confront organizations' expectations to be able to circulate information freely inside their fire walls and other security arrangements. Operations in the United States and other countries will often expect to exchange employee data with European operations. Wherever there is no finding of adequacy, however, sending data to third countries risks violating the data protection regime.

The difficulty of compliance hinges on interpreting the exception that allows transfers when "the data subject has given his consent unambiguously to the proposed transfer" (Article 26(1)(a)). The "has given" language suggests that the consent must be given before the transfer; it is apparently not permitted to make transfers based on an assumption that the employee will agree to them after the fact. But what action by the employee constitutes consent? Can an employee be assumed, simply by working for an organization, to have given permission to have his or her name included in its directory? If not, is it enough for the organization to give notice that an employee can refuse such a use, or must it get affirmative permission for the transfer?[1]

A related issue is how to define the permissible scope of consent to transfer. At the time of hiring a person, may a company get consent to use personal information for "all internal management purposes"? If this broad

---

1. A separate issue is what level of compliance is likely if organizations are not permitted to require employees to be included in directories, task force membership rosters, and other organizational activities.

scope of consent is permitted, organizations might get consent from most employees at the time of hiring, and compliance with the Directive will be relatively easy. Based on conversations with data protection officials, however, the likely answer is that data protection laws are not satisfied by this sort of total waiver allowing all internal uses of personal information, all around the world.[2] To comply with the Directive, every organization that sends employee data across borders will need to learn what sort of consent requests are sufficient.

As for consent to transfer data out of Europe, a senior European Commission official stated that consent would be valid under Article 26 only if the data subject were informed specifically that transfers would be made to countries that lacked adequate protection of privacy. This sort of specific warning might induce some employees not to agree to the transfers. In that event, organizations would need to develop procedures for ensuring that the data are retained in Europe.

A final problem concerning consent involves personal information that an employee ordinarily would not get to see. For instance, consider confidential investigations or performance reviews that are not ordinarily disclosed to the employee. It is far from clear under the Directive when and whether employees would have a right to access these records and what sort of consent might be required to waive that access or permit transfer to third countries.

Applying this analysis of consent to the categories of data, it is possible that employees retain at least the right to refuse to be listed in organization directories. Under a stricter reading the organization may be required to get permission before including a person's information in such directories. A similar conclusion applies to dissemination of an individual's resume or list of job skills. In these and related circumstances, the data subject often is understood only to consent to a particular use of the data. If the same data are later used for a different purpose, it may be necessary for the organization to gain consent once more. Here and elsewhere, there is unavoidable vagueness in terms such as "different use" or "different purpose." Controllers, however, are responsible under the Directive for not making the transfer unless proper consent has been granted.

---

2. This sort of global waiver, which would apply to uses that are unspecified even as to category, might be thought to run afoul of Article 6(1)(b) that data be "collected for specified, explicit and legitimate purposes and not further processed in a way incompatible with those purposes."

Additional considerations may limit the ability of an organization to transfer employee medical and other records across borders. Article 8 places special limits on processing sensitive data, including data concerning health, sex life, trade union membership, and racial or ethnic origin. The provisions in Article 8 governing sensitive data are complex; organizations processing such data should be alerted to the power of member countries to pass unusually strict rules regarding them. Processing sensitive data may be especially restricted because of the widespread European view that employees often lack bargaining power and thus are coerced by employers. This concern is perhaps most strongly built into German law, in which consents may not be considered voluntary unless agreed to by unions or work councils.

When unambiguous consent is not present, the organization may find other exceptions that permit transfer of the data to third countries lacking adequate protection. In some instances the transfer might be necessary for the performance of a contract, or the business information may be in a public register (Article 26(1)(b) and (f)). In addition, as proposed in the next chapter, it may be possible gradually to define certain named information as outside the scope of the Directive, especially where the information is processed for purposes of making a decision about the employer rather than the employee.

In summary, it is difficult to assess how burdensome it will be for organizations to get consent from employees to transfer personal data within the organization but across borders. As the burden becomes greater, we can describe some of the likely effects. There may be applications for which it is not worth gaining consent from each employee: directories and job skills databases might be developed for other countries but not for Europe. Information technologies such as intranets that are designed to create the free flow of information within an organization might not be usable in Europe for human resources applications. As a result, new information technologies might be adopted sooner in other countries than in Europe. Where managers are outside of Europe and cannot readily receive employee information, the limits on transfers may prove a disincentive to including European personnel on projects. In general, data protection rules concerning employees would simply be one additional cost to doing business in Europe; it might be easier for firms to place their employees elsewhere.

A great deal of clarification will be required under the Directive and national laws about how human resources records are to be treated. Organizations that have not paid close attention to data protection laws may suffer rude shocks when their standard practices turn out to violate European law. Human resources software may need extensive revision to comply with data protection rules. Running the server from the United States or routinely creating databases with employee data might very well be illegal. Because all organizations maintain human resources records, and a great many routinely transfer these records across borders, the treatment of employee records may be one of the most widespread and serious compliance problems under the Directive.

Auditing and Accounting

In an era of transnational business the accounting and auditing functions of companies require increasing transfer of information across borders. To carry out these functions, auditors and accountants must be allowed to examine the documentation of transactions. This documentation often includes personally identifiable information. The Directive thus challenges the ability of transnational firms to follow accepted and appropriate procedures for audit and accounting.[3]

A few examples can give a sense of how regularly auditors receive personal information. For companies that sell to people on credit, auditors necessarily learn the names of individual customers as they perform spot checks on accounts receivable.[4] Auditors also scrutinize the payroll. They might pay special attention to complex retirement plans and medical benefits, where payroll mistakes are especially likely but where sensitive information is often in the files. Audits of banks also include attention to individual loan files. Auditors learn personal information as they check to ensure that the files contain proper documentation. One might easily multiply these examples.

A next question is how often this personal information is transferred from Europe to the United States in the course of auditing and accounting

3. The discussion here concerns the ability of the accounting and auditing industry itself to transfer data to third countries. An entirely different issue concerns whether accounting and audit firms might be useful in performing special audits for compliance with data protection rules. For instance, a privacy code of conduct might specify that a third-party auditor would examine a company's compliance with the code.

4. Other examples involving consumers could include warranties, service contracts, affinity programs such as frequent flyer miles, and any other item appearing as an asset or liability on the company's balance sheet.

operations. Such transfers are already significant and are likely to increase, as shown by three overlapping categories of transfers. The first is the accumulation of information within a transnational company or group of companies. Managers in one country need to have effective control of their company's operations in other countries. The managers expect to receive reports from overseas operations and to perform audits to ensure their accuracy. Those audited might be in the same company as the managers, in an affiliated company, or in an outside company such as a subcontractor. By its terms the Directive appears to limit access to personal information by both internal and external auditors. A ban on transfers could undermine the ability of U.S. management to oversee European operations. Among other effects, this would tend to deter U.S. investment in Europe by making it riskier.

A second category involves transfers from a company to its external auditing firm or transfers among personnel of the auditing firm. A European company may wish to hire American auditors or, perhaps even more commonly, it may wish to hire auditors with operations in both Europe and the United States. Multinational teams of auditors are often appropriate for work on multinational companies, and information is ordinarily shared within the auditing team, perhaps through linked computer databases. A ban on transfers could obviously interfere with the ability of European companies to hire an auditing team with any members in the United States.

This control on hiring U.S. auditors becomes especially difficult in light of the third category, which involves transfers of auditing information to track international transactions. Somewhat different problems would arise for large and small companies. For large companies with extensive European operations, the history of the Bank of Credit and Commerce International illustrates the danger of confining auditing operations to separate countries. By shuttling assets among countries, BCCI was able to hide billions of dollars in losses and avoid legal action for years. In the wake of the bank's collapse, world banking regulators have adopted a system of "consolidated supervision," in which regulators in one country ordinarily oversee an international bank's consolidated operations.[5] As applied to nonbank multinational corporations, one would similarly wish to have con-

---

5. On consolidated supervision see Raj K. Bhala, *Foreign Bank Regulation after BCCI* (Durham, N.C.: Carolina Academic Press, 1994), p. 109.

solidated auditing. If the Directive blocks this consolidation, there may be an increased risk of BCCI-type scandals in the future.

For smaller non-European companies, or larger companies with limited operations in Europe, there would be no sensible way to justify hiring separate auditors there. An import-export company or a company with a modest sales force in Europe would expect to have unified auditing from its home office in the United States. Prohibiting transfer of personal information would prevent routine and desirable audits from taking place.

For all of these categories of transfers, the Directive may pose substantial obstacles if the United States or its accounting sector is not found to have adequate protection. Moreover, it is not clear that any of the exceptions in Article 26 can readily solve the problem. Auditing is governed by a contract between the company and the auditor; data subjects rarely have any reason to be aware that their files are being examined for auditing purposes. For this reason, it would seem odd to get unambiguous consent from the data subject, or to try to argue that the transfer is necessary for performance of a contract concluded in the interests of the data subject.

The most promising exception may be that the transfer "is necessary or legally required on important public interest grounds, or for the establishment, exercise or defence of legal claims" (Article 26(1)(d)). One might readily believe that important public interest grounds support having strong auditing procedures in place. One might similarly believe that proper auditing is necessary for a corporation to avoid legal claims that would otherwise result.[6] Despite the logic of these arguments, the vague terms of Article 26(1)(d) provide only modest comfort. Their applicability to auditing is not established, and if they apply, it may take considerable experience to determine what transnational transfers are permitted.

An alternative approach for auditing and accounting would be for the Europeans to recognize that industry practice is a sufficient safeguard to permit transfers to the United States. Auditing firms work under an expectation of confidential treatment of their clients' information, and data protection law could recognize the practical assurance of privacy offered by this tradition of confidentiality. Significantly, individual accountants are subject to discipline if they improperly disclose client confidential information.[7]

---

6. We discuss later, in the financial services section, the distinct issue of how accounting rules may justify public disclosure of information that would otherwise be considered private.

7. American Institute of Certified Public Accountants, *Code of Professional Conduct,* §301.01, Confidential Client Information, available at http//www.aicpa.org/about/code/et 301.htm.

If these established industry practices are not considered an adequate guarantee of privacy, accounting firms might agree to adhere to self-regulatory measures such as model contracts to provide an additional level of assurance to European authorities that good practices are being followed. We return to the general usefulness of self-regulatory measures in chapter 8 on policy recommendations.

Business Consulting

In many respects similar to auditing and accounting, business consulting to multinational corporations often involves transfers of personal data across borders. Information is transferred from the client to the outside consultant and among international teams of consultants. It is commonplace for a consultant to access the client's database remotely. A consultant in the United States thus might readily expect to draw upon data in a client's European operations. Within consulting firms, it is common to assemble a transnational team to work with transnational companies. Team members expect to be able to share information freely among themselves to get the job done, without concern for whether the information flows across a national border. On an even more mundane level, consultants travel a great deal on different jobs and might easily fly from Europe to the United States with data about identifiable individuals in their laptops. If the United States, or the relevant sector in the United States, is not found to provide adequate protection, the legality of all of these transfers would be subject to doubt.

Some areas of business consulting are especially likely to involve transfers of personal information. Consulting on personnel and employee issues often requires the consultant to have access to information about named individuals. The same applies for companies that sell to the general public and wish to receive advice about how to manage their customer accounts. By contrast, consulting on purely financial issues generally does not require the consultant to see personal information.

It is not clear what Article 26 exceptions would apply to business consulting. First, it may be more difficult to establish the "important public interest grounds" exception for consulting than for auditing. Second, perhaps consulting contracts could be considered necessary for the performance of a contract "in the interest of the data subject" (Article 26(1)(c)). The argument for such a position would stress that data subjects are benefited if the company handling their data is well run. The contract between the client and the business consultant would thus be "in the interest of the data subject." Third, a different way to comply with the Directive, while permitting consulting by persons outside of the European Union, would be to "scrub" the names out of the data provided to the consultants. This anonymization, however, may reduce the usefulness of the consulting to the client and may be expensive. Since consultants in the European Union would not similarly be affected by the ban on receiving named information, these costs of anonymization would be a competitive disadvantage for non-EU consultants.

Call Centers and Other Worldwide Customer Service

As a company offers ongoing service to a customer, it may need to transfer the customer's records to the persons providing that service. If the customer is in Europe, and the person providing the service is in the United States or another third country, problems can arise under the Directive.

An example is call-in customer service centers. The call-center market is growing rapidly, from an estimated $7 billion in 1998 to about $18 billion in 2002.[8] All of a company's call-in centers may be outside the European Union. Alternatively, calls may be routed outside the European Union during certain hours of the day or to handle an overload at European call centers. When the customer calls in, the customer's records will typically be pulled up by the person providing service, and the service can then be rendered. Similar examples of customer service include warranties and service contracts. In each instance, transfers of personal data may occur from Europe to the person in the United States or other country providing service.

Servicing customers internationally is likely to become increasingly common. International telephone rates are expected to decline with the development of new technologies and the promised liberalization of telecommunications regulation. Lower phone rates will expand the range of situations in which it makes sense for customers in one country to be serviced from another country. An especially important change will be toward servicing over the Internet. Customers will go to a company's Web page and send e-mail describing the problem. For instance, if software does not

---

8. Keith Dawson, "Can Outsourcers Best Handle Customer Service?" Teleservice News, June 8, 1998, p. 10.

work, the customer may e-mail from Europe to the United States, and customer records will be consulted by the employee providing the service.

Under the Directive it may be possible to get customer consent to transfer personal information to third countries (Article 26(1)(a)). The clearest case for compliance is probably when the customer is asked for consent at the opening stage of a service call, before an employee receives the data outside Europe. The customer can then refuse the transfer and can seek servicing in another way. As an alternative, the customer might be asked to consent at the time of initial sale to transfers of information in future service calls. Data protection authorities, however, might be especially skeptical about situations in which the customer is led to believe that he or she must consent to transfers as a condition for receiving the good or service. Authorities might be most skeptical when the seller has significant monopoly power, and the customer therefore has little effective alternative to having the data transferred to a third country. Here as elsewhere, guidance under the Directive and national law would be very useful to organizations in learning how to comply with data protection rules.

In some circumstances, the transfer would be necessary for the performance of a contract in the interests of the data subject (Article 26(1)(b)). Suppose that a customer wishes to use a warranty or service contract, and the only servicing center is outside Europe. For the company to fulfill its promises to the customer, the transfer must be made to a third country where servicing personnel can use customer records to assist them. As with other uses of this exception, the transfer is permitted only for information that is "necessary" to the performance of the contract, not for broader categories of information.

When neither of these exceptions readily applies, a company may choose to move its servicing operations into a member state or some other country that does have adequate protection of privacy. If this proves too costly, some forms of servicing may not be available to customers in Europe. The relative effectiveness of customer consent, use of the "necessary for the performance of a contract" exception, or movement of servicing operations into Europe is hard to assess without more detailed knowledge of the affected industries and their cost structures.

Article 7 and Article 26 Processing

A different way to understand the general effects of the Directive is to focus on the differences in the language of Article 7 and Article 26. Article 7 provides that personal data may be processed only if they meet one of the listed exceptions. For the most part, the exceptions in Article 7, which permit processing within the European Community, match the exceptions in Article 26, which permit transfers to countries that lack adequate protection. For instance, processing is permitted when there is unambiguous consent, when it is necessary for the performance of a contract, or to comply with legal obligations.[9]

The two Articles differ, however, in two potentially important respects. The relevant part of Article 7(e) allows processing within the Community that "is necessary for the performance of a task carried out in the public interest or in the exercise of official authority." The analogous provision in Article 26(1)(d) requires that transfers be "necessary or legally required on *important* public interest grounds" (emphasis supplied). There thus appears to be an ill-defined category of processing that is permissible within Europe because it is "in the public interest," but cannot be transferred out of Europe because there is no "important public interest ground."

A second potentially significant difference arises under Article 7(f), which allows processing that "is necessary for the purposes of the legitimate interests pursued by the controller or by the third party or parties to whom the data are disclosed, except where such interests are overridden by the interests or fundamental rights and freedoms of the data subject." No similar provision permits transfers under Article 26. Article 7(f) is potentially very expansive, because of the range of "legitimate interests" that might justify processing personal information. In assessing the effects of the Directive on transfers to third countries, however, any processing authorized exclusively under Article 7(f) creates a substantial problem. Data processed under Article 7(f) generally will not be transferable to third countries under Article 26.[10]

Discussions with data protection officials and other knowledgeable people suggest that not much attention has been paid to the issues arising under Article 7(e) and (f). It is not clear what processing would be permitted exclusively under these provisions. As the Directive is written into national law, however, and applied to concrete situations, the prominence of these provisions may rise. Any data processed within Europe exclusively

---

9. The precise language for exceptions (a) through (d) varies in a few places, but the main effect appears to be the same for both Articles 7 and 26.

10. To be legal, transfers would likely have to qualify under the contractual provisions of Article 26(2).

under these provisions likely will not be transferable to third countries that lack adequate protection.

Conclusion

This chapter has discussed certain issues under the Directive that will arise for many organizations, commercial and noncommercial. We have investigated effects on basic business functions such as employee records, accounting and auditing, business consulting, and customer service. We have also explored the implications of the differences between Article 7, which authorizes processing within the European Community, and Article 26, which permits transfers to countries that lack adequate protection.

Without ignoring the other significant compliance problems discussed in this chapter, the issue of employee records is likely to be of the greatest concern to the greatest number of organizations. If there is a restrictive understanding of consent by employees to transfers, many routine business practices may be considered illegal. Organizations would then face a difficult choice between complying with the strict consent procedures, despite the cost and loss of operational flexibility, or adopting procedures for blocking transfers out of Europe of records that may have legitimate uses in other parts of the organization.

6

The Financial Services Sector

Careful attention to financial services is important because the use of international financial services is nearly coextensive with international trade itself. Almost any international transaction requires international movement of financial information, often in personally identifiable form. In addition, capital is typically more mobile than labor and goods. International transactions are thus especially common in transactions involving capital. Moreover, the authors of this book have extensive backgrounds in the study of financial services. It is in this sector, therefore, that we have had a particularly rich context for assessing the effects of the Directive. By analyzing financial services in some detail, we can identify issues that are relevant to compliance in other situations.

This chapter moves systematically through financial services, including payments systems, sale of financial services to individuals and corporations, investment banking, compliance with securities and accounting rules, and individual and corporate credit histories. It concludes with a proposal to treat information about persons in their business capacity less strictly than information about persons in their individual or personal capacity.

Payment Systems

The transfer of information in a wire transfer or other international payment generally is permitted under the Directive. Problems arise, however, with respect to the transfer of additional information about payments, such as where mainframe processing takes place outside Europe for credit card payments made in Europe. Payments also raise the question of the extent to which additional, or secondary, use can be made of data once they have lawfully left Europe under one of the exceptions.

Imagine that a person in Europe wishes to wire payment to the United States. To make the payment work, the payor's name, account number, and size of the transaction must be transferred from Europe to the United States. The customer's bank can transfer the information out of Europe because transfers are permitted where they are "necessary for the performance of a contract between the data subject and the controller" (Article 26(1)(b)). In practice, however, the customer's bank may transfer payments information containing personal information to other banks within Europe. Along the way, various entities may handle the information. It appears that these entities could indeed transfer the personal information out of Europe, because the transfer would be "necessary for the conclusion or performance of a contract concluded in the interests of the data subject" (Article 26(1)(c)). Indeed, discussions with informed persons suggest that these exceptions in Article 26 may exist in large measure because of the efforts of banks and other entities engaged in international payments.

Similar analysis applies to credit card payments. Consider a European traveler in the United States who wishes to purchase a $500 item in New York. Authorization for the purchase must come from a computer system in Europe, and the question arises whether it is permissible to transfer the personal information to the United States. In this instance one might argue that the customer has given unambiguous consent to the transfer of information (Article 26(1)(a)). A strict interpretation of the Directive, however, might question whether proper consent has been given, because the customer might never have been specifically informed that personal data would be transferred to a country lacking adequate protection of privacy. Even if unambiguous consent does not exist for the transfer, however, other exceptions to Article 26 likely apply. Transfer of the authorization from Europe seems necessary for completion of the purchase and is in the interests of the data subject.

The outcome is the same when an American wishes to use a credit card to buy an item in Paris. A request for authorization must leave Europe and be received by a U.S. computer system. That transfer of the customer's data seems necessary for completion of the purchase and in the interests of the data subject. Transfer must also be permitted so that the merchant can receive proper payment from the customer, the customer's bank, and the merchant's bank.

Less clear is exactly what other data about the sale can be transferred back to the United States. Imagine, for instance, that the U.S. credit card company has a fraud protection program, where it routinely matches a customer's proposed purchases against a profile of the customer's buying history. To operate the program, the credit card company may wish to have more detailed information from the merchant than is required simply to ensure proper payment. If this information is not available, the credit card company may need to address the fraud problem in other ways, such as through higher annual fees or fees on transactions for which the antifraud information is not available. In terms of complying with the Directive, the credit card companies may seek unambiguous consent by the customer to the antifraud program; alternatively, the antifraud information might be considered necessary to the performance of the contract.

The Directive may cause particular problems when credit card processing is done outside of Europe for European transactions. For instance, a company with its mainframe in the United States may process a wide range of information that includes transactions and customers in Europe. In these instances, the transfer of data out of Europe may no longer be necessary to complete the transaction, as it was in the case of the European traveler who wished to get authorization for a purchase in New York. The centralization of processing in the U.S. mainframe may have many economic advantages. Setting up a new mainframe center in Europe may be prohibitively expensive. As discussed in the chapter on information technology, however, this sort of mainframe processing would likely be prohibited under the Directive; but it is an excellent place for a contract or code of conduct solution under Articles 26(2) or 27.

Another crucial issue for credit card operations is secondary use, that is, the use of personal information in ways other than the purpose for which it was collected. As a general matter, secondary use of data is probably more common in U.S. industry than in European countries that have well-established data protection regimes. Credit card companies in the United States, for instance, might track holders' purchases and sell lists of likely customers to direct marketers.

There is a significant argument that secondary use of this sort would indeed be permitted once the personal data have lawfully been transferred out of Europe. The plain language of Article 26 supports the position that personal data, once transferred to a third country under one of the exceptions, are no longer subject to the Directive. Notably, Article 26(1) provides that "Member States shall provide that a transfer . . . may take place" for the exceptions listed in Article 26(1). The mandatory "shall" supports the argument that compliance with an exception is sufficient to allow the transfer. (That language does not apply to transfers permitted under Article 26(2), the contracts provision.) This reading was confirmed by a senior data protection official of the European Commission in an interview. On this view, once credit card or other personal information is transferred to the United States under an Article 26 exception, the Directive, including its limits on secondary use, no longer governs processing of the data. The same data protection official made the point, very persuasive in this context, that this understanding of Article 26 weakens the claim that the Directive has extraterritorial effect on third countries. If the official is correct, once the data lawfully leave Europe, the Directive no longer applies.

Important caveats, however, should be noted. First, Article 26(1) also says that the derogations apply "save where otherwise provided by domestic law governing particular cases." Although the scope of member state authority here is not very clear, each country apparently retains some authority to limit the derogations in "particular cases." Second, some knowledgeable people suggest that Article 26 is limited by mandatory language in earlier articles of the Directive. For instance, Article 6(1)(b) says, "Member States shall provide that personal data must be . . . collected for specified, explicit and legitimate purposes and not further processed in a way incompatible with those purposes." Similar mandatory language exists for many of the other requirements of good data protection practices.[1] The question then arises how the mandatory language requiring good data protection practices, in Article 6 and elsewhere, is to be interpreted with the language in Article 26. For data that have lawfully moved to a third country, does Article 26 mean that the Directive no longer applies, or does Article 6 mean that European data protection rules are required in connection with those data? The answer to this question has considerable practical consequences. To return to the credit card example, if Article 6 controls, then the mainframe processing center in the United States would need to follow all European rules for handling data originating in Europe. For instance, data about an American traveler's purchases in Europe would presumably be subject to European rules. Information about European

---

1. Similar protective language, with terms such as "shall provide" or "shall prohibit," occurs in Articles 7, 8, 10, 11, 12, 14, 15, 16, 17, 18, 19, and 21.

purchases could not be combined with information about American purchases, at least unless the data subject gave unambiguous consent in advance.[2] Under this reading, where Article 6 trumps Article 26, the credit card company might need to set up separate databases and separate programs for processing, depending on whether the data originated in Europe.

Another important limit may exist even if we conclude that the Directive no longer applies once data have been lawfully transferred to a third country. At several points in our discussion, we highlight what self-regulatory measures can do to allow compliance with the Directive. Under the Directive, it appears that data protection authorities could condition approval of SRMs on assurances that processing in third countries will comply with data protection requirements. Organizations that rely *entirely* on the derogations in Article 26(1) for transfer of data to third countries may be able to rely on the reading of Article 26 confirmed by the European Commission official. That reading will not be sufficient, however, for organizations that cannot fit all of their transfers into the derogations and that seek to use SRMs. These organizations, if they rely on SRMs, may thus find their processing in third countries to be governed by European standards.

Sale of Financial Services to Individuals

People purchase a wide array of financial services products, including securities, mutual funds, and insurance, and they take out loans. Legal treatment under the Directive varies according to where certain actions take place.

First, suppose that the buyer and seller are both in Europe, and the transaction takes place entirely in Europe. The seller does data processing in the United States. This situation is the same as when a credit card company processes European transactions in the United States. For mainframe processing, we have suggested that the desirable approach is to use self-regulatory measures. Processing could then proceed in the United States with the specified privacy practices. Another possibility is to seek unambiguous consent in advance from the customer to transfer the data out of Europe.

2. More precisely, information about European and American purchases could not be combined if the processing center in the United States used the American data in any way inconsistent with European data protection requirements.

Next, suppose that the buyer and seller are in Europe, but action must be taken in the United States to complete the transaction. For instance, the decision about whether to underwrite the insurance or loan might be made in the United States, or the person may be purchasing mutual funds or securities that are sold only in the United States.[3] For these examples, the customer is dealing with a broker or other agent in Europe. The situation here would be like that discussed in connection with payments systems: transfer of the data from Europe seems necessary for completion of the contract and in the interests of the data subject (Article 26(1)(b) and (c)). Note that the scope of these exceptions is potentially narrow: only the information that is necessary for completion of the transaction can be transferred, so there are limits on the ability of the American entity to build a dossier on the customer.

Finally, suppose there is a direct sale with the buyer in Europe and the seller in the United States. For purposes of this discussion, assume that licensing laws do not prevent such sales of securities, insurance, or other financial services. The situation then becomes an example of direct marketing, as discussed in chapter 7. Although direct sales may take place internationally over the telephone or by mail, the number of international sales is likely to rise steeply because of the Internet. Sales of financial services will constitute one potentially significant part of the debate. The larger issue will be how direct marketing and Internet commerce will be handled more generally.

Sale of Financial Services to Businesses

Businesses as well as individuals purchase securities and insurance and take out loans. During the transaction the seller often learns personally identifiable information about key people in the company that is buying financial services. In general, the Directive applies in the same way to financial services purchased by businesses and individuals. The focus on business purchases, however, helps us appreciate how reinsurance and loan participations might be especially affected.

---

3. Various rules currently restrict the ability of citizens of one country to buy financial services from other countries. For instance, European citizens generally are not permitted to buy U.S. mutual funds. These sorts of rules may soon change, however, as negotiations continue to liberalize trade in services. The analysis here concerns what transfers of personal information are permitted under data protection laws when other laws do not prevent the transaction.

Reinsurance

Suppose that a European business buys insurance from a European insurance company. For large policies the insurance company may not wish to expose itself to the full risk of loss. It therefore may follow common practice and buy reinsurance, so that the reinsurance company pays for any loss above a specified amount.

To assess its own risk and set its prices, the reinsurance company may need to know a good deal about the insured entity and its important personnel. In various situations reinsurers receive a copy of the underlying insurance contract, which often includes personally identifiable information. For instance, reinsurance can be issued on a "key man" policy, with payment due if the president or other important person in a company is no longer able to work. The reinsurer for such a contract would wish to see medical and other information about this person.

For situations in which reinsurers receive personal information, the Directive poses obstacles to the sale of reinsurance by entities in the United States or other countries that are not found to have adequate protection. Sending the underlying insurance information to the reinsurer would appear to be a transfer permissible only under one of the exceptions in Article 26. In terms of getting unambiguous consent, the problem is that the personal information is about a particular employee; consent may need to be passed from the employee to the company to the insurer to the reinsurer. If the insurer is in Europe but the reinsurer is in a third country, the need for consent may be triggered only at the point that the insurer seeks to do business with the reinsurer. It may be difficult at that point to go back and get employee consent. The problem can be mitigated if employees routinely give such consent in the course of the insurance application.[4] According to at least one European official, that consent would specifically need to state that transfer may occur to a country that lacks adequate protection of privacy. As for other exceptions, it is far from clear that the reinsurance contract is necessary for the performance of a contract concluded in the interest of the data subject. After all, the insured is fully protected by the original insurance company, and the reinsurance contract simply allocates risks among various insurers. In short, it may be difficult to fit reinsurance within any of the derogations.

---

4. The analysis here suggests that additional boilerplate, gaining that consent, could be inserted into standard insurance contracts.

Participations

The same sorts of problems arise in the sale of loan participations. In this sort of transaction a bank may make a large loan to a corporation. Rather than take all the risk of the loan's going bad, the bank may sell off participations (parts of the loan) to other banks and investors. As with reinsurance, investors who are taking on risk will often wish to see the underlying documents, which may contain personally identifiable information. Once again, it is hard to see how transfers out of Europe of personal information would be permitted under the Directive.[5] An effect of the Directive could thus be to reduce the ability of banks in Europe to sell participations to non-European investors.

American banks might argue that the transfer is permitted under Article 26(1)(d), which permits transfers that are legally required for public policy reasons or for the defense of legal claims. American banks are under a general legal duty to act in a "safe and sound" manner, and detailed regulations exist to implement this general duty. American banks might thus argue that they are legally required to receive the underlying loan documents, including any personal data contained therein. Assessing this argument requires an interpretation of Article 26(1)(d). On the one hand, it is not legally necessary for the U.S. bank to buy the loan participation, so perhaps the exception does not apply. On the other hand, it may be legally necessary for the U.S. bank to get the underlying document if it is to buy the loan participation, so perhaps the exception does apply. Here again one gets a sense of the many unanswered questions that business must face in learning how to comply with the Directive.

Investment Banking

Investment or merchant banking constitutes a highly visible part of the financial services sector. For many of these banks' financial transactions, personally identifiable information may be included in documents and related databases. Many transactions are international and involve sharing information between European and American offices of one or more investment banks. The Directive may create other major problems with respect to market analysis and especially hostile takeovers. It also may cre-

---

5. For some transactions it may be possible to get consent in advance from each person named in the documents transferred to the third country.

ate other obstacles to the ability of European firms to raise money from United States or other third-country investors.

Market Analysis

An important role of investment banks is to analyze particular companies and industries. As they study a company, the bank's analysts often become aware of personally identifiable information. Transborder data flows may occur, for instance, when European companies send information to U.S. analysts or when analysts in Europe and the United States communicate about a company. By its terms the Directive governs flows of all named information to market analysts outside of Europe.

Companies often work closely with market analysts, because the companies believe that cooperation will tend to create stronger support in the market for their securities. These communications may include discussion of identifiable individuals, such as the possible successors to company leadership or the possible hiring of a key technology or marketing person. It is not clear that such communications are permitted under the Directive, especially when the information is sent to third countries. The identified individuals typically would not have given their consent to the communication in advance, unless prominent people in a company are assumed to have accepted the risk of publicity because of their high position. Perhaps communications with market analysts can be understood as fitting within Article 26(1)(c) of the Directive as transfers of information "concluded in the interest of the data subject." Even if such transfers are generally in the interest of the named individuals, because conversations with market analysts increase the stock price, there may be transfers for which this benefit does not exist. For instance, the analyst might make a sell recommendation for a security, which tends to be contrary to the interests of the individuals in the company.

Hostile Takeovers

One result of market analysis is the decision in some cases to pursue a hostile takeover of a target company. Because the action is hostile, it is difficult to say that transfer of the information is "concluded in the interest of the data subject" (Article 26(1)(c)) in the target company. In such a situation it thus appears that transfer to third countries of named information may not be permitted.

One possible solution is to say that the use of market analysis in the occasional hostile takeover can be permitted as part of the broader category of "market analysis," where "market analysis" is generally "concluded in the interest of the data subject" (Article 26(1)(c)). If this solution is not accepted, the transfer of personally identifiable information to the U.S. offices of investment banking firms would seem barred by the Directive (unless the treatment of such data in the United States is "adequate").

To the extent transfer of these data is barred, it will create an incentive for customers to employ investment banks in Europe whenever it will be useful to gain personal information about employees of the target company. Because many potential takeover targets have European operations or European subsidiaries, even if they are based elsewhere, this incentive to hire European banks may apply often.[6]

Another possible approach is discussed at the end of this chapter. A distinction can be drawn between processing data about people in their individual capacity and processing data about them in their business capacity. Market analysts gather named information that is used to make decisions about the *company*, not the individual employee. If this distinction is accepted under European law, market analysis and hostile takeovers would be far less affected by implementation of the Directive.

Due Diligence

Before a security can be publicly issued in the United States, the issuing company must use "due diligence" to ensure that its statements comply with U.S. securities laws. The purpose of these rules is to make certain that investors, especially small investors, receive accurate information about the issuing company. Failure to carry out due diligence can result in large liability for the directors, officers, accountants, lawyers, and investment bankers involved in the securities issue. To carry out these due diligence obligations, lawyers and other agents of the corporation typically examine enormous amounts of information, including personal information, that exist in the company's files wherever it does business.

---

6. In commenting on this section, one data protection official observed that U.S. investment banks would also have an incentive to find solutions to the apparent limits on their participation in hostile takeovers in Europe. As we discuss further in chapter 8 on policy recommendations, privacy advocates and data protection officials hope that the Directive will encourage U.S. and other companies to adopt stricter privacy practices or support reforms of laws and industry codes protecting privacy.

Can personally identifiable information be transferred from Europe to the United States in the course of due diligence? There would appear to be a solid argument that such transfers are "necessary or legally required on important public interest grounds" (Article 26(1)(d)). The transfer should also be legal in order to permit "defence of legal claims" by the parties that can be sued if they do not comply with the due diligence requirements (Article 26(1)(d)).

Private Placements and Other Sales to Europeans

Investment banks sell products to investors, who may be individuals or corporations. In many ways, the relationship is similar to direct marketing: the investment bank may keep records about customers to match its offerings with each one's taste. Under U.S. securities laws, public offerings are much more expensive to issue than "private placements" to sophisticated investors, some of whom are in Europe. Private placements are an important part of the overall market.

Investment banks thus face the familiar question: what information can be transferred to the United States about European customers concerning past transactions and customer preferences? For instance, if the customer knows the security is being sold in New York, does that constitute "unambiguous consent" for the data about the transaction to be kept in New York?

Other Issues for European Companies Raising Money in the United States

Apart from the due diligence requirements, there are other reasons companies with European operations may wish to convey information that is not already public to investors outside Europe. These investors may wish to see underlying documentation about the company and its key personnel. In many high-technology and other start-up companies, for instance, the track record of these people may be more important to investors than balance sheet information. The transfer of such information may not be strictly necessary under securities law, but may be important to the successful completion of the transaction. Is such a transfer, according to Article 26(1)(c), "necessary for the conclusion . . . of a contract concluded in the interest of the data subject"? If not, does this mean that the European company must gain unambiguous consent from each person named in the transfer in order to seek funding outside Europe?

Mandatory Securities and Accounting Disclosures

Corporations in the United States and Europe face a variety of obligations to disclose certain information, sometimes including personally identifiable information. Securities and accounting activities provide an excellent vehicle for examining the meaning of Article 26(1)(d), which allows a transfer where it "is necessary or legally required on important public interest grounds, or for the establishment, exercise or defence of legal claims." The terms of this exception are vague enough that it is difficult to determine what transfers would be permitted under it.

Legally Required Disclosures

Some corporate and securities provisions legally require disclosure of certain information. For instance, a rule of the U.S. Securities and Exchange Commission requires disclosure of the name and compensation of certain top officers of a corporation that publicly issues securities. Those officers may include Europeans. It would seem that the SEC requirements should constitute "important public interest grounds" that permit transfer of the personal information. The same result should apply to other SEC disclosure rules, such as the wide-ranging disclosure obligations at the time a public security is issued.

Disclosures Required by Accounting or Stock Exchange Rules

Companies in Europe and the United States are subject to a variety of accounting requirements for public disclosure. For instance, UK accounting rules require publication of information such as directors' remuneration, pensions, and loans from the company. Stock exchange or legal rules in Europe and the United States require publication of sales and purchases of stock by corporate officers. How does the Directive treat situations in which disclosure is not required by law but is required by stock exchange rules or under generally accepted accounting principles?

Disclosures That Are Not Strictly Required

A company may wish to disclose more information than is strictly required by legal, accounting, or stock exchange rules. One reason is that it may prudently wish to err on the side of disclosure. A policy of overdisclosure may reduce the risk of enforcement actions and avoid criticism that the company has underdisclosed. Another reason is if the company agrees with the public interest grounds that motivate the requirement and wishes to vindicate those grounds more fully through additional, voluntary disclosure. For instance, one could imagine that a company would disclose the remuneration of more of its officers than is strictly required. Can additional disclosure of this sort be justified as "necessary . . . on important public interest grounds" (Article 26(1)(d))? If not, the Directive might forbid transborder flows of personal information that goes beyond the strict requirements of legal, accounting, or stock exchange rules. In these cases, companies might seek to get consent from the individuals to disclose such information.

Individual Credit Histories

Lenders and other parties contribute information about individual consumers to credit agencies. Accurate and complete credit histories help consumers by allowing credit to be made available more freely and on better terms than if lenders faced greater uncertainty about an individual borrower's history. In an increasingly global economy, more people will engage in transactions in both Europe and the United States that are relevant to their credit history.

Providing Information to Credit Agencies

The Directive would seem to pose significant obstacles to the transfer of credit history information out of Europe. This is not surprising, because credit agencies assemble just the sort of detailed dossiers on individuals that are a chief concern of a data protection regime. A credit history may contain sensitive and embarrassing information. Mistakes in the file can harm people badly if as a result they are wrongfully denied employment or a home mortgage. For these reasons, one might expect in any data protection regime that credit histories would be regulated carefully.

Credit histories are especially strictly regulated in the United States under the Fair Credit Reporting Act.[7] Recall that Article 25 of the Directive permits adequacy to be shown sector by sector. Under the FCRA, indi-

---

7. 15 U.S.C. § 1681 et seq.

viduals have many of the rights that are embodied in the Directive, including the right to access their files and to correct mistakes.[8] In light of these detailed protections, there is a strong argument that the definition of adequacy in Article 25 is satisfied in the United States for individual credit histories. Even if there is no general finding that the United States has adequate protection, the category of individual credit histories might be included on any "white list" of categories where protection is adequate.

As an alternative, the major credit agencies may be natural parties to enter into data protection contracts, subject to approval by European authorities. The credit reporting industry is dominated by a small number of companies. These companies run the sort of mainframe systems that we have suggested are the most natural settings for contracts under Article 26(2) or codes of conduct under Article 27. Furthermore, because of the FCRA, credit reporting agencies in the United States already have in place many of the practices that the Europeans would wish to include in data protection contracts.[9]

Receiving Credit Reports

The discussion thus far on credit histories has focused on the permissibility of transferring data into credit agency databases. Somewhat different issues arise when information is transferred out of those databases. The information is no longer flowing into a small number of mainframe computers, each of which may be subject to a contract approved by European authorities. Instead, it is flowing to perhaps many entities, including potential employers and companies deciding whether to grant credit.

Once again, a strong argument exists that sectoral law under the FCRA should qualify for adequate protection. The FCRA sets various limits on who may legally access credit reports. The information, moreover, is sub-

---

8. For an examination of the 1996 revisions to the FCRA, see Peter P. Swire, "The Consumer Credit Reporting Reform Act and the Future of Electronic Commerce Law," *Electronic Banking Law & Commerce Report*, vol. 1 (November-December 1996), p. 4, available at www.osu.edu/units/law/swire.htm.

9. Even if the credit reporting sector in the United States is not found to be adequate, and contracts are not created in the area, other exceptions in Article 26 may apply. For instance, those wishing to transfer information to credit reporting agencies could get consent from the data subject. In addition, one could argue that such transfers are necessary for the performance of a contract concluded in the interest of the data subject. In this instance the contract would be between the credit agency and the entity that reports information to that agency. The benefit to the data subject would be an accurate and complete credit history, which would assist the data subject to receive credit in the future.

ject to the requirements that people can access and correct it in their own credit histories. The Federal Trade Commission has specified oversight power. In light of these protections, there should be a finding of adequacy.

Unambiguous consent may also be achievable when credit information is to be transferred out of Europe. The individual can consent to the transfer as part of the application for employment or for credit. Similarly, receipt of the credit report may be necessary for the performance of the contract: an employer or creditor may need to see the information before hiring the individual or making the loan. Here as elsewhere, however, compliance problems will mount if the Directive is interpreted to govern secondary use by those receiving the data in a third country. American employers and lenders will often be unfamiliar with European data protection law, and may not have any special procedures for handling personal data that are transferred out of Europe. If the Directive is understood to govern secondary use of data within third countries, then individuals may be unable to send their credit histories out of Europe, even when they specifically wish to do so. The burden of these limitations would likely fall most heavily on European residents, whose European credit history is likely to be most important to business decisions.

Corporate Credit Histories

Credit reports are also compiled on businesses. Most of the data are not personally identifiable. A commercial credit report typically includes, however, information about the people who conduct the business that is the subject of the report.[10] Could a commercial credit report on a European company that includes such information permissibly be sent to the United States? This question has considerable practical importance because it is common for U.S. companies to review commercial credit reports before doing business with other companies. European companies would be at a disadvantage if reports on them had no information on the business principals. They would lose business opportunities. Small and medium-

---

10. In many instances, the information in the commercial credit report would be of the sort that senior business executives would expect to be public, such as their title and work address. The analysis in the text primarily focuses on that sort of personal data. In other instances, "key executive" reports might provide more sensitive investigative information about lifestyle, health, and other topics. Because highly personal information is included in the report, the appropriate analysis would seem to be to treat such information as an individual credit history.

sized enterprises, in particular, would suffer because knowledge of the business history and qualifications of their principals often is as important to credit decisions as is knowledge of the performance of the business.

Data protection authorities may decide that information about business principals that is part of a commercial credit report should not be considered personal information at all. If, however, they do view the information as within the Directive, whether they give the information white list treatment would have to depend on company practices and industry codes, since there is no commercial credit analog to the Fair Credit Reporting Act regulating consumer credit reporting. Commercial credit reporting is essentially unregulated in the United States. The language of Article 25 of the Directive does, however, allow for data protection authorities to find adequacy based on "professional rules and security measures which are complied with in that country" (Article 25(2)). Moreover, Paul Schwartz and Joel Reidenberg, in their study of U.S. privacy laws conducted at the request of the European Commission, found that the leading U.S. supplier of commercial credit information maintains significant data protection for the information it collects about business principals.[11] Data protection authorities thus have an important basis for a finding of adequacy.

If there is no white list treatment for corporate credit reports, the focus may turn to consent by the data subject. One possibility is to find that a person's decision to conduct business publicly is in itself consent to permit collection of information about his or her business conduct. (A similar conclusion might apply, for instance, to information about senior officials in the context of hostile takeover or market analysis.) If there is no finding of this sort, the analysis becomes similar to the discussion of human resources records, where an important question is how broadly consent can be given. Compliance will be easier if a broad consent is permitted, perhaps by having executives agree that their personal information can be transferred "when it is in the corporate interest" or "for use in corporate credit reports." Such consent may be easy to secure from the sorts of important personnel whose data would appear in corporate credit reports. By contrast, if the consent must be more specific, or if it must be granted each time personal information is included in a credit report, the process would become more burdensome.

---

11. Paul M. Schwartz and Joel R. Reidenberg, *Data Privacy Law: A Study of United States Data Protection* (Charlottesville, Va.: Michie 1996), p. 287 (discussing Dun & Bradstreet).

Information on Persons in Their Business Capacity

In the discussion in this chapter about investment banking and commercial credit reports, a crucial first question was whether the named information is considered within the scope of the Directive. By its terms the Directive applies to all processing of personal information, except processing by "a natural person in the course of a purely personal or household activity" (Article 3(2)). This extremely broad definition means that the Directive, and its limits on transborder data flows, may apply to a wide range of information about individuals that is gathered in the course of business activity but not focused on individuals. As just discussed, commercial credit reports generally include information about the individual principals of the business. Investment bankers and other market analysts unceasingly gather information about important persons in the companies they are analyzing or considering for inclusion in possible transactions. For these industries, application of the Directive to transfers about business information could affect the essential flows of information needed to carry on the business of the investment bank or credit report company. Other examples of company information could be highly relevant to the discussion in chapter 3 about a company intranet. Consider a few examples of named information that might be subject to the Directive: the names of people who attend a business meeting, the names of people at other companies who might be useful to contact in connection with a company project, the name and work telephone numbers of purchasing agents and other business contacts at firms with whom the company does business. Such examples could readily be multiplied. Limiting transfers of this sort of information between the European and third-country parts of a company's operations could be a daunting task indeed.

The proposal here is to draw a distinction between processing data about people in their individual capacity and processing about them in their business capacity. In people's individual capacity, for instance, privacy rules may apply to information about them as employees (human resources records), borrowers (individual credit history), or consumers (direct marketing information). A chief goal of data protection law is to ensure that decisions about individuals are not made based on inappropriate or inaccurate data.

By contrast, different rules are probably appropriate for information gathered or processed about individuals in their business capacity. Consider, for example, a list of participants at a business meeting or the names of purchasing agents for business-to-business sales. In such instances there is a much smaller risk of decisions being made based on inappropriate or inaccurate information that would harm an individual. That is, the risk to privacy interests is lower. As seen in chapter 4, the volume of business-to-business electronic commerce is far greater than business-to-individual commerce. Applying strict data protection rules to the vast range of business-to-business transactions, which only incidentally include named information, would be an enormous regulatory effort only distantly related to the core concerns of privacy protection. Second, the named information can likely be used within the company for many legitimate purposes, so that the costs of regulating the use of the information may be higher. Third, the named information may be widely dispersed throughout the company and is not typically kept in structured databases of employment, credit, or marketing data. The overall burden on companies of restricting the use of information may thus be correspondingly great. Finally, companies already have a strong business incentive, without the need of data protection laws, to protect against disclosure of commercially valuable or embarrassing information. For all of these reasons, it likely makes sense to have fewer data protection restrictions on information that is processed about individuals in their business capacity.[12] After all, in most European countries, information about companies is not subject to data protection rules at all.[13] Information about persons, which is processed because of a decision concerning their employer, can be treated as information about that employer.

12. As with any distinction, there are likely to be some close or difficult cases. One example may be when a selling company learns adverse information about the purchasing agent of another company. The selling company may decide not to do further business with the other company, and the purchasing agent may be fired or suffer other consequences.

More broadly, further work would need to be done in understanding how the distinction should apply to information about a company's own employees. On one hand, payroll and benefits information seem to be an important target of data protection laws. On the other hand, there is often incidental information about an employee, such as attendance at a routine business meeting, where the information is primarily processed with respect to the employer's purpose rather than as information about the individual.

The existence of some close or difficult cases should not prevent recognition of a useful distinction. In most instances it is straightforward to distinguish between gaining information to make decisions about an individual and gaining information to make decisions about an individual's employer. Just as data protection law in most countries focuses on information about persons rather than companies, it can also distinguish between information about persons in their individual capacities and persons in their role as employees of a company.

13. Austria is an exception. Austrian data protection law applies to individuals, corporations, and other organizations. The proposed distinction would thus likely not apply to transactions processed under Austrian law.

Various legal strategies are available for incorporating the proposed distinction into the Directive. In some instances, information about people in their business capacity should be considered public knowledge. At least where information of the same sort is routinely published in the press, there is little expectation of privacy and the need for data protection rules seems relatively weak. In addition, a great deal of business information about individuals is gathered with consent: individuals participate in a business meeting, they benefit from having accurate information in a corporate credit report or business directory, or they want other companies to know how to contact appropriate people in their company. Derogations to the Directive would thus apply.

As another approach, third countries might be found to have adequate protection for this sort of information even where there is no finding of adequacy for information gathered about a person in his or her individual capacity. The risk to privacy interests is widely understood to be less if the data are gathered to make a decision about the employer rather than the individual. The Working Party's discussion of "adequacy" did not mention information processed with respect to a person's employer. The Article 25 definition of "adequacy," however, is designed to be considered in a contextual way, "in the light of all the circumstances."

One final way to incorporate the proposed distinction is to treat certain information as outside of the scope of the Directive. Article 3(1) states that the Directive applies to personal data "which form part of a filing system or are intended to form part of a filing system." Some of the information processed about persons in their business capacity is not intended to form part of a filing system. For instance, a list of employees who attend a business meeting or routine business letters that mention some fellow workers are probably not "part of a filing system." Even if the authors have such lists or letters on their hard drives, there is no structured system for keeping track of the files. By contrast, payroll information about employees is kept in a structured filing system and so would be within the scope of the Directive.

This interpretation of Article 3 may be useful in the medium term because it provides a legal basis in the Directive for excluding routine data processing that was likely not intended to be covered by the Directive.[14]

---

14. In conversations with data protection officials, there was substantial agreement that documents such as the list of persons attending a business meeting ought not be covered by all of the data protection rules in the Directive. Officials agreed in conversation, for instance, that people should not expect to have a right of access to every mention of their name in every memorandum throughout the files of their employer or companies that do business with their employer. There was no consensus, however, on how the problem should be analyzed as a legal matter under the Directive.

For the time being, it may be administrable to distinguish between "filing systems," such as payroll records, and "not filing systems," such as the occasional mention of a name in a company memorandum. In the longer term, however, it may become increasingly difficult to distinguish between data that are part or not part of a filing system. With modern computer technology, it becomes routine to place information in relatively unstructured databases, and then do searches of that database for each specific task. Today, it takes only an instant to search every file on a personal computer hard drive. As organizations continue to network their computers, it can become similarly easy for them to find whatever is on those computers, whether in a structured filing system or not. If the distinction breaks down between data that are or are not in a filing system, a different distinction may be needed under the Directive. We suggest that a good candidate may be between information about individuals that is processed in their business, rather than their personal, capacity.

7

Other Sectors with Large Transborder Activities

This chapter examines the effects of the Directive on other sectors where there are often transborder flows of personal data. Although our examination is by no means exhaustive, the sectors considered here should provide a good guide to the sorts of issues that would arise under the Directive for other sectors.

The chapter first explores effects on the press, where a strong tension exists between data protection rules and the rights to free expression. It then turns to effects on nonprofit organizations generally, on international education institutions, on international conferences, and on non-European governments. It analyzes effects on significant economic sectors, such as pharmaceuticals and medical devices, business and leisure travel, and Internet service providers. It then provides an extended discussion of direct marketing under the Directive, both in traditional forms and on the Internet. The chapter concludes with a survey of the effects on European individuals, businesses, and governments from restrictions on transfers of personal information to third countries.

The Press

A strict interpretation of the Directive could ban a great many practices by the press. The tension between the press and privacy laws is clear enough: an important responsibility of the press is to publicize personally identifiable information. In reporting on politics, business, entertainment, and sports, journalists routinely discuss named individuals. Often the reporting is done without the consent of the subject. Embarrassing information is disclosed about prominent politicians and movie stars. The experiences of Jackie Kennedy with papparazzi and the death of Princess Diana focused worldwide attention on unwanted intrusions by the media.

In the United States the First Amendment to the Constitution places many limits on the ability of government to prevent disclosure. European countries also have laws protecting free expression, although their scope is generally narrower than that of the First Amendment. Under Article 9 of the Directive, member states can make exemptions for the press, but the exemptions must be "solely for journalistic purposes" and "only if they are necessary to reconcile the right to privacy with the rules governing freedom of expression." This language seems to emphasize privacy rights and give relatively little scope to protecting free expression.

As governed by Article 9 the press will face compliance difficulties when it transfers personal information out of Europe. In addition to publication, such transfers occur when a reporter sends notes or a draft story from Europe to an outside country, discusses a story by e-mail or on the telephone with an editor in an outside country, or even gets personal information from someone in Europe while researching a story from an outside country. For many of these transfers none of the exceptions in Article 26 will apply. The transfer will be permissible only if it fits within the seemingly strict language of Article 9.

For press organizations, compliance with the Directive will require careful examination of national and EU rules governing freedom of expression, an important task beyond the scope of this book. Perhaps ironically, however, Article 9 may create opportunities for nonjournalistic organizations to receive information from Europe that might not otherwise be permitted. Transfers are apparently permitted if they are for journalistic purposes and within the rules governing freedom of expression. Consider, for instance, how the business press might be able to analyze personal information about a European company's management. That sort of journalistic reporting could presumably be sent to the United States, and subscribers in U.S. investment banks could get information from the press that they might not be able to receive otherwise. In this way the investment banks might be able to subscribe to newsletters, perhaps of very limited circulation, and receive information under Article 9 that would not be transferable under Article 26.

In an earlier age it was relatively simple to determine who qualified as a journalist. A journalist likely had a longstanding relationship with an entity that controlled an expensive printing press or similar technology. Today, with the spread of Web sites, Internet discussion groups, and desktop publishing, it seems everyone can be a publisher. A much greater number of persons and institutions might thus qualify as journalists or publishers and be subject to the protections of Article 9. By logical extension, those who report to publishers would seem to qualify as journalists. In short, a complicated political and legal debate will be needed about how to define who qualifies as a journalist and how to reconcile the role of journalism and free expression with privacy regulation under the Directive.

Closely related issues arise for companies that make journalistic and related information available to a wider audience. Some specialize in creating databases of publications, public records, and other information that is publicly available. Customers of these companies are able to search the databases for information on individuals. For instance, one might search for every mention of a particular individual in a wide range of European publications. For these companies, the relevant issue is not simply what qualifies as journalism in Article 9. What qualifies as public information? Depending on the answer, the data protection and Article 25 rules restricting transfers could no longer apply in many instances. Article 8(5), for example, places special restrictions on processing data related to criminal convictions. It is unclear what limits will exist on the ability of the press to republish information about such convictions, even when the accused was publicly named at the time of trial.

Some assistance for these companies comes from Article 26(1)(f), which allows transfers from a register that is intended to provide information to the public. This permission to transfer public records, however, does not define the circumstances that would make previously private information public. Under the First Amendment the usual American rule is that the government cannot restrict dissemination of information once it has been made public. Under the Directive, by contrast, there have been suggestions that the database search for all mentions of a given person would not be permitted.[1] In addition to clarification of the term "journalist," it will be important to clarify when information becomes public and thus no longer subject to data protection rules.

---

1. Our sources for this statement are two people who attended a meeting where data protection officials used this example.

Effects Generally on Nonprofit Organizations

The discussion so far in this book has focused on the effects of the Directive on corporations. By its terms, the Directive generally applies in the same way to nonprofit organizations, including charitable, political, religious, and educational institutions. Many of these can process member-related information without triggering the ultrastrict rules pertaining to sensitive data in Article 8(2)(d). But Article 25's prohibition on transfers to third countries applies identically to for-profit and nonprofit organizations.

The Directive may thus create problems for nonprofit organizations concerning their employee and membership records. Any organization with operations or headquarters in the United States will have to do the full analysis of whether they fit within the exceptions in Article 26. Prominent examples would include the Roman Catholic Church and other religious institutions, as well as any other nonprofit organization with personnel in Europe and elsewhere. Many of the issues will be the same as for human resources records of for-profit corporations. For instance, to make a transfer, nonprofits may seek unambiguous consent from data subjects. Some transfers may be necessary for performance of a contract, such as when personnel move from Europe to the United States. If none of the exceptions apply, the Directive would apparently prohibit transfer of personal employee data.

Nonprofit organizations stay in regular contact with their members to inform them of upcoming activities, raise money, and carry out many other activities. They use direct mail, telephone, and e-mail to contact members. The membership lists are similar to the employee directories discussed in chapter 4, and the Directive will apply to any effort to transfer out of Europe the lists or information contained in the lists. Special difficulties may arise when membership information is provided to third parties, such as often happens when nonprofits hire an outside organization to assist in fund-raising. The requirements of Article 14(b) will apply if fund-raising is considered to be "for the purposes of direct marketing." If Article 14 applies, members may need to be informed before personal data are disclosed for the first time to third parties.[2]

---

2. Here and elsewhere, an important question will be how general the notice can be to people that their information will be shared with third parties. For example, the nonprofit might be able to give notice simply stating that "information will be shared with third parties to assist in fund-raising and other operations." If this sort of notice suffices, it will be fairly easy to comply with the requirements in Article 14. But Article 14 might be read to require notice each time information is released to a

The number of nonprofit organizations in sports, industry, education, and the learned professions with international operations has grown strongly in the past few decades. Political and charitable organizations are increasingly prominent internationally in defending human rights, maintaining trade unions, and protecting the environment. If the Europeans seek to determine "adequacy" sector by sector, it will be difficult to define the range of organizations that deserve to be included, unless white list treatment is given to all nonprofits. Such a policy may be desirable, but it is not suggested by any language in the Directive.

The Internet will compound this trend toward internationalization as on-line communities multiply. Consider how the Directive would apparently apply to the membership list for a listserv or to the names of those who wish to participate in a scheduled on-line forum or chat session. Using the Internet, many new nonprofit alliances may be possible for those with shared interests. To the extent that each of these groups must comply with the Directive, there may be burdens on the ability of European residents to join such groups and share information within them. At a minimum, unambiguous consent may be required when personal information is shared outside of Europe.

International Educational Institutions

A growing number of universities and other educational institutions offer courses in both Europe and the United States. These institutions will face all the usual compliance problems for their human resources records. For instance, a university would need to make various disclosures to an American professor who teaches in Europe for a term and would need to get consent from the person before records concerning the term were returned to the United States. Additional difficulties might arise in the transfer out of Europe of confidential records, which might include teacher evaluations or investigative files about personnel. It is unclear whether employees can consent to transfer of records to which they have no access themselves.

---

third party, with notice of the identity of the party who is receiving the information. If this strict interpretation is adopted, it will become more burdensome for nonprofits to use outside organizations to assist them in fund-raising.

Student records would also fall under the Directive. Would those study-ing for a term in Europe need to receive notice of the proposed transfer of records back in the United States? Would they need to give consent before the transfer? Perhaps compliance is legal without prior consent because transfer of the records to the American institution is necessary to the per-formance of the contract between student and educational institution. That is, the records might need to be transferred to make sure that the student receives proper credit for studies completed in Europe.[3]

Student records may be one example for which there is a relatively strong argument that the United States has adequate protection. Under the Family Education Right to Privacy Act, popularly known as the Buckley Amendment, there are detailed rules about gaining parent or student con-sent before an educational institution can release grades and other infor-mation to outside parties.[4] The parent and student also have various rights to gain access to the student file.

International Conferences

An enormous number of conferences, arranged by both profit and nonprofit organizations, take place each year with participants from the European Union and the United States. Organizers typically amass a good deal of personal information about participants—address and phone num-ber, professional affiliation, participation in particular workshops or spe-cialized subgroups. Issues can arise under the Directive about the transfer of this personal information out of Europe.

Consider a common product of such conferences—a list of the names and addresses of participants. Unless one of the exceptions in Article 26 applies, the Directive would appear to prohibit the transfer of this list from Europe to a third country that lacks adequate protection. The prohibition would apparently apply to carrying an electronic copy of the conference

---

3. Further analysis may be required to ascertain *which* records are necessary to performance of the contract, and thus transferable. The number of credits received would seem necessary to determine whether the student qualifies for graduation in the United States. The grades might be transferable to determine grade point average or class rank, whose calculation is arguably a necessary part of the benefit a student receives from the contract. Would transfer of the names of the instructor and courses also be necessary? What about the instructor's comments about performance on a paper or in the course? Here as elsewhere, there are numerous concrete issues raised by the Directive.

4. 20 U.S.C. § 1232g.

listing in a person's laptop computer, e-mailing the listing from Europe to the United States, or posting the list of participants on a Web site.

One way around this strict interpretation is for the conference organizers to get unambiguous consent from participants before their information is included in conference materials. At least two problems would remain, however. First, conference organizers range from the professional to the occasional and ad hoc. By its terms, the Directive would apply even to a first-time meeting of persons sharing a professional interest. An American invitee to the meeting could be very surprised to learn that it is illegal to bring home the list of participants, and the meeting's organizers might not think to gain permission in advance for the transfer. Second, and more important, once again a clearer definition of "unambiguous" consent and of the permissible scope of consent is needed. Suppose the following notice is considered sufficient: "Personal information that you supply to the conference organizers may be shared with other conference participants." If that sort of vague notice suffices to comply with the Directive, conference organizers and participants will face fewer compliance burdens. As the detail in the required notice becomes greater, the burden of compliance will similarly increase.

Another way that transfer of conference information may be legal is under Article 9, which governs the press. Many conferences allow journalists to attend and to receive copies of conference materials, including lists of participants. In the United States the First Amendment offers journalists broad protection to report on events at conferences and to carry with them information about conference participants. As discussed earlier, Article 9 allows exemptions for journalistic purposes if they are necessary to reconcile the right to privacy with the rules governing freedom of expression. At least where a journalist would have the right to disseminate personal data about those who attend conferences, one wonders whether it may be permissible under the Directive for nonjournalists to transfer the same information out of Europe.[5]

---

5. The discussion in the text focuses on the use of information about conference participants by those associated with the conference. A separate issue concerns the release of that personal information to those unaffiliated with the conference. Direct marketers, for instance, might be interested in purchasing information about membership in a special-interest group such as a conference. Such uses of information would be governed by the general rules on direct marketing, discussed later.

Effects on Non-EU Governments

The Directive's terms apply in some circumstances to both EU and non-EU governments. As discussed in chapter 2 the Directive applies to all processing of personal data. It then exempts certain categories of government data processing, such as for public security, national defense, and regulatory functions (Articles 3(2) and 13).

The Directive would apparently apply to transfers of the employment and medical records of the personnel of the United States and other governments. Some personnel would fit within the exceptions for national defense or public security, such as military and diplomatic employees. For other employees, and for the families of U.S. employees, a different exemption would be needed. For U.S. nationals, there is a strong legal argument that the federal government is a sector with adequate protection because of the Privacy Act of 1974 and its requirement of fair information practices.[6] One problem in this regard is that the act's provisions do not apply to foreign nationals. Difficulties could arise, therefore, with records kept by the U.S. government about employees or other persons who are foreign nationals, such as when their employment or medical records are transferred back to Washington.

We do not suggest that any European government is likely to target the U.S. government for an early enforcement action. Enforcing against a national government would raise many special legal and political problems. The application of the Directive to the U.S. and other governments is nonetheless potentially interesting. Getting clarification about the application of the Directive to governments may provide precedents that would be informative about the legality of other sorts of transfers.

Research and Marketing for Pharmaceuticals and Medical Devices

The pharmaceutical industry faces some unusual issues under the Directive. Article 8(1) treats the "processing of data concerning health" as sensitive, subject to especially strict regulation. But Article 8(3) says those strict rules "shall not apply where processing of the data is required for the purposes of preventative medicine, medical diagnosis, the provision of care or treatment or the management of health-care services." Those exceptions

---

6. 5 U.S.C. § 552a.

apply only where the data "are processed by a health professional subject under national law or rules established by competent bodies to the obligation of professional secrecy or by another person also subject to an equivalent obligation of secrecy." These provisions seek to balance a patient's right to keep sensitive health information private against the need to use the information to save human life. Article 11(2) of the Directive, which indicates procedures for when information is provided to third parties, also has potential relevance to the pharmaceutical industry, because those procedures do not apply for processing done "for the purposes of historical or scientific research."

Transborder flows of personal data arise commonly in pharmaceutical research and marketing—clinical trials for a new drug or medical device, for example. Regulators in many countries require detailed clinical studies before a new product is approved. These studies often take more than a decade to complete, and information is commonly assembled from trials in many countries.

Pharmaceutical companies have a number of plausible arguments about how these clinical trials can comply with the Directive. Perhaps the clinical trials qualify as "preventative medicine" or one of the other terms in Article 8(3). If so, the information is not sensitive under Article 8, at least if all participating researchers are under "an obligation of professional secrecy." Perhaps the clinical trials qualify as "scientific research," so the notice and other requirements of Article 11 do not apply. Even more important for transborder flows, there may be a ready means of compliance for many clinical trials. Researchers can follow common practice and anonymize the names of the patients. The patient's name can be coded and secured within Europe. In this way, no personally identifiable information ever leaves Europe, and the transborder flow would arguably be legal under Article 25.

This sort of anonymizing may work well for trials when regulators wish to examine the statistical safety and efficacy of a drug or medical device. It may work less well, however, when the records must contain highly detailed information about each patient. This sort of information exists, for instance, in large databases of health records of the sort used for epidemiological and other important research. Detailed information also exists in reports of adverse effects that are routinely made to the drug companies and to regulators. It is indeed possible to anonymize the names in these reports. The difficulty is that they contain, by their very nature, a large amount of potentially sensitive information that, taken together, may be personally identifying. In studying why a patient had a bad reaction to a drug, for instance, it may be relevant that the person is HIV positive, has a rare blood type, or lives in a particular locale known for its air pollution. This information cannot be scrubbed out of the record without the risk of removing the relevant medical information. In addition, what is personally identifying and thus a candidate to be scrubbed can vary for each patient: one person has a rare blood type but the next person was exposed to particular environmental toxins.

Beyond these difficulties, troublesome issues may arise about what studies qualify as "preventative medicine" or "scientific studies" under Articles 8 and 11. For instance, a growing portion of medical and pharmaceutical research consists of cost-effectiveness studies as opposed to studies of the safety of the drug or device. As the focus shifts from medical effect to economic effect, it becomes less certain that a given study will qualify as medical or scientific. Yet knowledge about cost effectiveness is important to deciding appropriate patterns of medical practice.

A potential flashpoint for controversy is how to draw the line between research and marketing for pharmaceuticals, medical devices, and other medical care. Many of the major companies in these fields are now transnational, operating with increasingly unified computer systems. The marketing arms of companies may wish to have access to records of patients with certain characteristics. These records can allow the company to alert patients to potentially cost-effective or life-saving treatments. But still, patient records contain sensitive information. Overuse of the records may lead to a variety of bad consequences, including feelings of invasion of privacy and patients' refusal to report their conditions accurately to health care professionals.

The blurred line between research and marketing poses potential obstacles to the transfer of research information from Europe to the United States. There may be suspicion on the part of European authorities that sensitive medical information will not be handled carefully once it is transferred. One way to lessen this possibility is for the United States to move forward on sectoral legislation for health care privacy. The U.S. secretary of health and human services has submitted recommendations to Congress on the confidentiality of individually identifiable health information, as required under the Health Insurance Portability and Accountability Act of 1996. It is possible that this sort of legislation can resolve health care and pharmaceutical privacy issues. If no progress is made on such legislation, the sensitive nature of medical and pharmaceutical data may lead the Europeans to take early enforcement action in this area.

Business and Leisure Travel

The travel and leisure sector systematically involves transborder actions of identifiable individuals. Affected industries include airlines, railroads, cruise lines, charter buses, rental cars, hotels, and travel agents. The Directive can greatly affect how data will flow between Europe and the United States in connection with this vast volume of travel.

In considering the effects of the Directive, it is useful to contemplate the advantages to travelers of permitting flows of personal information. Detailed information can be a great help in providing customer service, to let the traveler receive the sort of personalized attention that might be available in his or her home town. Transfer of the information helps travelers get the service they prefer and reduces the need to state those preferences at each stop along the way. For the business traveler, for instance, it may be extremely helpful for the hotel to know what sort of office equipment should be available (for example, twenty-four-hour fax service), preferences on workout facilities (a pool or weight room), any food or beverages that should be in the room upon arrival, a smoking or nonsmoking room, and so forth. For the individual traveler, tastes and budgets vary enormously. A history of a traveler's past likes and dislikes may help identify local restaurants, lodgings, and tourist attractions that are most likely to be pleasing. In short, detailed information about an individual's preferences helps the travel industry provide personalized service and avoid imposing unpleasant experiences. The Directive will impose costs to the extent it prevents this sort of personalized service.

A safe and pleasant trip may be ensured by a range of industries. A successful trip often involves making good choices for transport, lodging, restaurants, and attractions. Although the Directive's impact on direct marketing will be discussed more fully later, the travel sector provides a commonsense example of benefits that can flow from direct marketing to consumers. Travelers' goals are to become well informed about a distant location, even before arriving there. Strict limits on direct marketing would prevent them from becoming aware of good choices. European destinations might lose the ability to inform Americans about attractive packages, and European travelers might be unable to find out about travel opportunities in the United States.

But the accumulation of detailed travel information into dossiers raises precisely the sort of privacy issues that are at the heart of data protection law. In today's mobile society a great many individuals use travel services for business, pleasure, or both. They may not wish to have detailed records retained of all their travel decisions, especially if the information is shared among many companies, often in many countries. The instinct of privacy advocates is that people should not have to submit to having a dossier compiled as a condition of being able to use travel services. From this viewpoint, data protection laws should help equalize the power balance between individual and company, making it easier for people to retain their privacy.

Reservation Systems

A substantial amount of information on individuals can be accumulated in travel companies' reservation systems. As already mentioned, travel agents or hotel chains may wish to keep detailed information about a traveler's lodging preferences. An airline might track information about seat preferences and travel history with the airline. Reservation systems may also accumulate information considered sensitive under Article 8, such as health information (for example, a medical condition requiring treatment during the trip) or religious information (a request not to be served certain religiously prohibited foods).

Although reservation systems, and accompanying issues of data protection, exist for many travel industries, attention thus far has focused on airline reservation systems. Notably, under Swedish national law authorities have prohibited transfer of customer data to the SABRE reservation system operated by American Airlines in the United States.[7] European authorities have reached a detailed agreement with the Amadeus system based in Europe, and negotiations are likely to continue with other major reservation systems. The European Commission has identified sensitive information in airline reservation systems as one of the five sectors to be studied in a special report by international privacy experts.

---

7. Under Section 11 of the Swedish Data Act, the Swedish Data Protectorate prohibited the transfer of computer reservation system information to the U.S. processing center of the SABRE system. The information in question included the customer's name, itinerary, address, telephone number, passport number, and method of payment, as well as potentially sensitive information about health or religion. Under the Data Protectorate's order, upheld by the courts, personal information could only be transferred to the United States when there was consent by the customers. Before consenting to the transfer, customers must be informed of "the information which is to be transferred; the way in which this will be done; the reason for transferring the information; the way in which the information will be processed; and how the information will be stored or deleted." See Decision of the Administrative Court of Appeal, Stockholm, Case No. 2104-1996 (April 23, 1997).

In some instances, personal data in reservation systems might be transferred from Europe to third countries under the derogations in Article 26, raising a series of by now familiar questions. When information is transferred to the United States, what sort of consent by the customer is "unambiguous"? What information is "necessary for the performance of a contract"? What restrictions on secondary processing, if any, exist once a transfer has been made to the United States under one of the exceptions to Article 26? For sensitive information, what additional steps must a company take under the Directive with respect to such data? Strict answers to these questions would mean a prohibition on many transfers of information from Europe to the United States. Information might then be unavailable to assist European travelers when they are in the United States, and information about Americans' travel in Europe would be unavailable for future reference when the traveler returns home.

Where the derogations do not apply, major reservation systems would seem good candidates for contracts or other sorts of self-regulatory measures (SRM). As with the mainframes discussed in chapter 3, large reservation systems are staffed by teams of computer professionals who would have the ability to modify the systems over time to comply with data protection requirements. But worldwide reservation systems are a prime example of possible extraterritorial effects of the Directive because the same protocols may be used for handling customer information throughout the reservation system. The rules applicable to European customer information, therefore, could become the rules applicable to U.S. and other customers.

In fact, unified networks such as the international reservation systems pose the most difficult extraterritoriality problems. European claims to apply data protection laws are strong because at stake is the handling of personal and sometimes very sensitive information about many Europeans. At the same time, concerns in the United States and other third countries about extraterritorial effects are also strong because the system that applies to European customers will likely also apply to many customers outside of Europe. When the same network applies to many Europeans and non-Europeans, each side can justifiably claim that it may be harmed by following the other side's preferred rules.

There is no magic way to resolve such a dispute over network configuration. In some instances, the network can operate differently in various locations. For instance, it may be possible to handle airline customer information so that the Directive applies only for flights that originate or conclude in Europe, but not otherwise. Alternatively, perhaps personal information can be handled differently for those whose trip originates or concludes in Europe than for those merely traveling through Europe temporarily. If the network can be fine-tuned in this way, the extraterritorial effects would be reduced. If not, some negotiation may be needed between the countries involved in recognition of the fact that any set of rules will have some extraterritorial effects.

Frequent Flyer Miles and Other Affinity Programs

The travel industry has a pervasive system of frequent flyer miles and other affinity programs. When a customer has signed up for an affinity program, it can make a strong argument that the customer has unambiguously consented to inclusion of the data in that company's database. As in other contexts, a chief compliance issue will be the specificity of the required notice. For instance, perhaps the notice might state that transfers may occur outside the European Union to countries that lack adequate protection. Where notice is not strong enough, severe consequences could follow. A person's frequent flyer miles accumulated in Europe might not be transferable back to the United States unless some other exception to Article 26 applies. When consent is not shown, the other exception that might apply is "necessary for the . . . performance of a contract" between the airline and the customer (Article 26(1)(c)). A very strict interpretation of "contract" might focus on the agreement of the airline to transport the customer, in which case transfer of the frequent flyer miles would not be "necessary" and thus would be forbidden. A broader interpretation would find that the affinity program agreement between airline and customer should constitute the relevant contract and that transfer of the frequent flyer information is necessary for performance of that contract.

The greatest threat to frequent flyer miles would be if the European Union were to take a strict approach toward secondary use of data. In this case complying with an exception to Article 26 would not be considered sufficient to permit a transfer to the United States. Those receiving data in the United States would also be required to comply with fair information practices with respect to the data. Where sufficient guarantees do not exist for these data protection practices, transfer of personal information, including frequent flyer miles, could be prohibited.

The legal issues grow a step more difficult in the common situation in which multiple companies share personal information about affinity programs. For instance, information about a person's flights may be shared among a number of airline partners. Hotel, rental car companies, and other travel-related industries often provide frequent flyer miles in addition to offering their own affinity programs. As information is transferred among these companies, including being sent from Europe to the United States, the controller or his representative must, no later than the time when the data are first disclosed, provide a variety of information to the data subject under Article 11. As the names of the partner companies shift and the categories of shared information change, this requirement of prior notice could become unduly burdensome.

When information is shared among companies, a somewhat similar problem arises under Article 14, which guarantees people various rights with respect to personal data that are transferred for "the purposes of direct marketing." A strict interpretation of the Directive might decide that information transferred among partners in affinity programs is done for just such a purpose. If so, customers might need to be contacted and given the opportunity to leave an affinity program each time a new partner is added. Such a requirement could be costly for modern affinity programs, which often span many industries over a wide geographic area and experience repeated changes in the list of participating companies. A predictable result of this approach would be to cut back on the size and range of customer benefits under affinity programs.

Internet Service Providers

Internet service providers (ISPs) connect individuals and businesses to the Internet, notably to browse on the World Wide Web. Often, they provide other services: they may enable users to send and receive e-mail and facilitate on-line chat. They may have proprietary content, such as when a magazine or other content provider gives an ISP the exclusive right to supply information on-line. They likely maintain their own elaborate Web sites, which may be popular destinations for nonsubscribers as well as subscribers. Increasingly, they sell advertising to various companies.

To operate their computer systems, ISPs often accumulate large amounts of personally identifiable information. They must bill subscribers. Sometimes payments are flat rates, but other times subscribers agree to pay for particular services, in which instance records must be maintained to match services to customer accounts. ISPs must have ways to route e-mails correctly to people. To fulfill their contracts with advertisers, ISPs have often agreed to have the payment depend on the number of "hits" on the advertisements; records are thus created that indicate each time an individual has visited a particular site where the advertisement is viewed.[8] Various other records might be created on the subscriber: decisions about privacy options, calls to customer service, and purchases made through the ISP, to name just a few.

A great deal of this personal information flows across borders. E-mail and chat systems operate globally; a company that helps operate them will thus gather identifiable data globally. Major ISPs that serve the European market, including America On-Line and the Microsoft Network, operate their computer centers in the United States. Interviews with industry representatives suggest that there are definite economies of scale to operating one computer center rather than building centers throughout the world. Some functions, such as chat, might only be technically feasible when run out of one computer center. It will be difficult or impossible to provide some services while preventing flows from Europe to third countries.

Our general analysis has been that this sort of processing is a strong candidate for having contracts approved under Article 26(2) or using a code of conduct under Article 27. Especially for the major ISPs, with many customers both in Europe and the United States, the number of such contracts would appear manageable from the point of view of data protection authorities and significant in terms of the amount of personal information that would be covered. Cutting off EU customers from these major services would seem needlessly harmful to them and EU commerce, especially if the ISPs agree to follow data protection rules for European customers. Because the major ISPs have a significant business presence in Europe, they would clearly fall within the jurisdiction of European countries, so there would seem little difficulty in enforcing European laws.

If these sorts of contracts are not approved by authorities, the ISPs can seek unambiguous consent for transfers to third countries (Article 26(1)(a)). Many observers have suggested that consent will be easier to give meaningfully on the Internet because of the possibility of interactivity—new questions can be asked of the customer based on responses to earlier questions, so that the person can specify exactly what privacy practices are preferred.[9]

---

8. According to interviews with people in the industry, these records often can be aggregated so that the "hits" cannot be traced back to named individuals. To track usage, however, there generally has to be an initial recording of a user's visit to a site.

9. This consent process can be speeded if the person builds privacy preferences into the Web browser.

Interviews with ISPs, however, suggest some practical limits to this. They report that many users are not very sophisticated with the technology. If the opening screens are too complicated, with many choices, the mainstream user may simply quit the service.

When contracts, codes of conduct, or consent do not apply, our analysis suggests that the Directive will not allow persons and businesses in the European Union to use ISPs that operate their computer centers in countries that lack adequate protection. For some functions, personal data might be anonymized before transmission to the third country. But for other functions this anonymization is likely to be very hard to do.

An additional issue for ISPs will be the extent to which they will be able to use the information they assemble for direct marketing to their subscribers. Each ISP that we interviewed independently expressed the opinion that business models are currently difficult to develop on the Internet. It may require a lot of one-to-one selling for many of the businesses to survive. Such selling often depends on having a substantial amount of information about the consumer. We return later to the issue of direct marketing, including direct marketing over the Internet. For now, we simply observe that ISPs are a natural locus for bringing sellers and buyers together, with the ISP using information it already receives to facilitate this process.

Retailing and Other Direct Marketing

The last sector we address is one that has received a great deal of attention in privacy debates. Retailing and other direct marketing to consumers relies heavily on accurate and timely information about consumers' tastes. Some areas of direct marketing have been discussed already, such as sales of financial or travel services. We now turn more generally to direct sales to customers through both the Internet and more traditional means.

For retailers and others using personal information, much of the discussion in other parts of this book applies in a straightforward way. For example, retailers operating stores both in Europe and third countries will face all of the potential problems that come from operating a mainframe or server outside of Europe. They will also face the same sorts of restrictions on transfers in ordinary business functions, such as on transfers of employee data or auditing data.

A substantial portion of direct marketing concerns sales to businesses.

As we have seen in other settings, the Directive does not distinguish between identifiable data provided in a corporate or personal setting.[10] The Directive would therefore apply, for instance, to a directory of executives in a particular industry, or to other marketing that identifies individuals in their business activities. This sort of business information may seem to call for less strict data protection practices, but there is no apparent provision in the Directive that would discriminate.[11]

Most of the discussion in this section focuses on what people commonly think of as direct marketing: sales directly to individuals. As Paul Schwartz and Joel Reidenberg have observed: "Fair information practice issues relate primarily to the activities associated with the creation and use of name lists. Fair information practices center on how particular individuals are targeted and how names are exchanged rather than the actual solicitation of particular individuals."[12] In our discussion, we first examine the effect of the Directive on traditional direct marketing, and then examine direct marketing in the Internet context. Effects in both areas may be significant. The electronic commerce setting, however, raises more profound issues for the future role of data protection regimes.

Traditional Direct Marketing

We use the term "traditional" direct marketing to distinguish it from direct marketing that uses the Internet. Traditional direct marketing includes gathering information from various sources, notably including a company's own customer lists and the rented or purchased lists of prospects from other companies. Traditional direct marketers may then contact customers through catalogues and other direct mail, telemarketing, and so on.

In our interviews there was a surprising consensus among companies and trade groups that traditional direct marketing has had only a small international component. A number of factors have created incentives to

10. Other examples of business-related information include personal data included in investment banking, a corporate credit history, business consulting, or identifiable business information included on a person's laptop computer.

11. As discussed later, Article 14 has certain requirements that apply to data used "for the purposes of direct marketing." One might interpret this language to apply only to data used for direct marketing to individuals in their personal capacity. In that case the requirements of Article 14 would not apply to marketing to businesses or marketing that uses information about individuals in their business capacities.

12. Paul M. Schwartz and Joel R. Reidenberg, *Data Privacy Law: A Study of United States Data Protection* (Charlottesville, Va.: Michie, 1996), p. 311.

conduct direct marketing country by country. Important practical reasons are that it is easier to work with one post office and to avoid customs restrictions. Cataloguers and other direct mailers work closely with each national post office to minimize costs, assure speedy delivery, and handle the inevitable glitches in delivery of mailings and merchandise. Conducting direct marketing across borders risks delay and other problems with customs and with clearing up problems that involve two or more post offices. The desire to keep close to the customer has been another reason for intranation direct marketing. Handling marketing at a national level allows use of the local language, payment with the national currency, and tailoring of advertising appeals and promotions to the local market. A final reason for marketing nation by nation is to comply with the variety of national laws on advertising and consumer protection. Data protection laws are simply one additional sort of national law that has varied across borders.

Despite this general pattern of direct marketing, the importance of transnational marketing has varied by industry. Interviews suggest that transnational marketing is more important for financial services, travel services, very high-end products, and magazines or other publications with an international subscriber base. For this sort of transnational marketing, information about customer transactions in Europe may flow back to databases in the United States or other third countries. Lists of customer prospects may also be developed based on transactions in Europe; either the raw data about these transactions or the prospect lists themselves may then be transferred to third countries. Within the European Community, the development of the internal market has gradually made it easier for companies to conduct direct marketing across national borders. Some major direct marketers have now centralized their European operations. The Directive will presumably continue this process because of its liberalization of the movement of personal data among countries in the European Community.

Article 14 provides some special rules with respect to direct marketing. It grants the data subject the right to object, on request and free of charge, to processing of personal data relating to him "which the controller anticipates being processed for the purposes of direct marketing" (Article 14(b)). The data subject also has the right to be informed before personal data are disclosed for the first time to third parties or used on their behalf "for the purposes of direct marketing." The data subject can exercise these rights free of charge. Article 14 applies to processing of direct marketing data both within Europe and as transferred to third countries.

The terms of Article 14 appear to create an important distinction between customer lists and prospect lists. When firms are acting for the purposes of direct marketing with respect to their own customers, they must grant the data subject the right to object. By contrast, when firms wish to make the personal data available to third parties for direct marketing, there is the additional requirement that the data subject be notified in advance. Using lists of prospective customers thus carries the potentially significant burden of providing notice in advance to each data subject. For both customer lists and prospect lists, these requirements apply only when the data are used "for the purposes of direct marketing" (Article 14(b)). The interpretation of this term could be important to determining how strictly the Directive will limit uses of personal data about customers.[13] Direct marketers in Europe also face additional requirements under national laws, some of which, as in Denmark, are especially strict.

To transfer direct marketing information to the United States and other third countries, firms must satisfy the requirements of both Article 14 and Article 26. Under both, the crucial way to comply is likely to be for the direct marketing firm to get consent from the data subject. Simply providing the customer the right to object is enough to allow direct marketing to existing customers when the personal data stay within Europe. Unambiguous consent by the customer will also allow transfer to third countries that lack adequate protection. As in many other settings, the burden of compliance will depend on how narrowly or broadly the term "unambiguous consent" is interpreted.[14] For the use of prospect lists, unambiguous consent must be granted prior to the transfer to third countries, and notice of the

---

13. For instance, does information used for customer service qualify as "for the purposes of direct marketing"? Such information might be included on the view that providing customer service is an important part of the next sale. The more expansive the interpretation of "for the purposes of direct marketing," the greater the restrictions on uses of customer data (Article 14(b)).

A similar issue arises when direct marketers accumulate a large batch of customer information, perhaps due to a sweepstakes or a coupon promotion. In some instances this batch of information is shipped to third countries for data input. Once the information is properly recorded and formatted, it is typically shipped back to the country where the promotion took place. This sort of transfer raises issues under both Article 14 and Article 26. Under Article 14 the question is whether it constitutes a transfer to a third party "for the purposes of direct marketing." If so, the data subject will need to be given notice of the transfer to a third party. Under Article 26 the question is whether subcontracting for data input counts as a transfer to a third country. Where effective security measures are in place, perhaps some mechanism can be worked out under the Directive for not counting this subcontracting as a transfer to a third country. It is not entirely apparent, however, what provision would permit such transfers except when there is unambiguous consent by the data subject.

14. See the discussion on transfers of employee data in chapter 5.

proposed use for direct marketing must be given in advance to the data subject. Here again, direct marketers who wish to use data will have an incentive to develop standard language and other practices that both comply with data protection laws and actually secure customer consent.

Some transnational direct marketing may be able to take advantage of the exception in Article 26 that permits transfers that are necessary for the performance of a contract. When the fulfillment center is outside Europe, such as when goods are shipped from the United States, the company can transfer the necessary personal data, primarily including the name and address of the recipient. Broader categories of data, which are not needed to ensure performance of the contract, would not fit within this exception. One possible compliance measure by firms would be to make a broader range of data necessary to the contract, such as when a warranty or service contract is serviced from the third country. In this way, all of the data needed for fulfillment of the contract could apparently be transferred.

In assessing the effects of the Directive on traditional direct marketing, an initial observation is that the laws of the member states to date have varied considerably. For the countries that already regulate direct marketing tightly, the Directive may change little. For other countries, including those that previously lacked data protection laws, the provisions of Article 14 appear significant, especially with respect to prospect lists. The effects of the Directive may thus be considerable for some direct marketing conducted entirely within Europe.

With respect to transfers to third countries, the effects of the Directive will largely depend on how difficult it is for companies to get unambiguous consent. Where such consent is impossible or too costly to secure, firms will have an incentive to move operations to Europe or to find ways to operate without the personal data.

Direct Marketing and Electronic Commerce

The Directive and other data protection laws on direct marketing will have potentially far-reaching effects on electronic commerce. In the American business press, a common vision of Internet commerce is of a future in which sellers and buyers find each other with unprecedented speed and precision. Sellers will be able to target buyers without the need for a costly distribution system of wholesalers and retailers. Buyers will be able to filter out the offers they do not want, and will use search engines to seek out exactly what they do want. Intelligent agents, used by either seller or buyer, will look at past buying decisions and extrapolate the individual's likely choices for the next purchase. In short, sellers will seek to move to a "market of one"; instead of the mass market of the past, advanced information processing will allow goods and services tailored precisely to the individual user.[15] For some products, it is fairly easy to imagine the advantages to the customer. For example, it might be desirable to receive a daily newspaper tailored to one's individual interests, with just the right blend of general news, sports, entertainment, and special topics of interest. Similarly, an internet service provider, on-line music store, or on-line bookstore might conveniently provide different information and promotions to customers with differing tastes.

Instead of a slice of utopia, however, it is perhaps not much of an exaggeration to say that this market of one is the nightmare of many persons active in data protection issues. Creating a market of one often means that the seller has an enormous amount of information about the data subject. Controllers of this information may be in a position to manipulate the desires and behavior of the data subject. Controllers may also release embarrassing and private information to third parties. From this point of view, fair information practices and restraints on direct marketing are essential to protect the individual's fundamental rights to privacy and autonomy. For instance, it would be vital to protect the right of the data subject to object to uses of data for direct marketing. Otherwise, the person would be put to the unfair choice of either allowing use of the data or giving up entirely the ability to engage in that sort of transaction.

Internet commerce will be the battleground between these optimistic and pessimistic views of the market of one. Consider some reasons why transnational direct marketing is likely to be far easier and more prevalent on the Internet than traditionally. The simplest and perhaps most profound difference is how easy and inexpensive it becomes for a seller to be in contact with buyers in another country. On the Internet the goods and services sold are often electronic or easy to ship, so there is less need to rely on the national postal service.[16] On the Internet it is often possible to be close to the customer even when physically remote. It is already routine to see Web sites available in multiple languages. In the future the trend will be

15. See Don Peppers and Martha Rogers, *The One to One Future: Building Relationships One Customer at a Time* (Doubleday, 1993).

16. Some leading current areas of Internet sales include software and information services, which are downloadable electronically, and books and music, which are easily shipped.

for a site to take account of all available information about the customer—nationality, past purchasing history—to tailor offerings more precisely than has been possible in mass mailings. On the Internet it is far from clear when European countries will have jurisdiction to enforce data protection and other laws. It is also unclear how effectively customs, value-added taxes, and other taxes will be collectible on Internet transactions. The jurisdiction and taxation issues may provide important advantages to direct marketers operating outside Europe.

All these reasons suggest that transnational direct marketing is likely to become enormously more important on the Internet than traditionally. Under the Directive Articles 14 and 26 apply equally to traditional and Internet direct marketing. They place significant limits on the ability of direct marketers to transfer information to third parties and to third countries that lack adequate protection. Direct marketers often will be required to give advance notice to customers about transfers to third parties and will need to receive unambiguous consent before transferring personal data to third countries. The market of one will only be permitted when the data subject has given repeated consent to accumulation of personal information.

In contemplating the future of Internet commerce, there are sincere and important disagreements about how to balance the advantages of the market of one with the disadvantages of widespread flows of personal information. There are important questions ahead about the extent to which this balance should be made at the level of national or European law, at a broader level of multilateral legal agreement, or in the technologies adopted. Although the Directive by its terms appears to govern Internet direct marketing, it is far from clear that European law will be effective at shutting off flows of personal information over the Internet. The Directive is an important step in Europe's effort to regulate electronic commerce, but it is far from the final word.

Effects on Europe of Restrictions on Transfers

This chapter completes our description of the sector-by-sector effects of the Directive. In much of the discussion to this point, we have emphasized the effects that a strict application of the Directive would have on organizations and individuals in the United States and other countries outside Europe. We now examine a closely related topic, the effects that restrictions on transfers would have on organizations and individuals in the European Union.

From Europe's perspective a principal benefit of restrictions on transfers would presumably be the protection of individuals' privacy. As discussed in chapter 2, data protection authorities fear that their entire regulatory effort will fail if personal information about Europeans moves offshore into data havens. The Article 25 adequacy requirement is thus seen as a necessary component of a successful privacy regime. This benefit would accrue predominantly to European individuals rather than businesses.

A second benefit, for at least some Europeans, would be the protectionist advantage the restrictions would provide against competition from the United States and other countries. This benefit would accrue predominantly to European businesses and workers. The legal analysis of protectionism, as governed by World Trade Organization rules, is discussed in Chapter 8. Here we focus on economic and practical effects of a protectionist barrier, namely the limit of transfers of personal information to third countries.

We can distinguish two types of protectionist effects. The first is one in which a company based in Europe gains business at the expense of a firm based in a third country. For instance, suppose that a company in the United States finds it too expensive to comply with the Directive, perhaps because it is not worth the effort to reconfigure its computer systems for the small portion of its business that takes place in Europe. In this event a European firm might win business that otherwise would have gone to the U.S. firm. A second sort of protectionist effect is if the firm based in the third country decides to move operations to Europe. For instance, a company that processes all sales in the United States might set up a second processing center in Europe that complies with European data protection rules. In this event the same firm makes the sale, but the data processing and associated jobs shift from the United States to Europe.

Under standard economic analysis, protectionist rules can provide benefits for the firms and individuals that gain business because of the rules. In our examples, these benefits could flow to the European firm that replaces an American firm or to the European workers who get the new jobs when operations are moved to Europe.

Also under standard economic analysis, however, the overall costs of protectionism generally outweigh the benefits. The loss to consumers is usually greater than the gain to producers. In the first example, European purchasers had previously preferred the goods or services of the U.S. firm.

Because of the burdens of regulation, however, European purchasers now shift to goods or services that they previously did not prefer to buy, perhaps because they once cost too much or were of insufficient quality. In the second example, the firm had earlier decided to conduct operations in the third country, presumably because it was more efficient to do so. When the regulations prompt operations to shift to Europe, then the inefficiency of having duplicate facilities is passed on to customers, typically in the form of higher prices.

For both examples, it is important to note that the purchasers are often businesses rather than consumers. Protectionism can make the inputs for manufacturers and other companies more expensive. One result is that consumers in Europe will ultimately pay higher prices. Another result is that the higher cost of imports will make it more difficult for European producers to compete in world markets—they will have to overcome protectionist barriers that may not apply to their competitors.

In applying this general analysis of protectionism to the specific issues of data protection, we will consider what sorts of opportunities for businesses and individuals would be cut off by limits on transfers of personal information out of Europe. At issue is trade in which personal information flows from Europe to third countries and the processing in the third country does not have "adequate" protection.

Intraorganizational Data Flows

The disruptive effects of restrictions will increase depending on the tightness of the link between the processing of data in Europe and third countries. Some of the tightest links will be where data flows within a company or other organization. For instance, in our discussion in chapter 3 about corporate intranets, we quoted an American industry person as saying, "Without the intranet, you can't run your European sales offices or subsidiaries as part of the company." Seen from the perspective of a company based in Europe, this also means that a company cannot run its U.S. or other third-country operations as part of the company. For all of the many transnational companies that have operations in Europe and elsewhere, limits on transfers of data out of Europe could mean obstacles to processing many sorts of intraorganizational information. Our discussion elsewhere in the book suggests some important examples.

—Human resources records.

—Internal directories of e-mail, phone numbers, and membership on task forces.

—Internal organizational statements and policies that contain named information.

—Accounting and auditing reports.

—Instructions and reports from European management to operations in third countries.

—Salesperson reports from Europe to third countries that contain named information.

—For religious and other nonprofit organizations, member information.

This functional description of intraorganizational data flows can be complemented by a list of some technological ways that organizations might transfer information from Europe to third countries.

—Mainframes. Any organization using one mainframe to service both Europe and third countries can expect to have large transfers of named information out of Europe. Large transfers are also likely where there are multiple mainframes for backup and other purposes.

—Client-server systems. If the server is in the third country, flows of named information from the clients in Europe can be blocked. If the server is in Europe, processed data, such as reports from management, may not be available to clients in third countries.

—Intranets. As already described, it is not apparent if an organizational intranet can be operated cost effectively while limiting transfers from Europe to third countries in compliance with data protection rules.

—E-mail and computerized facsimiles. Within an organization, named information can easily be transferred from Europe to third countries via e-mail or fax.

—Laptops. To the extent that transferring laptops from Europe to third countries is covered by the Directive, the employees of organizations would face restrictions on transferring personal data out of Europe by laptop or diskette.

Data Flows between Organizations

Organizations based in Europe would also face disruptions to the extent that there are restrictions on the flow of personal data between organizations. Disruptions would occur whenever a business or individual would have had an opportunity to enter into a transaction but could not do so because of the restrictions on transfers of named information. Once again, the degree of disruption would depend on the tightness of the link between the processing of data in Europe and third countries. At one extreme are transnational networks in which the sharing of data is pervasive. At the other are transactions in which no personal information is ordinarily shared. Data protection rules would have little or no effect on the latter sort of transaction.

Substantial attention has recently been focused on network externalities or network effects, defined as markets in which the value that purchasers place on a good increases as others buy the good.[17] Network effects are familiar from the fact that telephones, e-mail, and fax machines all become more useful the larger the number of other people that have compatible equipment. The World Wide Web itself is far more useful because of the enormous number of people who use its standard programming language and protocols. In software, there are arguably important efficiencies from having many people use the same operating system, so that software designers can design their products for that system and users can learn how to work it without the need to learn different programs.[18]

Where network effects exist, losses are caused by barriers placed between two parts of the network. The network is then not as large as it otherwise would be, and its value to users is reduced by this smaller size. One example of this problem would be if it were forbidden to send e-mail containing personal information from Europe to third countries. Our discussion of e-mail in chapter 3 showed why many e-mails would apparently violate the plain language of the Directive, even though early enforcement actions against ordinary e-mail users are unlikely. A possible limit on e-mails, however, does illustrate how network effects can exist; e-mail, although still very useful, would be significantly less useful to Europeans to the extent that e-mail messages could not be sent out of Europe.

Another example of network effects occurs for corporate extranets and other business-to-business electronic commerce. As discussed in chapter 3, many procurement actions involve the exchange of named information between the buying and selling companies. The electronic linkages can be very tight between organizations engaged in electronic commerce. A limit on transfer of named information out of Europe could have a correspondingly disruptive effect. European companies wishing to purchase from third

<hr>

17. Mark A. Lemley and David McGowan, "Legal Implications of Network Economic Effects," *California Law Review*, vol. 86 (forthcoming).

18. Lemley and McGowan, "Legal Implications" (discussing possible efficiencies of having a Microsoft monopoly on an operating system).

countries or sell to third countries might find that they cannot use state-of-the-art electronic means to do so.

Throughout the book, we have highlighted other effects that would be caused by limits on transfers between organizations, from Europe to third countries. A partial list, with emphasis on effects within Europe itself, would include:

—Auditing and accounting. Operations in Europe may face obstacles in exchanging auditing and accounting information with operations in third countries.

—Business consulting. Transfers of European corporate information to consultants elsewhere could be banned. European consultants could be prohibited from making reports to clients in third countries if the reports contain named information.

—Call centers and other worldwide customer service. Information about European purchasers may not be available in call centers in third countries. Call centers and other service operations based in Europe would be limited in what information they could disclose to persons in third countries.

—Payments systems. Problems may arise when the major processing center exists in Europe (with limits on information that it can send) or in the third country (with limits on the ability to send transactional information to the processing center).

—Reinsurance and loan participations. Difficulties may face European insurers who want to purchase reinsurance from third countries or banks that want to sell loan participations to third countries.

—Investment banking. Limits on market analysis within Europe would tend to reduce the efficiency of European capital markets, as would limits on takeovers. European firms that wished to use investment bankers in third countries could face significant obstacles in doing so.

—Individual credit histories. Limits on transfers of information to credit agencies could deprive European individuals of the ability to develop an accurate and complete credit history, thereby increasing their cost of credit.

—Corporate credit histories. Businesses, especially small- and medium-sized enterprises, often must establish credit histories to qualify to do business with other corporations. Limits on the use of corporate credit histories would reduce European businesses' ability to establish new business relationships with third countries.

—Press archives and look-up services. Data protection authorities have discussed whether limits should apply on information services such as Lexis/

Nexis. Such limits would mean that persons in third countries might be able to conduct research that would not be available to those doing research in Europe.

—International conferences. Those participating in conferences in Europe may face restrictions in bringing information home. These limits would not apply to conferences held in third countries.

—Pharmaceuticals. Data protection rules may make it more costly or impossible to include European residents in pharmaceutical research. Drugs might therefore be tested on non-European populations, which may differ in medically significant respects from European populations.

—Business and leisure travel. Europeans may face restrictions or higher costs in receiving travel services in third countries because of limits on the transfer of personal information to travel service providers.

In addition to these and other sectoral effects, our discussion of the market of one shows the general pattern of how purchasers in Europe may be affected by limits on the transfer of personal information to third countries. The market of one holds out the possibility of advantages to purchasers, who become aware of precisely the opportunities that they are most likely to prefer. Large flows of personal information are likely necessary to create the market of one. Difficult judgments will need to be made by countries about how to balance the advantages of opening up these opportunities against the disadvantages of loss of privacy. When the purchasers are businesses, the lost opportunities may especially not be worth the price. When the purchasers are individuals, privacy arguments are more powerful.

Dynamic Effects

There is an additional, more explicitly dynamic, element of the effects on Europe of limits on transfers to third countries. From the European side, an important possible advantage of the Directive is the incentive it creates for third countries to strengthen their privacy laws. If the United States and other third countries do indeed pass strict new laws, there will be no reason to impose limits on transfers from Europe to these countries. The adverse effects that limits would have on Europe, which we have listed here, would not apply.

For proponents of the Directive, this optimistic view of its effects on third countries can be combined with the consumer confidence argument analyzed in chapter 4, which held that good data protection laws will increase electronic commerce by assuring consumers that it is safe to do business on the Web. From this view the Article 25 restriction on transfers is one more good rule that encourages Europeans to do business. By prohibiting transfers to unsafe locales, Article 25 might facilitate a fair and reliable commerce.

Although the Directive creates some pressure on third countries to tighten privacy laws, and may help some European consumers to be more confident in engaging in electronic commerce, there are significant counterarguments. The evidence at this point is that the United States and other important third countries are *not* going to adopt comprehensive privacy laws on the European model in the near future. Our discussion of the consumer confidence argument, furthermore, showed that it was subject to strong critiques, including that it would not apply to the business-to-business sales that predominate in electronic commerce.

In considering the dynamic effect of the Directive there is also the possibility that strict data protection rules in Europe, coupled with less strict rules in other countries, will pose a competitive disadvantage for Europe. The risk is that Europe will fall behind in creating the information society. Innovation in information products and services might be easier in countries with fewer restrictions on the flow of information. Innovators in the less regulated countries will not need to spend as much time seeing how their products mesh with the complex regulations of the Directive. In addition, any such reduction in innovation may prove especially costly in information markets. First-mover advantages in such markets are often believed to be considerable, so that the first entrants into a market often gain enormous market share.

Conclusion

This chapter has examined various sectors that may be affected by the Directive, including the press, nonprofit organizations, international conferences, international educational institutions, non-EU governments, pharmaceuticals, Internet service providers, business and leisure travel, and direct marketing. Although these sectors do not by any means exhaust the range of actors affected by the Directive, we believe our analysis provides guidance for how to analyze the issues that will arise for other sectors. The chapter concludes with an examination of some specific effects that may be felt within Europe if there are limits placed on transfers to third countries.

8

Policy Recommendations for Privacy Issues

Our principal task in the previous chapters has been descriptive, to probe the meaning of the Directive and understand what effects it will likely have on the United States and other third countries. In this chapter we turn to our policy recommendations. We first examine the information cultures of Europe and the United States and show the dilemmas facing both the European Union and the regulated community as implementation of the Directive begins. We next show how effective self-regulatory mechanisms as model contracts can play a crucial role in escaping from the dilemmas. In looking at policy options facing the European Union, we discuss the likelihood that the United States will not be found generally adequate, even though particular sectors are probably adequate. We then look at reasons from the EU perspective why there should be an openness to the use of self-regulatory measures (SRM) and examine a number of places where it will be important to clarify the meaning of the Directive.

After recommending that the United States create an Office of Electronic Commerce and Privacy Policy within the Department of Commerce, we conclude by discussing the role the World Trade Organization might play as a forum for resolving individual trade disputes and as a more general forum for resolving privacy debates.

Information Cultures and the Dilemmas of Enforcement

Much of the debate about the Directive comes down to a choice between broad laws, the European tendency, and narrow laws, the American

152

tendency.[1] Under the European Directive, many routine and desirable trans-fers of information would apparently be restricted. For instance, as written the Directive would appear to hinder pharmaceutical research, could pose a major obstacle to investment banks' collection of important information about companies, and would call into doubt many mainframe and intranet applications that involve processing data in the United States or other third countries. In contrast, U.S. privacy laws have been sharply criticized for being haphazard, incomplete, and lax.[2] It strikes many people as odd, for instance, that video rental records are often regulated more strictly than sensitive medical data.

The differences in laws are to a significant extent a reflection of differ-ent information cultures. Americans historically have a strong suspicion of government and a relatively strong esteem for markets and technology. The United States has an almost religious attitude toward free speech rights under the First Amendment, and a strong tradition of keeping government records and proceedings open to the public. Europeans, by contrast, have given government a more prominent role in fostering social welfare but have placed more limits on unfettered development of markets and tech-nology. Many European governments regulate themselves less strictly than the United States does for open meeting and freedom of information laws. European governments are often more strict, however, in regulating the press and other private sector uses of information.

The Directive, which will be effective October 1998, has precipitated a clash between the differing information cultures. In the European view the United States has disappointingly weak protection of individual rights to privacy. To protect these fundamental rights, it is better to err on the side

---

1. See Alan Westin, ed., *Data Protection in the Global Society* (American Institute for Contemporary German Studies, 1996) (contrasting U.S. and European approaches to privacy regulation).

The distinctive American information culture even extends to what secrets are disclosed in the course of litigation. See Geoffrey C. Hazard, Jr., "From Whom No Secrets Are Hid," *Texas Law Review*, vol. 76 (1998), p. 1665. Professor Hazard quotes the U.S. Supreme Court: "Mutual knowl-edge of all relevant facts gathered by both parties is essential to proper litigation." *Hickman v. Taylor*, 329 U.S. 495 (1947). He then notes: "Such, however, is not the basis of procedural policy in any other country in the world."

2. For instance, Spiros Simitis, Germany's first data protection official, described the American approach to data protection as "an obviously erratic regulation full of contradictions, characterized by a fortuitous and totally unbalanced choice of its subjects." Spiros Simitis, "New Trends in National and International Data Protection Law," in J. Dumortier, ed., *Recent Developments in Data Privacy Law* (1992), pp. 17, 22, quoted in Robert M. Gellman, "Fragmented, Incomplete, and Discontinu-ous: The Failure of Federal Privacy Regulatory Proposals and Institutions," *Software Law Journal*, vol. 6 (1993), pp. 199, 203.

of protective regulation. In the American view the Directive's regulations mean that many organizations will have to carry out costly compliance measures when there is little or no social harm caused by unregulated practices. It would be better to seek other ways to protect against violations of privacy without subjecting so many organizations to strict legal mandates. Our discussion of the market of one in chapter 7 was intended to give a sense of ways in which a more open flow of information could have important benefits to people.

Beyond this clash of information cultures, there is tremendous uncertainty about how strictly the Directive will be enforced. When it was promulgated, there was a hope among at least some Europeans that the United States and other third countries would create new privacy laws that would meet the adequacy test. It is now clear that comprehensive privacy laws, whether or not desirable, are unlikely to be passed in the United States very soon.

This lack of new legislation has left the European Union in a dilemma. On the one hand, it has taken a stand that privacy is a fundamental human right requiring careful legal protection. To protect these important rights, the Directive requires that transfers of information to third countries be allowed only when they are adequately protected. The consequence of this position is that violations of adequate protection are to be taken seriously. Companies and other organizations must comply with the Directive and national laws as written. As many senior EU officials have stated, the political will of Europe should not be doubted in this matter. Access to the enormous EU market will depend on compliance with data protection laws. Regulators also must take a tough stance on privacy to push organizations based in Europe to live up to their obligations.

This book has treated the passage of the Directive and the statements of officials as sincere and serious expressions of EU law and policy. We have pointed out many places where the Directive is unclear or appears to prohibit routine and desirable uses of personal information.[3] The dilemma facing the European data protection regime then becomes clear. On the one hand, the regime is designed to protect important human rights. On the other hand, no European official wishes to create a major trade war or prohibit practices that are desirable or vital to European and other economies.

---

3. A list of applications needing clarification is given later in this chapter in the discussion of policy recommendations to the European Union.

The desire to avoid confrontation and economic harm results in quite different statements from those supporting the European regime. The United States is told that it should not be alarmist about the Directive. Data protection laws have existed in Europe for many years and have caused few problems. The history of data protection enforcement is described as one of sensible and incremental implementation, with encouragement of good privacy practices but few penalties on individual organizations. Therefore, organizations that are "good" on privacy should not worry about technical violations of the language of the Directive. In the mildest form of this view, the Directive is described as simply one more effort to encourage organizations based in Europe and elsewhere to make progress in protecting privacy.

The problem of course is that Europe cannot strictly enforce the letter of the Directive and at the same time announce that organizations can routinely ignore it. It violates the rule of law and fundamental fairness to enforce a law strictly against some while allowing others to violate the same law in the same way. This sort of enforcement would be the opposite of transparent—reading the rules would give people no opportunity to know what is permitted or forbidden. A particular worry is that enforcement of a very broad law will be done selectively and unfairly. An often expressed concern of U.S.-based firms is that they might be targeted for enforcement, even when they follow the same privacy practices as their Europe-based competitors. This targeting may fit the perception that American companies are less careful on privacy issues, and the focus may be politically popular in Europe.

The dilemma of the European Union is mirrored in the dilemma of the organizations expected to comply with the Directive. If the Directive is going to be enforced as written, these organizations will have to take immediate measures to comply. New consent forms must be drafted, operations of mainframes and other information processing might be shifted to Europe, and internal procedures must be amended. Policies for company intranets and extranets must be adopted. A comprehensive internal audit must be done of flows of personal information from the European Union to the United States, the third world, and all other countries that arguably lack adequate protection. Some product lines that require intensive use of personal information in order to be profitable might have to be dropped. National laws within the European Union will have to be carefully examined (even though some have not yet been adopted), so that there is compliance with each country's requirements. Privacy advocates might view these developments with delight. Businesses may not yet be prepared to go so far.

If, however, the Directive is primarily hortatory, these crash efforts to comply will seem expensive and unnecessary. Many businesspersons have expressed the view that "they just can't do that"—the European Union will simply not be willing or able to enforce the Directive as written. The budgets and staffs of data protection authorities are limited. Because so many categories of data and so many organizations are affected by the Directive, some organizations might decide not to comply. They might correctly judge that the risks of expensive enforcement actions are low. Privacy practices might be adopted when they help profits, but not otherwise. Of course, in this scenario organizations will knowingly engage in routine violations of a law. But some might rather do that than undergo the expense and disruption of complying.

The challenge for policymakers and the regulated organizations is how to steer a sensible course between the unattractive options of harsh enforcement and public flouting of the law. A related challenge is how to vindicate privacy values while controlling the burdens of compliance. In particular, there may be opportunities to reduce compliance burdens when there is little risk to privacy.

In seeking to address these challenges, our first goal has been to offer an accurate description of the potential effects of the Directive on various industries and in various situations. The previous chapters of this book have examined how data protection laws may work. With these surveys in mind, we are in a better position to recommend specific steps that businesses, the European Union, and the United States can take to avoid destructive conflict and meet the goals of each.

Our recommended resolution calls for significant action by all parties. The proposals here address the challenges, build on the self-interest of each party, and focus on important risks to privacy while seeking to keep compliance costs manageable. They promote transparency and fairness by bringing the actions of the regulated into closer agreement with announced law and policy. Finally, the proposals show a workable way to avoid destructive conflict about privacy between Europe and the United States and provide a model for addressing the issues of electronic commerce and Internet governance that loom ahead.

Effective Self-Regulatory Measures

Many organizations operate in Europe and in third countries, including the United States. This book has discussed some of the ways they routinely transfer personal information from Europe to third countries. These organizations face many uncertainties about what data processing is permitted within the European Union. The uncertainties multiply as data are transferred to third countries, where there will often not have been any EU decision on whether protection is adequate. To reduce these uncertainties, we strongly recommend that the organizations involved in significant transfers to third countries consider adopting effective self-regulatory mechanisms to govern such transfers. We also strongly recommend that EU countries find that such measures, when properly drafted, constitute adequate safeguards of privacy under Article 26(2), so that compliance with them would protect a company from enforcement actions.

A decisive advantage of self-regulatory measures is that they enable organizations that wish to comply with the Directive to do so. There is no need to wait for the national legislature to pass a comprehensive privacy law. There is no need to wait for data protection agencies, which may be heavily burdened in implementing the Directive, to give prior consent to each transfer or category of transfer. Organizations that wish to be good citizens on data protection can take responsibility for adopting good privacy practices. By contrast, if compliance with self-regulatory measures is not considered enough to comply with the Directive, there will be far weaker incentives for organizations to seek to comply. If even substantial and good-faith efforts by controllers still leave organizations in violation, practical managers may decide that the effort to comply is not worthwhile.

In considering the role of self-regulatory measures, a word about terminology is in order. "Codes of conduct" usually refer to industry association or sectorwide provisions. "Principles" or "policies" usually refer to rules adopted by individual companies. "Contracts" usually refer to individual company arrangements, such as an agreement about the terms for transferring data from a company in Europe to another in the United States. "Model contracts" refer to efforts to provide standard terms for transferring data. These model contracts might be adopted verbatim by companies, or the model contract terms might be incorporated into individual contracts with some supplementation or modification to take account of the parties' special situations. For all of these self-regulatory measures, one can imagine a scale between the hortatory (encouraging parties to follow good privacy practices) and the binding (providing for legally enforceable punishments for failure to comply). In terms of the Directive, the central question is when an SRM constitutes an adequate safeguard under Article 26(2).

In seeking to answer this question, a useful starting point is the working document released by the Article 29 Working Party in early 1998 entitled *Judging Industry Self-Regulation* (hereafter called *Industry Self-Regulation* or the working document).[4] We will then turn to the similar discussion in the April 1998 Working Party document entitled *Preliminary Views on the Use of Contractual Provisions in the Context of Transfers of Personal Data to Third Countries* (hereafter called *Contractual Provisions*).[5]

The working document tries to assess the extent to which self-regulation in a third country helps to establish adequate protection under Article 25. In doing so, some parts assume that an *industry* is adopting a code, rather than a particular company. For instance, it asks what fraction of an industry has agreed with a code and whether members of an industry are aware of a code's existence. Our discussion here contemplates the possibility of having an industry code of conduct, a contract signed by particular companies, or both.

An industry code of conduct can be highly useful even if it does not fulfill all of the requirements for establishing Article 25 adequacy for an entire industry or profession. Agreeing to comply with a code may have various sorts of legal significance. First, including a code in a contract might increase the possibility that a data protection authority will approve the contract. Second, a data protection authority may adopt a general position, announced in advance, that agreement to comply with a code or model contract provision is considered an adequate safeguard. Third, senior European Commission officials have explained in public meetings that all transfers after October 1998 will *not* need to be approved in advance by data protection authorities. Required preapproval would create impossible administrative tangles. Organizations therefore will need to determine what sorts of procedures to adopt in light of the many areas of uncertainty in the application of the Directive. Compliance with a code of conduct or model contract that has been developed in consultation with data protection officials would seem to offer a good measure of practical protection against subsequent enforcement actions.

The working document sets forth specific expectations about how strict

4. Working Party on the Protection of Individuals with Regard to the Processing of Personal Data, *Judging Industry Self-Regulation: When Does It Make a Meaningful Contribution to the Level of Data Protection in a Third Country?* (January 14, 1998), available at http//europa.eu.int/comm/dg15/en.

5. Working Party on the Protection of Individuals with Regard to the Processing of Personal Data, *Preliminary Views on the Use of Contractual Provisions in the Context of Transfers of Personal Data to Third Countries,* DGXV D/5005/98 (April 22, 1998).

self-regulation should be in order to help permit transfers to third countries, notably including the contribution of a code to "a good level of general compliance." In examining these expectations, one general point to keep in mind is that the legal standard is whether there are "adequate safeguards" in connection with the transfer. As discussed earlier, this legal requirement is less strict than a requirement that "equivalent" safeguards be available in the third country. The SRM must provide significant privacy protections that are adequate, but transfers should not be considered illegal simply because the protections are not the same as in Europe. In discussing the working document, we will look to its discussion of remedial and punitive sanctions, outside verification of compliance, and support to individual data subjects, including dispute resolution. We will then examine some promising ways that self-regulatory measures can protect important privacy values while reducing the compliance burden on organizations.

"Remedial" and "Punitive" Sanctions, and Outside Verification of Compliance

In discussing self-regulatory measures, a leading concern of European regulators has been to ensure enforceability. In the words of one European Commission official, self-regulatory efforts "must be manifestly enforced or enforceable in practice, and they must offer a genuine means of redress to individuals who may suffer as a result of the code being breached."[6] On this topic the working document is interesting because it expects both "remedial" and "punitive" sanctions for violation of a code of conduct. A "remedial" sanction requires the controller, in the event of a violation, to bring its practices into compliance with the SRM that it has adopted. Such a remedy would seem to be a natural consequence of adopting an SRM.

The working document, though, also seems to require that a company expose itself either to "punitive" sanctions or mandatory external audits. The use of the term "punitive" creates a potential problem. To American ears, the term invokes punitive damages in a state tort suit. Such damages can be awarded at a jury's discretion for behavior that it finds wanton or willful. American businesses are understandably leery of exposing themselves to punitive tort damages in light of widespread publicity about runaway jury verdicts in the millions of dollars.

---

6. Letter from Ulf Bruehann, Directorate General XV of the European Commission, to Robert Vastine, January 1998.

The working document, however, appears to use "punitive" in a less draconian fashion. Punitive sanctions are those that "actually punish the controller for its failure to comply." Such sanctions have "an effect on the future behavior of data controllers by providing some incentive to comply with the code on an ongoing basis. . . . The absence of genuinely dissuasive and punitive sanctions is therefore a major weakness in a code." There is no mention of the potentially enormous jury damages available in an American tort suit, and such damages are rare in European law.

After discussions with knowledgeable persons, it seems possible that more modest sanctions would satisfy the working document's definition of punitive. For instance, under the U.S. Fair Credit Reporting Act, any person who willfully violates the act is liable for "any actual damages sustained by the consumer as a result of the failure or damages of not less than $100 and not more than $1,000."[7] These statutory damages are significant in the historical context of fines levied in Europe for individual violations of data protection rules. Fines at this level, which might apply to each violation, might thus meet the working document's definition of punitive. If so, transnational companies may be able to accept punitive damages as proposed by the Europeans. As additional evidence of the existence of punitive sanctions, companies in the United States that agree to bind themselves to self-regulatory measures and fail to honor their commitments may be exposed to suit for unfair and deceptive trade practices under the Federal Trade Commission Act and similar state laws.

It is also possible to argue that punitive damages are not a necessary part of an SRM. The test for adequacy under Article 25(2) is "in the light of all the circumstances" and the requirement is to show "adequate safeguards." For any one element of an SRM, therefore, a company can argue that a less strict provision is justified than is suggested in the working document. With respect to punitive sanctions, a company could argue that focusing only on legal, punitive remedies ignores other reasons that a firm would not wish to have an enforcement action even for purely remedial sanctions. It could, for example, face severe penalties in the marketplace from bad publicity—loss of goodwill from customers, employees, and regulators—that can create strong incentives to comply in the absence of punitive sanctions. In addition, within the European Union there has been limited reliance on punitive sanctions. One might thus question whether

7. 15 U.S.C. § 1681n.

punitive sanctions are as essential to adequate compliance as suggested in the working document.

Organizations wishing to make this argument that punitive sanctions need not be included in the code will have to make a practical judgment about how the overall SRM can be shown to European authorities to be adequate. It may well be possible to omit one or a few of the apparent requirements laid down in the working document and similar statements by European officials. Other compliance provisions might make up for aspects of an SRM that are less strict than the working document contemplates. Nonetheless, a useful strategy in drafting an SRM may be to determine where it is possible to meet the stated requirements of the working document. If punitive sanctions can be included in a manageable way, disagreements between companies and European officials can be saved for other instances when it is more difficult or expensive to comply.

Along with sanctions, the working document contemplates "the existence of a system of external verification (such as the requirement for an audit of compliance at regular intervals)." The document treats verification as important but less "crucial" than "the nature and enforcement of sanctions in cases of non-compliance." Where there are no punitive sanctions, "it is difficult to see how a good level of overall compliance could be achieved, unless a rigorous system of external verification (such as a public or private authority competent to intervene in case of noncompliance with the code, or a compulsory requirement for external audit at regular intervals) were put in place."

In drafting any SRM, a central question will be how to assure regulators that there will be a good level of compliance. Some companies have suggested that external audits are too expensive. If so, some other means will need to be found to satisfy European regulators. One possibility is to include punitive sanctions. Other possibilities would be to establish institutional controls or submit to the jurisdiction of a European data protection authority. The overall goal is to design a package of provisions that, taken together, meets the definition of adequate protection of privacy.

Support for Individual Data Subjects

The working document stresses that "a key requirement of an adequate and effective data protection system is that an individual faced with a problem regarding his/her personal data is not left alone, but is given some institutional support allowing his/her difficulties to be addressed. This institutional support ideally should be impartial, independent and equipped with the necessary powers to investigate any complaint from a data subject." These requirements seem natural in the European system with its national data protection authorities. Indeed, in Europe, institutional support for the complaints of data subjects is probably far more common than seeking punitive sanctions.

It is far more challenging, however, to satisfy the language of the working document when no supervisory authority exists, as in the United States. It is not yet clear how best to address this issue. One possibility may be for a company to agree to submit to the jurisdiction of the supervisory authority in one or more EU member states for independent support. In other words, a U.S. corporation that receives data from Europe might designate a national authority as having certain powers to investigate complaints about data processing. Another possibility would be to designate some other institution in the United States or Europe to play this role. A third possibility is to decide that the proposed SRM will not provide the sort of institutional support that is provided by supervisory authorities in Europe. In support of this third possibility, companies might take the position that it is unfair for them to have to create (and perhaps fund) an independent agency of the sort that is supported by general taxes in Europe. The companies would then point to other safeguards and argue that, taken as a whole, the SRM provides adequate protection. As stated in connection with punitive sanctions, however, a judgment must be made about whether this issue is one on which the SRM should depart so visibly from the expectations of the working document.

A related issue is how to design the process for resolving disputes between individuals and companies that have adopted the SRM. In Europe such disputes are handled under national law. The options here are analogous to those just discussed. First, one could try to bring disputes within the jurisdiction of one or more of the member states. In many ways this is the most appealing solution. European authorities would have jurisdiction over personal data originating in Europe. Disputes concerning a person in Europe would be handled in that person's own country, typically in the person's own language. From the company's perspective, being brought under the country's jurisdiction might also be the best solution. The pattern in European data protection law has often been to announce strict rules that appear to prohibit desirable practices but to have considerably more flexibility in practice. If an American processor of data from Europe is treated the same as a European processor, under the same national law, these possibilities of flexibility might be built into the enforcement of the model contract or code of conduct. The contract or code would not need to specify all of the possible areas of flexibility, because the American company would receive the same treatment as a European company. In addition, there is an important protection if the national authority decided to be especially strict in enforcing against the American company. Unjust discrimination of treatment could give rise to a claim in the World Trade Organization. There is thus a significant legal limit on the possibility of discrimination against processing done in third countries.

In drafting the SRM a different approach would be to establish a new dispute resolution process or designate that cases would go to some existing system. One potentially attractive model could be the arbitration system administered by the National Association of Securities Dealers. The NASD system handles a large volume of consumer disputes each year, and the contracts that funnel people into the system have been specifically upheld in a U.S. Supreme Court decision.[8] Finally, one might propose that no dispute resolution is necessary under the SRM, or that companies could handle complaints as an entirely internal matter. It is doubtful, however, that European officials would find that this offers adequate protection of privacy.

The April 1998 Working Party Document on Contractual Provisions

After the text of this book was substantially completed, the Working Party released *Preliminary Views on the Use of Contractual Provisions in the Context of Transfers of Personal Data to Third Countries* in April 1998. The document suggests that the Working Party is noticeably more open to the use of contracts than it appeared to be in its 1997 *First Orientations*, where contract solutions were only "rarely" to be allowed. *Contractual Provisions* emphasizes that there are particular practical difficulties in investigating noncompliance with a contract, especially when the third country has no supervisory authority. "Taken together, these two considerations mean that there will be some situations in which a contractual solution may be an appropriate solution, and others where it may be impossible for a contract to guarantee the necessary 'adequate safeguards.'" In short, contracts will be available in "some situations," which would seem to be more often than

8. *Shearson/American Express, Inc.* v. *McMahon*, 483 U.S. 1056 (1987).

"rarely." Furthermore, conversations with senior data protection officials in the late spring 1998 confirmed a greater willingness to develop contracts than was apparent a year earlier.

The *Contractual Provisions* document closely follows the approach laid out in the January 1998 working document. Once again, adequate protection requires a good level of compliance in practice, support available to individual data subjects in the exercise of their rights, and appropriate means of redress when the principles are not complied with. When data are transferred to a third country, individuals must retain their data protection rights, including the principle that "data should be processed for a specific purpose and subsequently used or further communicated only insofar as this is not incompatible with the purpose of the transfer."[9] Concerns are expressed about the resource challenges facing EU agencies in overseeing contracts, and "it is probable that in most situations a contractual solution will need to be complemented by at least the possibility of some form of external verification of the recipient's processing activities, such as an audit carried out by a standards body, or specialist auditing firm."

Contractual Provisions parallels the analysis in this book in suggesting that contracts will likely be most feasible and effective for mainframe applications: "Contractual solutions are probably best suited to large international networks (credit cards, airline reservations) characterised by large quantities of repetitive data transfers of a similar nature, and by a relatively small number of large operators in industries already subject to significant public scrutiny and regulation." Enforcement will also be easier when the recipients of data are affiliates of European operations: "Intracompany data transfers between different branches of the same company group is another area in which there is considerable potential for the use of contracts."

In short, *Contractual Provisions* is an important and pragmatic step by the Working Party toward developing self-regulatory measures that can be the basis for compliance by companies that do business both in the European Union and in third countries. American companies, however, may continue to find the requirements laid out in the document to be substantially stricter about data protection than the companies' current practices. A lengthy process of negotiation and learning is likely as data protection officials and companies seek to implement workable self-regulatory measures in specific situations.

9. Working Party on the Protection of Individuals with Regard to the Processing of Personal Data, *First Orientations on Transfers of Personal Data to Third Countries: Possible Ways Forward in Assessing Adequacy*, XV D/5020/97–EN final (June 26, 1997).

Institutional Controls as a Mechanism for Compliance

One promising route for compliance in self-regulatory measures may be through what are sometimes called "institutional controls," policies and procedures adopted by companies to protect personal information. Institutional controls are not simply a matter of a company's asserting that it will achieve good privacy practices. Institutional controls would describe the specific steps taken by a company to help achieve data protection goals. Examples would include policies adopted by senior management, training programs for personnel, and specific security measures adopted with respect to access to personal data.

The Directive offers textual support for the importance of institutional controls. Article 25(2) says that "particular consideration shall be given to . . . the professional rules and security measures which are complied with in that country." Effective institutional controls would seem to qualify as such "professional rules and security measures." In some instances, the institutional controls may simply be codification of good practices already in place.

Two useful precedents for such controls come from the protection of trade secrets and from banking regulation. There are obvious analogies between protection of trade secrets and protection of personal information. In both settings a company may have information that it does not wish to have released except under authorized circumstances. In both settings the legitimate need to use the information may require that a substantial number of people in the company have access to it in appropriate situations. The regulatory challenge, then, is how to allow access to the information where appropriate while otherwise preventing its disclosure.

Interviews with high-technology companies suggest various ways to protect trade secrets. Here is the relatively strict procedure followed at one major U.S. corporation for persons with access to trade secrets. A new employee is required to read the company's detailed trade secrets agreement and sign it in the presence of a witness. The employee must watch a video describing trade secrets procedures and is required to view it again at regular intervals, perhaps once a year. Regular reminders about trade secrets and other intellectual property protections are sent to employees. Access to trade secrets is generally based on "need to know," with different passwords required to gain information on various parts of the company's intranet.

In U.S. banking regulation, institutional controls are an important element of each bank's compliance program. A required part of each bank examination is the "adequacy of and compliance with internal policies."[10] The assessment of management "takes into account the quality of internal controls, operating procedures and all lending, investment and operating policies; and the involvement of the directors and shareholders."

The trade secret and banking precedents suggest several advantages of including institutional controls in an SRM. First, the precedents show that both companies and regulators have found institutional controls to be a useful part of an overall compliance strategy. Second, U.S. managers may find it an easier and more familiar task to implement a company's own privacy procedures than to comply with the vague, multifaceted test for "adequacy" in Article 25. Individual managers can be assigned responsibility for following the company policies, with their job performance evaluated on the level of compliance. Third, because adequacy is assessed "in light of all the circumstances surrounding a data transfer" (Article 25(2)), the use of institutional controls can be a component of an overall package that assures European authorities there is adequate protection. In particular, the existence of internal controls can help show that there is a "good general level of compliance." Fourth, attention to institutional controls may be useful in working with European data protection officials. The debate until now has often focused on abstract discussions about human rights to privacy or the differing privacy cultures in Europe and the United States. When the Directive goes into effect, it becomes more urgent to focus attention instead on what policies and procedures a company might reasonably be expected to adopt. Regulators might thus provide useful and detailed guidance about what sorts of procedures are considered most important for compliance. These procedures can then be built into widely available codes of conduct, model contracts, or other self-regulatory measures.

Because institutional controls have not been a prominent aspect of compliance with data protection laws, how to build institutional controls into an SRM would need to be resolved in consultation with European authorities. Some important issues would include:

—What sort of institutional controls should be adopted? To what extent can they be added to existing security procedures or to procedures for

---

10. U.S. banks are rated under the "CAMEL" system: capital adequacy, asset quality, management, earnings, and liquidity. Institutional controls come within the "management" part of bank examinations. Quotations here are from the Federal Deposit Insurance Corporation, *Manual of Bank Examination Policies, Basic Examination Concepts, and Guidelines*, available at http://www.fdic.gov/banknews/manuals/exampoli/.

protecting trade secrets and other intellectual property? How, if at all, should the institutional controls vary by industry or by type of information system?

—How would the policies be communicated and carried out within the organization? What personnel would be included in the data protection compliance program? What measures, such as password protection of databases containing personal information, might be used to limit the number of personnel?

—What benefits would the institutional controls create in terms of protecting personal information and achieving other corporate goals?

—What costs would the policies create? What would the policy cost and would it hinder achievement of other corporate goals?

—Of great importance to European authorities, what sorts of verification would exist that policies are being followed? Do professional organizations or other bodies exist that can help ensure compliance? If the existence of institutional controls is to be useful in persuading authorities that adequate protection exists, the controls must be credible.

—What sorts of sanctions, if any, would exist for failure to implement the institutional controls? For instance, if a company promises to institute a training program for employees, would there be any sanction for failing to follow through?

In summary, companies might agree to follow certain policies and procedures as part of their compliance with data protection rules. They might, for example, provide training programs for employees and security procedures for access to databases containing personal information. One possible risk is that they could be exposed to double sanctions: once for improper handling of a person's information and again for failure to follow the company's stated procedures. But the risk to an organization of additional sanctions might be outweighed by what institutional controls could provide in assuring regulators of the adequacy of an organization's processing of data.

Focusing on the Greatest Threats to Privacy

From a company's perspective, a self-regulatory measure becomes more burdensome as it applies to more and more kinds of data processing. From the perspective of European regulators, an SRM is less likely to be widely adopted or complied with if it becomes too burdensome. Both sides thus have a significant incentive to have an SRM focus on the sorts of processing that pose the greatest threats to privacy. Indeed, in a study prepared for the European Commission, Yves Poullet and Bénédicte Havelange suggested that the strictness of data protection rules should vary with the level of risk to privacy.[11] They did not, however, show how to carry out a flexible program in a practical way.

We advocate a risk-based approach with three elements. First, it is possible and desirable to identify certain categories of data processing that are low risk. For low-risk data processing, the rules in an SRM would not need to be as strict. In some instances, personal information in a low-risk category would ordinarily be transferable even to third countries that lack adequate protection.

Second, stricter rules may be appropriate for "sensitive" personal data, as defined in Article 8 of the Directive and under national laws. In discussing categories of processing that are generally low risk, data protection officials have emphasized that special protection is often needed for information about topics such as racial and ethnic identity and religious affiliation. For categories of transfers where an SRM would not generally apply, there could be special provisions limiting transfers of sensitive information.[12]

Third, the presumption of transferability would not apply where there is specific intent by the user to circumvent data protection rules. This exception addresses the concern that companies would use low-risk categories of processing to evade the stricter rules that apply to higher-risk categories.

The advantages of adopting this categorical approach to processing could be substantial. Self-regulatory measures could focus on the sorts of processing that are of greatest concern to data protection officials. Other sorts, which raise few privacy concerns, would not need to be governed by the measures. At the same time, the measures would apply to the unusual cases in which low-risk processing turns out to pose greater risks to privacy, namely, for sensitive data and deliberate evasion. Discussions could be held with data protection officials to help define what sorts of rules might be appropriate concerning these situations.

Turning to possible categories that pose a low risk to privacy, one can begin with laptop computers. Data protection officials are split about

11. Yves Poullet and Bénédict Havelange, *Preparation of a Methodology for Evaluating the Adequacy of the Level of Protection of Physical Persons with Respect to Data Processing with a Personal Character,* ETD/95/B5-3000/165 (European Commission-DG XV, December 1996).

12. Such limits might be especially appropriate where there are systematic or substantial transfers of sensitive personal data. Such language might permit the occasional or incidental transfer of sensitive data, for example when a company lists the religion of a business contact to avoid violating that person's dietary restrictions at meetings.

whether the Directive could be used to block transfer of laptops to countries that lack adequate protection. To clear up the uncertainty, an SRM could state that laptops are not subject to data protection rules unless they contain significant amounts of sensitive data or are being used deliberately to evade protection rules. Thus employees ordinarily could carry laptops on company business. They could not, however, use them to transfer databases of sensitive medical information out of Europe.

Another candidate for the low-risk category is information processed about persons in their business capacity. The focus of data protection laws concerns people in their capacity as private individuals so that information is not misused against them as employees, or borrowers, or consumers. But there are low risks to individual privacy (and likely large burdens on companies) if the full sweep of data protection law applies to information that is gathered about individuals in their business capacity. For instance, e-mails, computer-generated faxes, and many transfers on company intranets contain information in which the names are relevant for the business of the employer. Information about individual employees, such as purchasing agents and many others, is routinely exchanged with other organizations in business-to-business sales and in many other contexts. Categories of transfer might be defined where the risks to privacy are low and strict data protection rules need not apply.[13]

This proposed policy builds on the risk-based approach that has been recommended to the European Commission by its consultants Poullet and Havelange. It is difficult to assess at this time the extent to which European officials will be open to its use in general or in the particular instances suggested here. If they are receptive, perhaps after some modification further categories might be identified as posing low risks, especially if there are high compliance burdens on companies. In such instances, it may be appropriate to try to define the categories with some precision so that the SRM can be amended in a way that is as simple as possible to apply.

13. Discussions with European data protection officials indicate a willingness to consider some of these sorts of information as outside the scope of the Directive. Less clear at this time is the legal route for defining what categories of named information would have to be governed by data protection rules. The proposal here is to exclude some categories explicitly in the SRM. Another possibility is to interpret various terms of the Directive or national laws in ways that would not require privacy practices to apply to certain categories of named information. As discussed in chapter 6, one candidate could be the Article 3 definition of the scope of the Directive, applying only to data "which form part of a filing system or are intended to form part of a filing system." One way to exclude data from the Directive is to say that they do not "form part of a filing system," such as when data are collected about a person in his or her business capacity.

Codes of conduct, model contract provisions, or other self-regulatory measures can help transnational organizations manage their risk as the Directive goes into effect. In the spring of 1998, model contract initiatives were being conducted by the International Chamber of Commerce and by a group headed by noted U.S. privacy expert Alan Westin.[14] Regulators gain important assurance that fair information practices will be followed. Regulated organizations get clearer notice of what actions will constitute compliance.

Policy Recommendations for the European Union

In discussing policy options for the European Union, we first examine the extent to which the United States, or sectors in the United States, should be found adequate. Then we make a strong recommendation that the European Union accept well-drafted self-regulatory measures to provide European and American institutions with a workable way to comply with the law. Finally, we identify places in the Directive where the language is open to multiple interpretations.

The Adequacy of Protection in the United States

How well is personal information protected in the United States? The European Union has made and continues to make substantial efforts to answer this question. Notably, the European Commission sponsored a comprehensive study by Paul Schwartz and Joel Reidenberg, published in 1997, of public and private sector privacy protection in the United States.[15] The findings are complex. Data privacy in the United States is covered by intricate legal rules at both the state and federal level. American privacy protections are based on common law and statute law and vary in the extent to which the laws match the privacy practices expected by the Directive. Amidst this complexity, however, Schwartz and Reidenberg single out certain sectors for particular criticism, including direct marketing and medical information.

---

14. One of the authors (Swire) has participated in the process led by Alan Westin, conducted through the Center for Social and Legal Research in Hackensack, New Jersey.

15. Paul M. Schwartz and Joel R. Reidenberg, *Data Privacy Law: A Study of the United States Data Protection* (Charlottesville, Va.: Michie, 1997).

A useful document for comparison was written by Ronald Plesser and Emilio Cividanes, who assembled a list of U.S. laws that govern the use of personal information.[16] Some of these laws have become familiar in the data protection debate. The Federal Trade Commission Act and similar state laws, for example, authorize suits when unfair or deceptive trade practices have been uncovered. For companies that promise to abide by privacy codes, the FTC Act creates substantial remedies.[17] Other U.S. laws have been less often mentioned in privacy debates. The Electronic Communications Privacy Act provides stricter legal regulation of unauthorized access to e-mail than may exist in Europe. Protections in the U.S. Constitution, as supplemented by the Privacy Act and antiwiretap laws, often give citizens stronger legal rights against government wiretapping and data processing than exist for EU member states. American data security practices are likely better on average than those found in Europe. The press is also particularly prominent in protecting privacy.

In public conferences and private meetings, EU officials have heard about the strengths of the U.S. privacy protection system. It seems fair to conclude, however, that European data protection officials will *not* find that the United States generally has adequate protection. In early 1998 the European Commission named consultants in several countries, including Robert Gellman in the United States, to study the adequacy of protection in five areas: management of a multinational company's human resources; medical research and epidemiology; subcontracting agreements; electronic trade and global communications networks; and sensitive data in air transport reservation systems.[18] By choosing these five, the commission has prob-

16. Ronald Plesser and Emilio W. Cividanes, "Data Protection in the United States," in Charles E. H. Franklin, ed., *Business Guide to Privacy and Data Protection Legislation* (Paris: International Chamber of Commerce, 1995), pp. 473–536. For a wide-ranging comparison of U.S. and European privacy laws, see also Fred Cate, *Privacy in the Information Age* (Brookings, 1997).

17. Section 5 of the Federal Trade Commission Act provides authority for the commission to act against "unfair or deceptive acts or practices." 15 U.S.C. § 45(a)(6). The most common remedy for violations of section 5 is a cease and desist order, and such orders have been upheld by the courts. See, for example, *Warner Lambert Co. v. Federal Trade Commission*, 562 F.2d 749 (D.C. Cir. 1977); *J.B. Williams Co., Inc. v. Federal Trade Commission*, 381 F.2d 884 (6th Cir. 1967). Congress has added two provisions to the FTC act that allow the commission to obtain economic redress for consumers. Section 19 of the act authorizes the commission to file a civil suit in district court to seek restitution from a firm that has previously been found guilty of an unfair or deceptive trade practice and which has a cease and desist order entered against it. 15 U.S.C. § 57b(a)(1). Section 13(b) allows the FTC to seek ancillary relief in an injunctive suit including monetary awards to reimburse consumers. 15 U.S.C. § 53(b).

18. Mr. Gellman was for a number of years a senior staff person in Congress on data privacy issues and has written widely on privacy issues.

ably signaled that they are among the sectors that concern it most. These sectors would seem to be at particular risk of being labeled inadequate. Alternatively, individual companies in these sectors might be targeted for early enforcement actions. Data protection officials have also mentioned direct marketing and insurance as industries that may be early targets for enforcement. More generally, any industries that transfer a large volume of named information to third countries can expect to attract regulators' attention.

Some sectors do have significant privacy legislation and can make an especially strong case for the existence of adequate protection. Notable examples include individual credit histories, telephone records, student records, U.S. government records under the Privacy Act, communications governed by the Electronic Communication Privacy Act, cable television records, and video rental records.[19] Other sectors may not have legislation in place but may have other institutional measures for ensuring protection. For instance, accountants and lawyers may be expected to treat personal information received from their clients with great care. Confidential agents wish to retain a strong reputation for discretion, and professional groups can impose sanctions for violations of client confidences. Schwartz and Reidenberg found Dun & Bradstreet, the leading company in corporate credit histories, to have especially good privacy practices.[20]

The European Union and Model Contract Provisions

We have provided important reasons for transnational companies to adopt self-regulatory measures that provide significant privacy protection for data transferred out of Europe. Now we turn to the somewhat complex signals that European officials have sent with respect to the EU's willingness to accept contractual solutions.

In the summer of 1997 the Article 29 Working Party issued *First Orientations on Transfers of Personal Data to Third Countries—Possible Ways Forward in Assessing Adequacy.* The report focused on assessing "adequacy" under Article 25. Concerning the interpretation of "adequate safeguards" in Article 26(2), it stated that "contractual solutions have inherent problems, such as

---

19. In compiling this list we are not stating that the legislation provides precisely the same protection required for processing personal data in Europe. The legally relevant inquiry is whether there is "adequate" protection in the United States, and the existence of U.S. legislation could be highly relevant evidence of such adequacy.

20. Schwartz and Reidenberg, *Data Privacy Law,* p. 287, n. 104.

the difficulty of a data subject enforcing his rights under a contract to which he is not himself a party, and . . . they are therefore appropriate only in certain specific, and probably relatively rare circumstances."[21]

This statement prompted concern that the European Union would not recognize the need for contract provisions in very many cases. Over time, however, European authorities have seemed more willing to consider using self-regulatory measures in a broader range of circumstances. For one thing, it is possible that there will be greater flexibility from political officials whose responsibilities extend beyond data protection. Some flexibility of this sort has been suggested at meetings involving EU and U.S. officials.[22] In addition, it now seems that EU officials, both in and out of the Working Party, are likely to be more accommodating to the use of SRMs than suggested by the 1997 Working Party report. Notably, the April 1998 *Contractual Provisions*, although quite strict in certain respects, appears to contemplate a significant role for model contracts, especially with respect to large companies and companies transferring data to affiliates.

As it has become more clear to the Europeans that the United States and other countries will not pass comprehensive privacy laws, European officials have become more willing to find workable contract and other SRM solutions. Otherwise, many companies may find it hard to carry out routine data processing after the effective date of the Directive. It is in the interest of everyone concerned to find practical solutions. The European authorities wish to protect the handling of their citizens' data while avoiding widespread data blockages. The private sector wishes to have a manageable way to comply with the law. Because of the reality that significant and desirable data flows to third countries will otherwise not comply with the Directive, it is of great practical importance to arrive at a sensible policy on model contracts and other SRMs.

---

21. Working Party, *First Orientations*.

22. As of summer 1998 we can report two instances in private meetings in which a senior European Commission official has suggested more flexibility. First, one senior official stated categorically in a meeting with U.S. government officials and private sector representatives that there would be no interference with the transfer of laptop computers out of Europe. At the same meeting, however, a data protection official specifically said that transfer of laptops could pose a problem if they contained sensitive information or were being used to avoid data protection rules.

In a second instance the same senior official suggested that Article 3 might be interpreted to exclude some categories of business use of named information. Under this approach, discussed in chapter 6, these categories might not constitute "personal data which form part of a filing system or are intended to form part of a filing system," and so would be beyond the scope of the Directive. By contrast, members of the Working Party have specifically objected to excluding these categories of data from the scope of the Directive.

Interpreting the Directive and Promoting Transparency

We now turn to questions about how to resolve uncertainty under the Directive. Throughout the book we have pointed out places where the text does not provide clear guidance and is open to multiple interpretations. In large measure this lack of guidance is the inevitable result of a new legislative framework. This structure governs many sectors and data processing practices. In applying the new rules, regulators will often need to make decisions about how the Directive and national laws apply in specific situations. At the level of legal doctrine, ambiguities gradually will be resolved and new distinctions will be made. The European Commission and national authorities will provide guidance, and the Working Party will examine difficult issues.

It becomes clear that nothing magical or irrevocable will happen when the Directive goes into effect. The enactment and implementation of national laws will continue. There will be many interpretive questions concerning intra-EU data processing as well as transfers to third countries. Where the law is apparently quite strict, it may take considerable time for organizations and regulators to come to an understanding about what practices will actually change. The uncertainties are compounded by the constant change in data processing technology. The Directive itself recognizes that data protection laws will need to evolve, "taking account of developments in information technology and in the light of the state of progress in the information society" (Article 33).

It is thus understandable why there are so many uncertainties about the interpretation of the Directive. We should not underestimate, however, the problems and risk that such uncertainty poses for organizations that are expected to comply with the law. To take one important example, consider the situation facing a company investing in its next-generation information processing system for Europe. If the company follows its traditional practices, there is the distinct possibility that it will not be in compliance with the new rules. It may then be required to retrofit its information system, perhaps at considerable expense, to meet new requirements. If, however, the company believes the Directive is as strict as it might appear, it will face other problems. The company may implement compliance programs that are more expensive than its competitors use and may decide not to pursue some innovative and potentially profitable ways of using information. In this information age a business may run significant risks if it decides not to use information in ways that turn out to be legal and in fact desirable. Faced with all of these uncertainties, there is an incentive for companies doing business in Europe to delay implementation of new information processing systems.

For data protection authorities, there are similarly important reasons to clarify the meaning of the Directive. In terms of the example just discussed, reducing uncertainty will tend to encourage investment in new information technologies, presumably an important goal. Reducing uncertainty will help concentrate efforts on areas with the greatest concerns about privacy. More generally, reducing uncertainty will increase transparency, or the ability of those affected by a rule to know what the rule is and how it operates.

With the reasons for clarifying the law in mind, we are now in a position to survey some of the particular areas where people in good faith can interpret the Directive differently. In the course of the book we have sometimes suggested how to choose among the possible interpretations. In interpreting a complex creation such as the Directive, moreover, it is helpful to remember that there are often alternative means to the same goal. For instance, one could give a broad scope to the Directive, while remaining flexible in creating exceptions. Another means, which might have roughly the same practical effect, would be to give the Directive a narrower scope, but provide fewer exceptions. Those involved in elaborating the interpretation may have subtle reasons for choosing among these approaches or for preferring to create flexibility under one Article rather than another.

Appendix B addresses the various sectors governed by the Directive and highlights compliance issues. Here follows a list of some of the issues we have considered.

—The meaning of "unambiguous consent," "necessary for the performance of a contract," and the other exceptions in Article 26(1).

—The applicability of model contracts or codes of conduct under Article 26(2). These could be especially important for mainframe-type transfers of information.

—The ways to handle more distributed processing of data, notably through organizational intranets.

—The regulation of e-mail and computerized telecopies when transferred to third countries.

—The regulation of Web sites, and the situations in which sites physically located outside the European Union are considered to be within the scope of the Directive.

—The treatment of laptop computers and personal organizers.

—What rules apply to the transfer of personal information to confidential agents such as accountants, lawyers, and business consultants. More generally, how subcontracting of information to other entities will be handled.

—The international use of call centers and other services provided to individuals.

—The legal treatment of processing permitted under Article 7 but not Article 26.

—The rules governing secondary use of information once it has lawfully left the European Union.

—The treatment of reinsurance and loan participations.

—The treatment of information in investment banking, corporate credit reports, and other instances where data are processed about an individual in his or her business capacity.

—Disclosures that are not mandated by law, such as where they are required by accounting or stock exchange rules, or where the corporation wishes to make greater disclosure than strictly required by applicable rules.

—Rules about who may send information to credit reporting agencies and who may receive credit reports.

—Possible conflicts between journalism and protection of privacy as governed by Article 9.

—The extent to which nonprofit organizations, international educational institutions, international conferences, and non-European governments are subject to enforcement under the Directive.

—What rules should apply to pharmaceutical research and other medical information.

—Rules applying to business and leisure travel, including affinity programs and travel reservation systems.

—Special rules for telecommunications data, as affected by the specific Directive on telecommunications.[23] Additional analysis, not undertaken in this book, will be needed to understand the effects of that Directive on transfers of telecommunications-related data to third countries.

—Rules applying to direct marketing, including the definition of "for the purposes of direct marketing" under Article 14 and the decisions about when a transfer is to a third party for purposes of Articles 11 and 14. More

---

23. "Directive 97/66/EC of the European Parliament and Council of 15 December 1997," concerning the processing of personal data and the protection of privacy in the telecommunications sector. Located at http://www2.echo.lu/legal/en/dataprot/protection.html.

generally, how to weigh the advantages of the "market of one" against the risks to privacy.

As lengthy as this list is, it leaves out many of the particular interpretive problems that will arise as the Directive and national laws are implemented. Data protection authorities can be enormously helpful in educating the public and the regulated organizations about the meaning of various passages. For example, with respect to consent by data subjects, the European Commission or national authorities might create a "best practices" area on a Web site and in print. This material could include sample language that clearly passes muster under the consent requirements. It can present a convenient place for reporting any actions by national authorities concerning specific policies for securing data subject consent. Similar publicity might be useful for contract provisions or other self-regulatory measures that have been reviewed by authorities. Through this and related means the data protection authorities can help those organizations that wish in good faith to comply with applicable law.[24]

Policy Recommendations for the United States

In this book we have suggested that there are important similarities between the privacy regimes in Europe and the United States, even when the systems differ in important particulars. Since the seminal 1890 article on privacy by Samuel Warren and Louis Brandeis, the United States has been an important source of ideas for common law and other privacy rules.[25] America has major privacy legislation in particular sectors, and new initiatives are being seriously considered for maintaining the privacy of medical records and children's privacy. The sectors chosen for legislation match the sorts of data and decisions that the United States has considered sensitive. The United States also has long-standing consumer protection and anti-fraud laws that overlap significantly with privacy protections. The Federal Trade Commission Act and similar state laws provide important remedies for situations in which an organization promises to use information in a certain way and then fails to do so. Even where these laws do not apply, private tort and contract remedies may be available when an organization's

24. For those interested in following data protection developments, one source is the PrivacyExchange Web site established by Privacy and American Business, available at www.PrivacyExchange.org.

25. Samuel D. Warren and Louis D. Brandeis, "The Right to Privacy," *Harvard Law Review*, vol. 4 (1890), p. 193.

practices are deceptive or unfair, such as when a customer would not reasonably expect the disclosure of personal data to occur and is thereby harmed. The effect of these laws is the protection of many of the sorts of information that are covered by the Directive.

Beyond these remedies the United States has institutional protections against privacy abuses, which often do not exist in similar form in other countries. There are constitutional and statutory protections against many governmental invasions of privacy. The First Amendment and a robust press mean that bad privacy practices can be loudly denounced, and organizations often respond quickly to this sort of publicity. There has been rapid innovation in information technologies, and there is considerable political ferment about ways to build privacy protections, including encryption, into the standard operating procedures of the Internet. Self-regulatory codes to protect privacy are also becoming stricter.

All this is not to say, however, that the United States and Europe agree on all privacy issues. One critical difference is that America does not have the general presumption that data should be used only for the purpose for which they are collected.[26] It is roughly accurate to say that Americans are more concerned with wrongful decisions and harmful effects than with the wrongful processing of information itself. A second difference is that Americans seem to have a less adverse reaction to "automated individual decisions," as governed by Article 15 of the Directive. Similarly, there is no general American recognition of the right of the individual to have "knowledge of the logic involved in any automatic processing of data concerning him," as provided in Article 12. A third difference concerns the required deleting of data. There has been little support in the United States for rules along the lines of Article 6(e), which states that personal data must be "kept in a form which permits identification of data subjects for no longer than is necessary for the purposes for which the data were collected or for which they are further processed." To American sensibilities, this sort of rule might easily seem an unnecessary regulatory intrusion into how an organization should manage its own information.

Recognizing these important areas of similarity and dissimilarity, we turn to recommendations for U.S. policy. Our principal proposal is to create a more structured institutional home within the U.S. government to consider issues arising from the private sector use of personal information.

---

26. Article 6(b) requires that personal data must be "collected for specified, explicit and legitimate purposes and not further processed in a way incompatible with those purposes."

We advocate formation of an Office of Electronic Commerce and Privacy Policy (OECPP).[27] This office would make and coordinate policy with respect to privacy and electronic commerce but would not be a regulatory or enforcement agency.

The Domestic Case for a Privacy Office

Purely domestic reasons for creating a privacy office include growing public concern about privacy issues, the expertise such an office could provide, the way the office could facilitate self-regulatory efforts and coordinate with state and federal agencies, the possibility of better articulation of public policies on privacy issues, and the special role of such an office in handling Internet-related issues.

There is undoubtedly strong public concern about privacy issues in the United States, especially with respect to the Internet. Eighty-seven percent of U.S. computer users report that they are concerned about privacy (56 percent are "very concerned").[28] Computer users have much less confidence in the privacy practices of on-line services and companies offering products and services over the Internet than they do in institutions such as banks, hospitals, and employers.[29] Privacy concerns about the Internet are significantly more acute among those who do not regularly use computers.[30] Of those who are not likely to access the Internet in the next year,

27. Another possible name, which we discarded upon further consideration, was the Office of Privacy and Electronic Commerce (OPEC).

28. Computer users were asked: "How concerned are you about threats to your personal privacy in America today?" The 1998 results were consistent with similar surveys in recent years. Alan F. Westin and Danielle Maurici, "E-Commerce & Privacy: What Net Users Want" (Privacy and American Business and Price Waterhouse, June 1998), p. vii.

29. A 1997 survey by Privacy and American Business and Harris reported: "A great majority of computer users are 'very' or 'somewhat' confident that employers (80 percent), hospitals and clinics (79 percent), and banks (77 percent) use the personal or confidential information people give them in a proper manner. Only 48 percent of computer users express the same confidence in companies providing online services, 46 percent in companies providing direct Internet services, and 40 percent in companies offering products and services on the Internet. Credit bureaus and credit card companies enjoy a similar level of confidence, with 47 percent and 46 percent, respectively." *Privacy and American Business Survey Report*, vol. 4, no. 3 (1997), pp. 6–7.

30. The 1997 Privacy and American Business and Harris survey asked, "When you communicate or send a message how concerned are you that the content of what you're communicating will be read by some other person or organization without your knowledge or consent?" For those who use e-mail, 22 percent were "very" concerned, and 59 percent were either "very" or "somewhat" concerned. For those who do not use e-mail, the figures were higher—47 percent were "very" concerned and 81 percent were either "very" or "somewhat" concerned (p. 5).

greater privacy protection is the factor that would *most* likely convince them to do so, outranking other factors such as reduced cost, ease of use, security of financial transactions, or more control over unwanted marketing messages.[31]

These polls show that concerns are both persistent over a number of years and stronger than they have been. To the extent that the polls accurately reflect public sentiment, there is a powerful basis for government attention to privacy issues—democratic accountability to citizens' views calls for attention to privacy problems.

Although it is not altogether clear why people are more concerned about privacy on the Internet, one can make a few informed comments. Privacy problems of course can arise through mail-order or telephone sales. The seller might be previously unknown to the buyer, and might misuse the data or transfer personal information to third parties. On the Web, however, many people perceive the risk as greater. It is more routine for the Web site operator or the seller to be previously unknown to the buyer. Often it is impossible to determine from the Web page itself who the operator is or where it does business. Perhaps most important, the very use of the computer reinforces the lesson of networked processing, that the costs of collecting, processing, and reselling data are rapidly declining. As people contact distant Web sites they feel intuitively that the data sent to the site can easily jump to other sites around the world, outside of the users' knowledge or control. As an additional concern, many users do not yet feel familiar with computer technology. They feel more at risk because they do not understand what personal information is actually being transferred and they fear, sometimes correctly, that information is secretly being gathered about their purchases, desires, and actions.[32]

---

31. Of five factors presented, nonusers rated their positive likely effect on using the Net as follows: privacy of personal information and communications would be protected, 44 percent; security of financial transactions on the Internet was assured, 40 percent; use became less complicated, 40 percent; more control over businesses sending unwanted marketing messages, 36 percent; and cost was reduced, 35 percent. Westin and Maurici, p. viii.

32. On the telephone the seller gains only the information that the potential buyer verbally expresses. By contrast, cookies can allow a Web site operator to gather a significant amount of information in ways that are often unknown and unsuspected by the purchaser, such as the list of pages that the purchaser has visited and how long was spent on each page. This information, combined with the likely decision by the purchaser to reveal his or her identity at the time of sale, can be substantially more revealing than the actual words communicated directly from the purchaser to the Web site operator.

For these or similar reasons, it is clear that the rise of the Internet has increased U.S. political concern about privacy. But there has not been a high-profile, unified office in the U.S. government for addressing privacy issues. The president's special advisor, Ira Magaziner, has been a leader in expressing administration policy on electronic commerce and privacy issues. Such leadership in the White House, though, cannot be counted on in the long term because new issues gain priority. The Federal Trade Commission has been active in addressing many privacy issues. Its jurisdiction over unfair and deceptive trade practices, however, does not extend far enough to cover many privacy concerns. The National Telecommunications and Information Administration (NTIA) of the Department of Commerce has also addressed privacy issues. The name of the NTIA, though, does not mention privacy, and its work on these issues could alter with a political change.

In the absence of a solid institutional home for privacy, the rise of the Internet creates the impetus for a permanently established organization, such as the OECPP, to work on privacy issues. One hope for such an office is expertise. As Paul Schwartz has written, "the data protection commission develops expertise in a critical area that is subject to dazzling technological developments. The commission's knowledge is to be made available to government, business, and private citizens."[33] Lack of an office could squander the expertise developed when privacy is an especially hot issue. Without such an office, there may be drastic fluctuations in staffing on investigations of privacy issues, as has occurred before.[34]

In addition to providing expertise, a privacy office could be an important contact point with other U.S. entities on privacy matters. The office could express concerns about privacy abuses and state aspirations for good practices. It might encourage self-regulation, as has been done in recent years by the White House, the FTC, and the NTIA. An ongoing government office with an institutional interest in privacy could reduce the likelihood that self-regulatory codes will be less vigorously enforced if and when public attention shifts to other matters.

In a similar way, the office might coordinate among federal and state agencies and be constructive in development of the law. Federal agencies

---

33. Paul M. Schwartz, "European Data Protection Law and Restrictions on International Data Flows," *Iowa Law Review*, vol. 80 (March 1995), p. 493.

34. Robert M. Gellman, "Fragmented, Incomplete, and Discontinuous: The Failure of Federal Privacy Regulatory Proposals and Institutions," *Software Law Journal*, vol. 6 (1993), p. 199.

face significant privacy issues in the areas they regulate. A list would include banking, telecommunications, transportation, health care, and children's privacy. State government agencies also face a long list of privacy issues. In addition, there is a complex process for creating uniform state laws for emerging electronic commerce transactions. As proposals move forward for amending the Uniform Commercial Code in the United States, a knowledgeable federal agency might be very useful on privacy issues.

A Privacy Office and International Concerns

The case for creating a federal privacy office becomes stronger once international factors are considered. Anne-Marie Slaughter and Abram and Antonia Chayes have documented how a larger and larger portion of important regulation is being handled between regulators who have the same functional responsibilities in different countries.[35] One well-known example is the Basel Accord among bank regulators, which sets minimum levels of capital for banks operating internationally. Other examples include the International Organization of Securities Commissioners, coordination among environmental protection agencies, and cooperative criminal law enforcement. This growing "transgovernmentalism" is in contrast to supranational, multilateral organizations—the United Nations, the International Monetary Fund—acting through formal treaties. These continue to be significant, of course, but they have lost some initiative to the increasingly dense networks of regulators in each field.

Data protection officials around the world meet together regularly and continually share information and views.[36] Until recently, the United States sometimes did not send any official representative to such meetings. More recently, U.S. officials have attended the data protection commissioner meetings, but the status of the U.S. participation has not been regularized. The meetings of international commissioners are especially important because of the increasingly global nature of information flows, especially for electronic commerce, and the consequent large spillover effects of national and EU data protection laws.

---

35. Anne-Marie Slaughter, "The Real New World Order," *Foreign Affairs*, vol. 76 (September–October 1997), pp. 183–97; and Abram and Antonia Chayes, *The New Sovereignty: Compliance with International Regulatory Agreements* (Harvard University Press 1995).

36. Peter Swire has been asked by the Berkman Center for Internet and Society at Harvard Law School to conduct research, due to be completed in early 1999, on the history and current functioning of the network of data protection regulators in different countries.

Creation of the OECPP could provide an institutional home for continuing contacts with data protection officials in other countries. The lack
of such an institutional home has been a steady source of complaint by
these officials. Creation of the OECPP would reduce the risk of having
drastic staffing fluctuations in parts of U.S. agencies dealing with privacy
issues. The OECPP could also provide more effective advocacy in international meetings for U.S. views on privacy. As American officials become
more familiar with other government regulators and their positions, it is
likely that U.S. interests can be expressed in more nuanced and effective
ways. Sustained participation by U.S. officials would reduce the risk that
the United States and its economic interests would be harmed by lack of
familiarity with other countries' positions.

One particular benefit of the OECPP could be to back self-regulatory
measures as a means for meeting the goals of the EU Directive. Where U.S.
companies have entered into measures that are binding in Europe, it may
be useful to have U.S. officials who develop expertise in the area. These
officials may serve as a source of information about how and to what extent
European individuals and authorities can get remedies under U.S. law. This
sort of cooperation among governments may be helpful in assuring European officials that there will be effective enforcement against U.S. companies who have obligated themselves to follow a self-regulatory measure but
who fail to do so. Without some such office, European officials may be less
willing to accept self-regulatory measures because of their unfamiliarity
with enforcement issues under U.S. law.

Finally, creation of the OECPP would also likely be a significant help
in reducing the risk of tensions with the European Union over its implementation of the Directive. The European Union has strongly emphasized
the need for some U.S. governmental entity to deal with data protection
issues, participate in international meetings, and serve as a point of contact
for problems as they arise.

In short, there is a solid case for creating the OECPP for domestic
U.S. reasons, and discussions with knowledgeable observers suggest that
creation of the office could help the United States and its economic interests receive more favorable treatment during the implementation of the
Directive. Although there is little reason to believe that the European Union
will find that privacy protection in the U.S. is generally inadequate, there
are many concerns about how the Directive will be interpreted and how
adequacy will be evaluated in various sectors. U.S. views can probably be
more effectively presented if the OECPP existed. First, its existence would

be taken by the Europeans as a sign of U.S. good faith. Second, it would have the institutional base to advocate U.S. views effectively on the many transnational issues arising in data protection.

The OECPP and Electronic Commerce

In European countries, data protection agencies are institutionally separate from the parts of the government that are directly concerned with fostering and regulating electronic commerce. Within the European Commission, electronic commerce is handled primarily in Directorate General XIII while data protection is handled primarily in Directorate General XV. But we suggest that the U.S. government should have an office that addresses both privacy and other matters related to the Internet.

First, creating the OECPP would be an authentic expression of the political sentiment in the United States. American political and popular concerns about privacy are closely linked to the Internet and global commerce and to new telecommunications technologies.

Second, privacy and electronic commerce have been linked in the U.S. government initiatives led by Ira Magaziner. The links are also recognized in the EU white paper on electronic commerce. In this period of rapid change, it makes sense to have an institution at the national level that is keeping track of both privacy and electronic commerce issues. The OECPP could provide needed staff for White House initiatives involving privacy.

Third, electronic commerce will create major, ongoing issues, of which protecting privacy is one important example. Some other electronic commerce matters will include deterring and remedying fraud by buyers and sellers over the Internet, protecting intellectual property, modifying systems of taxation, creating effective new payments systems, and coordinating law enforcement across borders. The expertise of many parts of the government will be required to address such a daunting range of issues. Having an office devoted to electronic commerce, however, can create expertise at handling the many links among them. The OECPP can help lead cross-agency task forces. It can serve as a point of contact for states as they pursue commercial law reform, and help identify areas where federal statutory preemption may indeed be appropriate.

Fourth, the OECPP can see that international discussions treat the various matters connected with electronic commerce in a more integrated and expert way. There is a pressing need to make sure that an international regime can develop in the medium term that will allow electronic commerce to flourish while preventing fraud, guaranteeing accurate payments, protecting intellectual property, and strengthening privacy. International discussions about these matters should not be handled solely by privacy commissioners; instead, they should be broadened to reflect the proliferation of issues that are inextricably linked with how electronic commerce will process personal information.

As we discuss in chapter 9, electronic commerce will make it far more common for individual consumers to purchase goods and services directly from other countries. A legal regime must develop to allow resolution of the disputes that will inevitably arise. In these new sorts of international transactions, use of personal information will be only one of the many concerns that may be handled differently in different countries. The international discussions about protecting privacy should thus be part of a broader dialogue about electronic commerce.

Which Government Agency Should House the Office?

We believe that the new privacy office should be housed in the Department of Commerce. The department already has considerable expertise in matters of privacy and electronic commerce. The National Telecommunications and Information Administration has taken a prominent part in discussions on privacy issues. In light of our recommendation to include responsibility for electronic commerce policy issues in the same office as responsibility for privacy matters, Commerce is the logical choice.

There would be no need for a new statute to allow the OECPP to operate within the Department of Commerce. Politically, it may be relatively easy for the president to create the office within an executive branch department, especially since the new office would be consistent with administration views on how to proceed with addressing privacy and electronic commerce issues. Placement in Commerce, with its experience in business issues, may also mute the otherwise strong political opposition that might be expected from the U.S. business community.

By having privacy responsibilities given to an office with "privacy" in its title, and in light of its responsibilities to interact regularly with international privacy regulators, the OECPP would have institutional incentives to take privacy issues seriously. At the same time, its position in the Department of Commerce would make it familiar with the concerns of industry. By being informed about both privacy and electronic commerce matters, the OECPP could help achieve the Clinton administration's goal of pursuing the protection of privacy while encouraging the development of electronic commerce.

If responsibility were placed either in the Office of Management and Budget or in a newly formed part of the Executive Office of the President, there could be limits on the ability to staff the office successfully. The Clinton White House, for example, has announced a tight ceiling on total staff for the Executive Office of the President. Such limits would constrain the activities of a privacy office. Nonetheless, one argument for placing the office in OMB is that the budget office already oversees the public sector Privacy Act, so perhaps one office should handle both public and private sector privacy issues, as in Europe. In response, it seems, at least in the United States, that privacy issues in the public and private sector should be handled separately. The government is subject to constitutional law, the demands of law enforcement, and a variety of special statutes. Private sector issues are closely linked with the development of electronic commerce, which is more logically handled by the Commerce Department.

As for the European concern about having a single privacy agency to contact, any such problems should be manageable. For business privacy, contacts would be with Commerce; for government issues and law enforcement, contacts would be with OMB and the Department of Justice.

In principle, it is also possible to consider giving the Federal Trade Commission expanded authority to deal with matters of privacy. After all, the agency has already taken the lead in attracting attention to consumer privacy issues, acting under its general grant of power to enforce the laws against unfair and deceptive trade practices. Furthermore, the FTC is an independent agency, which is the form used by EU countries for data protection.

Nothing in our proposed creation of an OECPP within the Commerce Department would take away from the FTC's power to deal with unfair and deceptive trade practices. Instead, the OECPP, as we envision it, would amass expertise on privacy issues and coordinate with state and foreign governments, advocacy groups, and the private sector to deal with these matters.

Although we are not necessarily opposed to granting the FTC greater powers to protect privacy, there would be important political and practical obstacles to such an effort. Expanded powers would require statutory action by Congress, which would take far longer than producing an executive order creating an office in the Department of Commerce. And there is no guarantee that a Republican-controlled Congress will pass significant national legislation that regulates business in new and potentially far-reaching ways.

Objections from Those Who Would Want Stronger Action

Some may object to the creation of a privacy office unless it has strong regulatory powers. For them, the OECPP would be simply a dummy agency to hide the lack of U.S. political will to do anything effective about invasions of privacy.

This objection is really a claim that a comprehensive regulatory approach to protecting privacy is better than the action the United States has generally taken to date. Washington has emphasized market-based and self-regulatory measures to govern the use of personal information. That emphasis is consistent with American caution about allowing government regulation to intrude into the marketplace, especially in rapidly changing, high-technology areas. When there has been evidence of specific abuses, legislation has been created to address them. Nothing in the creation of the OECPP would prevent such sector-specific legislation from being adopted in the future when it is needed.

A second objection is that the proposed office would be part of the Commerce Department, an executive branch agency, rather than be an independent agency such as the Federal Trade Commission. The Directive insists that supervisory agencies in the member states be independent agencies. As a political matter, however, it would be difficult to grant extensive new powers to the Federal Trade Commission or some other independent agency. The FTC has had its regulatory jurisdiction closely monitored by Congress. Indeed, there have been serious initiatives, especially by Republican-controlled Congresses, to cut back the FTC's jurisdiction.

Besides, the difference in behavior between independent and executive branch agencies in the United States is probably less pronounced than sometimes believed. Both are subject to congressional oversight and budget authority. The leaders of both sorts are the result of the same political process; they are named by the president, subject to Senate approval. Academic studies have found little difference in the way the two sorts of agencies operate.[37]

Independence is also less of a concern for the proposed OECPP than for European data protection authorities. In Europe the same agency oversees privacy protection in both the public and private sectors, and there is

---

37. Peter Strauss, "The Place of Agencies in Government: Separation of Powers and the Fourth Branch," *Columbia Law Review*, vol. 84 (1984), pp. 573, 596; and Peter P. Swire, "Note, Incorporation of Independent Agencies into the Executive Branch," *Yale Law Journal*, vol. 94 (1985), pp. 1766, 1772.

a reasonable argument that independence helps it criticize other government agencies more freely. In the United States the Office of Management and Budget would remain the lead agency in applying the Privacy Act and its provisions regulating the public sector. The OECPP's work would focus on information practices in the private sector, and so it would not be filling the same watchdog function with respect to other government agencies.

Objections from Those Who Want No Office

Those who disapprove of more active government intervention to protect privacy believe that the creation of a privacy office would be the first step toward the eventual establishment of a regulatory agency. But the proposed OECPP here can be created by presidential order; regulatory authority would require that Congress make a statutory change, a much less likely political event. In addition, the Department of Commerce does not historically have a strong regulatory mission; putting the office in Commerce reduces the likelihood that there will be large new regulatory authority except where Congress specifically approves.

A related objection is that creating the OECPP, even without regulatory authority, legitimates the government's intrusion into privacy issues too strongly, moving the United States too far toward the European policies for protecting privacy. In this view, creating the OECPP would be caving in to the European Union on privacy issues. Instead, the United States should continue its opposition to a greater government presence in resolving privacy issues.

Our analysis, however, has provided entirely domestic reasons for supporting creation of the OECPP. We have also explained why creating the office is in the long-term international interest of the United States, notably the OECPP's role over time in dealing with transgovernmental privacy and electronic commerce issues. The belief that creating the OECPP would help resolve tensions in implementing the Directive is only one of many reasons for taking action.

The World Trade Organization and Privacy

The title of this book, *None of Your Business*, suggests two ways in which restrictive data protection laws might clash with free trade agreements that have been signed by the United States, the members of the European Union, and most other countries in the world. First, the United States and other non-EU countries may argue that the Directive is an improperly extraterritorial enactment and that it is none of Europe's business to dictate how personal information should be handled outside Europe. Second, there is a suspicion among some that the Directive may serve protectionist goals, saying "none of your business" to non-European companies that face the barrier of having to comply with complex European privacy laws. The last part of chapter 7 examined the economic and other effects on Europe of potentially protectionist laws regulating transfers of personal data. We turn now to the legal analysis of potentially protectionist measures.

Since shortly after World War II, the General Agreement on Tariffs and Trade (GATT) has been the principal vehicle for creating and enforcing the international free trade regime. In 1994 the General Agreement on Trade in Services (GATS) was signed, with provisions directly relevant to the Directive. In 1995 the World Trade Organization (WTO) was established, with broader scope and enforcement powers than had existed under GATT.

The WTO can be involved in resolving data protection issues in two ways. First, a European data protection law can be challenged by third countries under the WTO trade rules. If the challenge succeeds, diplomatic pressure can be applied to the offending country to change its behavior, and trade sanctions can also be imposed by the country that brought the challenge. Second, privacy laws might become part of WTO negotiations. In this way the WTO might become a useful forum for resolving disagreements about data protection rules. Ultimately, new privacy rules might even be included in treaties that are negotiated through the WTO.

In our discussion, we first analyze the law as it would apply in a challenge to a European data protection rule. This challenge may be more than hypothetical. In February 1998 comments, Ira Magaziner, a Clinton adviser, said, "We don't accept the EU direction. We don't accept the legitimacy of them trying to impose it on us." He added that the Clinton administration would "be very firm about this. If we have to go to the WTO, we will."[38] After we discuss the legal implications of "going to the WTO," we then discuss advantages and disadvantages of using the WTO as a forum for resolving international disputes over privacy protections.

Data Protection and Free Trade Rules

Data protection laws at the national or EU level may violate the free trade rules administered by the World Trade Organization. To understand

---

38. Comments of Ira Magaziner, February 6, 1998, at a conference of the Brookings Institution and the Cato Institute, as reported by Declan McCullagh for the *Netly News*.

the possible problem, consider two business consulting firms, company U located in the United States and company E in the European Union. The consulting work requires examination of personal information in the client records. The companies are selling identical services to the European client and process personal information in the same way.

If there is a finding under Article 25 that the United States (or the relevant sector) lacks adequate protection, this sale may be permitted for the European company but forbidden for the U.S. company. In this simple example, the Directive seems to work in a protectionist way, favoring European service providers at the expense of sellers from outside Europe. The United States might begin an action before the WTO, complaining about the finding of inadequacy and the restriction on imports of consulting services into Europe. The United States might seek a WTO finding that a European country was not meeting its treaty obligations.

Before turning to the special provision concerning data protection, it is useful to consider the legal standards that apply generally under GATS, as enforced by the WTO. First, the most-favored-nation provision in Article II of GATS essentially prohibits Europe from discriminating among third countries. Under the provision Europe would risk WTO sanctions if it gives permission for data transfers to one country but not to another similarly situated country. The risk to Europe would increase if it gives permission for transfers to one country but denies permission to another country that has stricter data protection laws and practices. This situation might arise, for instance, if the European Union permitted transfers to former colonies in the third world, while denying transfers to the United States. If the United States has stricter data protection laws and practices than the former colonies, it might have a strong case in the WTO for violation of the most-favored-nation provision.

Article XVII of GATS states the second general principle, that the European Union must give "national treatment" to non-EU countries. The basic idea is that foreign companies should be treated as if they were companies of the importing nation. A company should not be put at a disadvantage solely because it is not from the importing nation. The general principle is limited in Article XVII to situations in which a country has undertaken a specific obligation to give national treatment.[39]

---

39. An additional research task, not undertaken here, is to examine the EU "schedule of commitments" to see what relevant national treatment obligations European countries may have incurred.

Going beyond these general GATS provisions, however, we must look to the specific exception for data protection rules. To provide more scope for nations to enact data protection laws, Article XIV of the GATS states:

> nothing in this Agreement shall be construed to prevent the adoption or enforcement by any Member of measures . . . (c) necessary to secure compliance with laws or regulations which are not inconsistent with the provisions of this Agreement including those relating to: (i) the prevention of deceptive and fraudulent practices or to deal with the effects of a default on services contracts; (ii) the protection of the privacy of individuals in relation to the processing and dissemination of personal data and the protection of confidentiality of individual records and accounts.

The language in Article XIV(c)(ii) provides a significant legal defense against a claim that the Directive or national privacy laws violate GATS or the free trade regime more generally.

The data protection exception is limited, however. Article XIV also states that the exception is subject "to the requirement that such measures are not applied in a manner which would constitute a means of arbitrary or unjustifiable discrimination between countries where like conditions prevail, or a disguised restriction on trade in services." This language, then, provides the specific legal standard for judging whether the Directive or national data protection laws violate GATS: are such measures "arbitrary or unjustifiable discrimination" or "a disguised restriction on trade in services"?

Because there is no law interpreting Article XIV, our analysis must necessarily be tentative and exploratory. Returning to our example of company U's consulting service, the United States would claim that Article 25 is being applied in a discriminatory way or is a disguised restriction on trade in services. After all, the same services are being sold to the customer, and personal data are being handled in precisely the same way in both companies.

One response by the European country could be to dispute the claim that the information is being processed in the same way. From the European perspective, a crucial ingredient of fair information practices is that a legal regime is in place to prevent abuses in the handling of personal information. Even if companies U and E happen to handle personal information in the same way, Europeans might explain that it is justifiable (that is, not discriminatory) to treat them differently.

In our discussions with trade experts, we have heard considerable skepticism expressed as to whether such a European position would survive

WTO scrutiny. The form of the argument is that the importing country (in Europe) could ban exports from the other country (the United States) because of the inferior or different legal regime in the other country. This sort of argument, if accepted, could be expanded to an enormous number of trade disputes and could potentially undermine much of the free trade regime.

A more tenable European position would emphasize that the data protection exception in Article XIV(c)(ii) must be given some significant effect. Legitimate data protection rules, which further important public interests, should be permitted under the WTO regime. The burden should be on the United States and the U.S. company to show, in exceptional circumstances, that there is actually "arbitrary or unjustifiable discrimination" or a "disguised restriction in trade in services." From the European point of view, because the Directive imposes the same requirement of fair information practices on all those who process personal data, there should be no finding of discrimination.

The outcome of any WTO adjudication would depend on the facts of the particular case. We can nonetheless now identify four situations in which a claim in the WTO would seem to be relatively strong. A first situation would be one in which direct evidence exists that a particular data protection law is indeed a "disguised restriction in trade in services." Despite concerns expressed by American business, our research has not uncovered any situation where deliberate protectionism seems to explain a European privacy rule. Once the Directive goes into effect, however, the temptation may exist for European producers to use data protection laws to reduce foreign competition. When such deliberate protectionism can be shown, the WTO might readily find a violation of GATS.

A claim before the WTO would also be supported if a third country has strong legal and practical protection of privacy but is nonetheless found inadequate under Article 25. In such circumstances, the finding of inadequacy could be an "arbitrary or unjustifiable discrimination." The category of winning claims would not be limited to countries having equivalent protection to Europe. "Adequate" protection is understood to be less rigorous than "equivalent" protection, so a third country may have a winning WTO claim even if the protection is not as strict in all respects as that in Europe. Furthermore, under the most-favored-nation rule, a WTO claim would be stronger if Europe allowed transfers to other countries that have weaker data protection regimes.

A third situation, which may have considerable practical importance, would occur if certain individuals receive adequate protection in the third country, even though that country does not generally have an adequate privacy regime. Suppose, for instance, that company U adheres to a model contract for protecting privacy and that the model contract provides protection of individual privacy rights substantially equivalent to the protection offered under EU law.[40] The contract, for instance, might permit the same enforcement actions by the individual as authorized under that individual's national law. In this example, the individual would be just as protected whether the data are processed in Europe or the third country. Under these circumstances, if the European Union does not find adherence to the contract to be adequate, there would seem to be a strong argument of "arbitrary or unfair discrimination" against sales of services by company U. This analysis provides another important reason for the European Union to approve model contracts that provide adequate protection. Failure to do so would expose it to challenge in the WTO for discriminatory treatment against those who process data outside Europe.

A fourth situation, which may be difficult to prove in practice, would involve instances in which the data protection rules place a significantly disproportionate burden on non-EU service providers when there is no adequate nonprotectionist justification. Here is one possibility (it would require considerable empirical support to make a persuasive case before the WTO). Suppose it can be shown that U.S. companies subcontract out many aspects of their operations that are ordinarily done in-house in Europe. In various circumstances the Directive and EU national laws limit transfer of personal information to third parties. These laws increase the cost of using subcontractors and may make certain business arrangements uneconomic. If the difference in the U.S. and EU use of subcontractors is substantial but the effect on privacy rights of using subcontractors is minimal, there may be a valid claim before the WTO for discrimination or disguised restriction on trade in services.

---

40. The legal argument against the European position is strongest when the code of conduct or model contract offers "equivalent" protection to Europe. In such an instance the individual would, by definition, enjoy the same protection in either country. Failure to permit transfer to the third country might readily be seen to meet the "arbitrary or unjustifiable discrimination" test in Article XIV. If the legal protection meets the somewhat less strict adequacy test, discrimination may be somewhat more difficult to establish: there may be some discretion for the European Union in defining the level of adequacy. The European practice, however, would also be subject to the most-favored-nation provision. If some codes or model contracts were approved and others with similar protections were not, the Europeans might be exposed to the argument that they were impermissibly treating one country more favorably than another.

The WTO as Forum for Resolving Data Protection Issues

The WTO might become embroiled in privacy issues when it is called on to adjudicate a dispute. More broadly, it might help bring about international discussions or write additional privacy provisions into future WTO treaties. There are advantages and disadvantages to involving the WTO as either a judge of disputes or a forum for multilateral discussions of privacy laws.

One advantage of the WTO's significant involvement is simply that it exists as a forum for resolving privacy disputes. With the passage of the General Agreement of Trade in Services, service industries, which often use personal data intensively, are included within the WTO framework. The organization has a dispute resolution process, and the major countries involved in the privacy debates have agreed to participate in that process. The WTO thus offers the prospect of an authoritative resolution of privacy disputes.

The WTO could also provide an international forum for harmonizing the legal treatment of privacy protection. Harmonization may be desirable because of the increasingly global handling of personal information. There are important aspects of extraterritoriality to data protection law—European laws can affect practices in the United States and around the world. To reduce the tensions that arise from conflicting legal regimes, it may be desirable to harmonize at least some privacy rules. Decisions in the WTO can help move this process along.

From the U.S. perspective, an additional advantage of recourse to the WTO may be the organization's historic focus on free trade. Because it exists primarily to combat protectionism, the protectionist aspects of data protection laws are likely to receive close scrutiny. The WTO may thus limit any temptation by countries to use data protection rules to favor domestic industry.

But there are reasons to be cautious about giving the WTO a leading role in resolving privacy disputes. In the resolution of a dispute, it is far from clear that the organization is the most appropriate and expert decisionmaking body. It must decide how the challenged rule fits within WTO rules, rather than whether the privacy law is actually desirable. Privacy advocates might fear that the WTO would interpret the privacy exception in Article XIV narrowly. As a result, many data protection laws might be prohibited. Conversely, those regulated by data protection laws might fear that the exception would be interpreted broadly. If so, the WTO would give its apparent blessing even to rules that companies believe are badly drafted or ill-advised. No matter how the WTO decides a given dispute, however, the decision would be based on interpretation of GATS language rather than on explicit consideration of the public interest.

As for using the WTO as a forum for negotiating future privacy rules, there are several possible disadvantages. For one thing, WTO negotiations take a considerable amount of time; they would be of only limited use in solving problems arising in the early stages of implementing the Directive. Next, negotiations in the WTO are at least as hard to predict as a WTO decision in a particular case. They might result in relatively market-oriented rules. The United States and most developing countries do not have comprehensive privacy laws, so most WTO members have reasons not to agree to European-style privacy laws. But the European Union and some other major countries do have national laws that are stricter than those in the United States. For that reason, negotiations could result in a more law-centered emphasis than the United States, with its emphasis on self-regulation, would prefer.

Another concern is that the WTO negotiation process probably works better for more purely economic issues. As attention shifts to more contested issues involving social values, such as protecting privacy, it is less clear whether the forum is well equipped to resolve international conflicts. For example, there have been sharp controversies about how to "green the GATT," and these environmental concerns have been difficult to accommodate within the WTO framework.[41]

The WTO is also open to the criticism that it is not participatory enough. In discussions about environmental and other issues, nongovernmental organizations and other affected parties have felt excluded from a WTO process that is premised upon negotiations among sovereign nations. If the WTO becomes a central place for resolving privacy disputes, it is unclear whether and how privacy advocates, industry, and other nongovernmental entities might be included in the discussions.

In assessing these advantages and disadvantages, we can reach a number of conclusions. First, the interpretation of Article XIV will depend heavily on the facts of a given dispute. We have been able to identify several situations in which a claim would be especially strong. The failure of authorities to permit self-regulatory measures may itself present a strong WTO

41. Daniel C. Esty, *Greening the GATT: Trade, Environment, and the Future* (Washington: Institute for International Economics, 1994).

case. The threat of a WTO claim thus presents an important additional reason for European authorities to find ways to accommodate self-regulatory measures where adequate protection exists.

Second, the WTO serves a clearly useful function in limiting the extent to which data protection laws can be used for protectionism. International disagreements about privacy laws are done in the shadow of the law—the WTO free trade rules put nations on notice that they cannot be blatant in discriminating against foreign companies.

Third, the WTO will likely address a range of electronic commerce issues in the future. In our discussion about the Office of Electronic Commerce and Privacy Policy, we explained why it is useful for data protection issues to be negotiated internationally along with electronic commerce issues. For some electronic commerce issues the WTO is probably the best forum. For example, in early 1998 the Clinton administration launched an initiative to keep certain electronic commerce transactions free from customs duties. As proposed, the measure would apply to transactions involving electronic information sent over the Internet, such as music or architectural designs.[42] This effort to reduce customs at national borders is consistent with the core historical mission of the WTO to reduce barriers to international trade. The organization is thus a particularly appropriate forum for addressing customs issues.

It is more difficult to assess the extent to which the WTO will turn out to be a useful forum for negotiating disputes about data protection. Multilateral discussions on privacy issues can also take place through the Organization for Economic Cooperation and Development, in international discussions about electronic commerce, and through the regular meetings of data protection commissioners. We are inclined to be cautious about expanding the reach of WTO treaties into complex issues such as privacy protection that are only modestly related to free trade and protectionism. WTO treaties are difficult to update quickly, and binding WTO privacy rules might soon become out of synch with technological and marketplace realities. In short, although discussions in the WTO are probably one helpful way to address privacy issues, we are not convinced that binding international rules, administered through the WTO, should be implemented by treaty.

42. Remarks of U.S. Ambassador Rita Hayes, "Global Electronic Commerce: Duty Free Treatment for Electronic Transmissions," February 19, 1998, reprinted in *BNA Electronic Commerce & Law Report* (February 25, 1998), p. 263.

9

The Internet,
Electronic Commerce,
and World Data Flows

We have now concluded the principal task of the book: describing the effects of the Directive and recommending policy solutions for privacy and transborder data flows. In this chapter, we explore some broader implications of our study for the future of the Internet, electronic commerce, and world data flows.

International Sales to Individuals

Concerning world data flows and electronic commerce, our research underscores what is crucially different about the Internet. Far more than before, people will routinely buy goods and services across national borders. In chapter 6 we observed that direct marketing has so far had only a small international component. True, transnational marketing has been important for travel services and sectors offering some very high-end products. But the dominant reality has been that individuals (except in border regions) rarely buy directly from a seller in another country.

This reality, meanwhile, has been accompanied by an enormous growth overall in international trade. Until now, international trade has overwhelmingly featured business-to-business transactions. Goods and services have generally been imported by businesses, and the ultimate sale to consumers has been made by companies licensed to do business in the consumer's country. Business-to-business sales will continue to increase rapidly in the emerging world of electronic commerce. Indeed, as chapter 3 showed, in purely financial terms, business-to-business sales over the Internet are much larger today than business-to-individual sales, and this predominance will certainly continue.

Although business-to-business sales in electronic commerce are and will remain larger than business-to-individual sales, the greatest legal and policy ferment will occur for the latter, especially internationally. An important reason is that for business-to-business sales commercial practices are already in place, using bills of lading, letters of credit, and the other accepted tools of international transactions. International banks and other intermediaries are experienced at facilitating these transactions. When disputes arise, businesses can appeal to national laws and to a well-established system of commercial arbitration. Indeed, our policy discussion in chapter 8 relied heavily on the possibility of business-to-business contracts to handle major transfers of personal data from Europe to third countries. Notably, the contracts can solve problems concerning jurisdiction and choice of law by specifying in advance what nation's rules will apply to disputes that arise under the contract.

The situation changes substantially when a business sells to individual consumers across national borders. European and American law often treats consumer contracts differently from business-to-business contracts. In general, consumers are less able to waive their legal rights because of public policy concern about contracts of adhesion and the unfair bargaining power of the seller. Consumer contracts are more likely to be subject to mandatory rules in the consumer's jurisdiction, making it more difficult for the contract to specify alternative choices of law. When disputes arise, there is no significant history of international arbitration of a consumer's dispute with a merchant. If disputes go to court, the process may be lengthy and expensive, and there is no certainty that the judgment of one country (such as the consumer's) will be enforced in the other country (such as the seller's). Nor have intermediaries arisen to create a dependable structure for transactions between a seller and a consumer in a distant country.

These contract interpretation issues suggest some obstacles to international sales to consumers over the Internet. Moreover, other legal and policy problems multiply when international transactions are done with individuals rather than businesses. Existing problems often become more acute, and enforcement far more difficult, when international transactions involve millions of individuals rather than thousands of businesses. Let us consider the sorts of social harms that are likely to become more prominent as the Internet expands the ability of individuals to access Web sites and transactions in other countries. Countries will vary in which items on the list they consider social harms, but each has enacted laws concerning at least some of these items.

—Privacy and data protection. The Internet creates the possibility of Web sites outside Europe that can process personal information about people in Europe. Companies can enter into business-to-business contracts that provide for adequate safeguards. Other Web sites, however, may be outside of Europe's jurisdiction and might not follow data protection rules.

—Consumer protection laws generally. Countries now have a host of consumer protection laws covering fraud, proper advertising, usury limits, installment contracts, rebates, and many other topics. There will be a growing demand to enforce these sorts of laws internationally as more consumers do business on the Internet. Enforcement will be especially difficult when the buyer and seller are not aware of each other's nationality. Problems will also arise when the site sells downloadable goods such as software, music, or information. In such instances there are no parties involved in physical shipment of the goods who are ready targets for regulation.

—Professional licensing. The Internet makes it far easier for a person to purchase professional services—legal advice, medical advice, psychological counseling, financial services—across borders. Jurisdictions may find it increasingly difficult to prevent outside persons from offering services without a license.

—Labor laws. The Internet makes it easier for employers to hire people in distant countries, either full time or on a contract basis. This sort of employment might raise difficult legal issues both in the employer's country (laws against hiring nonunion employees, for example) and in the employee's country (enforcing laws that protect employees, such as antidiscrimination and minimum-wage laws).

—Intellectual property. As copying of valuable information becomes easier, for both small corporations and individuals, the difficulty mounts for owners of intellectual property who wish to control dissemination of that information. Owners of intellectual property often can enforce laws more effectively when the purchasers are large corporations. One reason is the risk that a disgruntled employee will blow the whistle on an employer's large-scale violation of copyright or other rules. This could mean substantial expense to the employer.

—Taxation. Today, international tax enforcement can focus on the relatively limited number of businesses that engage in import and export. But tax authorities fear they will not have any similarly effective way to track Internet transactions involving a much larger number of sellers and individual buyers.

—Gambling. Countries vary widely in their approval of Internet gambling. It may be very difficult for antigambling countries to prevent their residents from gambling at a site located in a country where the activity is legal.

—Pornography. The Internet allows people around the world to access pornography, including child pornography, that is forbidden in the person's home country. Countries that wish to restrict pornography will face great challenges in preventing their residents from viewing material that is lawful in the country hosting the site.

—Hate speech. Some countries, such as Germany, have strict rules forbidding certain forms of hate speech, including Nazi propaganda. Such laws become much more difficult to enforce if free speech protections in other countries allow posting of Nazi or other material to the Internet.

—"Treasonable" or other politically censored speech. Singapore, China, and other countries have laws forbidding certain sorts of political speech. The Internet makes it more difficult for these countries to exclude such speech.

—Digital defamation. On the Internet, everyone can be a publisher. It becomes easy and cheap to have a Web page that can be accessed from around the world. Some of these pages, perhaps many, will contain malicious and untrue statements. Countries will vary in what must be proved to establish a claim for defamation.

This list suggests the array of harms that might occur as people gain the ability to visit Web sites from around the world. On many of these subjects, national legal regimes will have major disagreements. A central issue then becomes the extent to which a nation (or group of nations) can act effectively to protect against the harms that it considers important.

Elephants and Mice

In considering this issue, we suggest a distinction between large players, "elephants," and small and mobile "mice." The style of enforcing regulation against elephants and mice differs significantly. Elephants are large, powerful, and practically impossible to hide. Consider a transnational corporation that has major operations in a country. If that country has strict regulations, the corporation's actions are highly visible, and it may become an enforcement target if it flouts the law. At the same time, elephants are enormously strong and have all sorts of effects on the local ecosystem (potentially crushing trees and smaller animals). If a particular regulation angers an elephant, it may have the ability to change the rule.

The situation is far different for mice, which are small, nimble, and breed annoyingly quickly.[1] A good example on the Internet might be pornography sites. A profitable site can establish itself quickly, perhaps using bootlegged pictures that belong to other owners. If the site is closed down, the operator can simply open a new one under a new name and perhaps in a new jurisdiction. The same pictures might be back on the Net the same day. Would-be regulators can run around furiously with a broom but with little chance of getting rid of all the mice.

Our metaphor of elephants and mice helps explain what sorts of sites are most subject to successful national regulation. When the perceived harm is caused by elephants, the country has an especially good chance to stop the harm. But it will often be very difficult to stop perceived harms that are caused by mice. Inventors will keep trying to devise a better mousetrap, but with little hope of complete success. Drastic measures such as using strong poisons might get rid of the mice, but the poisons may also kill the many things we cherish. A national ban on Internet access would stop the harms, but it would also stop all the good things the Internet can provide.

Applying the metaphor to privacy, mainframe processors of information—credit card companies, airline reservation systems, telephone companies, Internet service providers, and the human resources databases of major companies—are the easiest elephants to identify. Even if they ship data to third countries, they typically have large operations in Europe and are clearly subject to enforcement actions there. These firms cannot hide; data protection authorities will be on the lookout for big databases that lack adequate protection. But these sorts of companies could also afford to participate in lobbying on the Directive and the implementation of national legislation. The companies have thick skins. They can defend themselves vigorously and can afford to pay fines if necessary.

---

1. The metaphor of the mice was suggested in part by the Stainless Steel Rat series of novels by Harry Harrison. These novels, set in the future, describe the intelligent hero as a stainless steel rat who can move through the walls of high-technology society, breaking the rules and evading capture.

This analysis suggests that national data protection rules might work reasonably effectively where the data are primarily in the hands of the largest companies. If few people outside of mainframe centers ever get access to personal data, that sort of data can be well protected. Similarly, we would expect the Web sites of elephants to comply relatively well with national laws and to install relatively strict privacy policies. Failure to do so will predictably lead to media and regulatory scrutiny.

But it will be extremely difficult for national regulators to effectively govern data processing by the mice of the electronic world. Many sites are run by individuals or small companies. A country may lack jurisdiction over the site. Even if jurisdiction can be established, there may be no effective way to identify or punish the wrongdoers. Individual users might reveal personal information to such a site, perhaps because of a fraudulent promise to keep information confidential or under the mistaken impression that the site will comply with data protection laws. As each crumb of information is received, the mouse might transfer the information to its favorite nest. Databases filled with these crumbs might especially develop in countries that lack privacy laws.

Our metaphor of elephants and mice applies similarly to other items on the list above. Consider intellectual property. The elephants of the world will generally comply with copyright and other requirements. If an elephant is doing something it should not, it can be very obvious. For instance, large companies that break copyright rules are subject to retaliation (and expensive damages) from any employee who becomes disgruntled and blows the whistle on the offending practice.[2] By contrast, mice might find stealing more profitable than paying for their food. For many owners of intellectual property, a crumb here or there is not worth the chase, especially when the chances of catching the pest are so slight.

This analysis of intellectual property is borne out in practice. For software, large companies routinely pay for site licenses, while individual users are more likely to pass bootleg copies amongst themselves. The biggest threat to content providers is when their most valuable material is subject to easy copying by mice. Examples include music companies and *Playboy* magazine, which mostly sell to individuals rather than large corporations

---

2. There are other reasons why large companies may comply more with intellectual property rules than other companies. Large companies have in-house expertise in how to comply with such rules, and know how to get permission to use other companies' intellectual property. Large companies can afford to pay licensing fees. They also often own intellectual property of their own and so have a vested interest in the system of property rules.

that respect copyright. These content providers seem to be at risk of being nibbled to death.[3] In response, the companies have taken vigorous action to close down Web sites that violate their copyrights and have appealed to users not to patronize sites that provide bootleg copies.[4]

What are countries to do when mice cause harm? Because it is so hard to find and catch the mice, the focus of legal regulation predictably falls on other groups—users, Internet service providers, payment intermediaries, or offshore countries that shelter the mice.[5] First, a country can punish users, such as anyone caught gambling or accessing pornography. If a society has a strong enough consensus against the particular behavior, punishing users may be legitimate. This approach does not work, however, for privacy issues. It makes no sense to punish people for giving their own personal information to a Web site.

A second target can be the Internet service provider, who can be held liable if the allegedly harmful material is accessed through its service. ISPs are firmly rooted in the customer's locality and so are subject to jurisdiction and enforcement actions. Governments may thus find it overwhelmingly tempting to regulate ISPs. There are reasons, however, to be extremely cautious before instituting regulation. Harsh rules on ISPs may sharply increase the price and reduce the access to the many good things on the Internet. In addition, it is far from clear that they have any effective ways to screen out "bad" content while permitting "good" content. The poison set for mice may also kill off our favorite pets. And, even as the pets die off, new mice might emerge that are resistant to the poison. Search engines will let people find the hidden bad sites they seek. Mirror sites will let users get to bad sites that are supposedly banned by the ISP. And clever editing on the bad sites will let the prohibited words or pictures get through the ISP's filters (for example, they could take one letter out of the vulgar words that trigger the filters). In time, filtering technology may improve beyond its current crude state, but until it does, efforts to regulate at the ISP level will often be a nasty combination of overbroad and ineffective.

---

3. We take no position on whether such a death would be desirable for *Playboy* or any other content provider. We simply describe the difficulty facing an owner of intellectual property that is subject to widespread copying by small Web sites that are accessible worldwide. On the problems facing producers of music CDs, see Jason Chervokas, "Internet CD Copying Tests Music Industry," *New York Times*, April 6, 1998, p. D3.

4. See, for example, *Playboy v. Webbworld, Inc.*, 968 F. Supp. 1171 (N.D.Tex. 1997); *Playboy v. Russ Hardenburgh, Inc.*, 982 F. Supp. 503 (N.D.Ohio 1997); *Playboy v. Frena*, 839 F. Supp. 1552 (M.D.Fla. 1993); and *Playboy v. Chuckleberry Publishing, Inc.*, 687 F.2d 563 (2d. Cir. 1981).

5. Jack L. Goldsmith III, "Against Cyberanarchy," *University of Chicago Law Review* (forthcoming).

A third sort of target for regulators is the institutions that transfer money to the Web site operators. Some annoying mice give away information free over the Web. Others, however, are vulnerable to the extent that regulators can stop the consumer from paying the Web site operator. Suppose, for instance, that it became illegal for a U.S. bank to transfer money on behalf of an individual, directly or indirectly, to a gambling operation outside the United States. We are not advocating such a law, and great enforcement difficulties can be imagined, but the law does illustrate how interruptions in financial flows might cut off sustenance to mice.[6]

A fourth target for regulators can be any offshore country that shelters the mice. The business opportunities of a mouse are constrained in a country where the activity is illegal. It is difficult and dangerous to become large and public enough to attract customers while remaining small and hidden enough to avoid the police. It is thus very tempting for mice to find a safe nest in an offshore country. And it is consequently tempting for the European Union, the United States, or other continental countries to exert pressure on the offshore haven. In the future, as various countries try to take advantage of global telecommunications to become offshore havens, diplomatic maneuvers involving onshore and offshore countries are likely to become complex.[7]

Self-Regulation, National Regulation, and Supranational Regulation

The discussion of elephants and mice sheds some light on the extent to which privacy and other rules should be set by self-regulation, at the national level, or in international organizations. Where the perceived harm is caused by elephants, there is the hope of reasonably good compliance with rules: large companies are likely to respect the intellectual property of others, and large databases are the most easily monitored for privacy viola-

---

6. If such a law were passed, the gambling operations would presumably try to hide their identity, perhaps by having payment move through apparently clean front operations. Cutting off payments to the gambling operations would then closely parallel cutting off payments to drug cartels or others considered criminal by the onshore country. A chief goal of money laundering laws is to make it difficult to transfer funds to front operations. For analysis of these issues, see Peter P. Swire, "Offshore Banking, Privacy, and the Future of the Internet," available at http://www.osu.edu/units/law/swire.htm.

7. For an illuminating discussion of tax havens and the countermeasures by fiscal authorities, see Caroline Doggart, *Tax Havens and Their Uses*, no. 113-34 (London: Economist Intelligence Unit, 1997), chap 5.

tions. Elephants are also subject to heightened enforcement under both national regulation and self-regulation. National law enforcement will often target them because of the possibility of whistle-blowers and because the violations are potentially on the largest scale. At the same time, self-regulatory efforts typically feature the same large companies. Self-regulation often occurs when a group of large companies agrees to set rules. But it is difficult for regulators to find and punish the mice of the world, and mice often hide rather than expend resources on joining self-regulatory efforts.

This analysis suggests more of a similarity between binding national laws and self-regulatory efforts than has usually been recognized. Under either approach, the largest companies are subject to particular pressure to comply. Under either approach, the smaller companies often calculate that the risk of enforcement is less than the expense of complying. Put another way, even binding national regulation is implemented largely through self-regulation by individual organizations. If the mice are adept at hiding and do not wish to comply, it is very hard to force compliance.

When the mice are hiding in other countries, there is a strong temptation to seek a supranational solution. In that way, rules can be harmonized among nations, and mice may have nowhere to hide. We suggest being cautious before imposing binding, supranational approaches for the Internet. The World Trade Organization, for example, is not well suited to handling matters that stray far from its historical mission of lowering trade barriers. As attention shifts to contested social values such as privacy and pornography, it is far from clear that the WTO is well equipped to resolve international differences.

It is particularly risky to impose supranational solutions for areas such as the Internet that are experiencing rapid technological change. A useful example is the current controversy about whether to seek international agreement on digital signatures. Briefly put, digital signatures use mathematics or other means to help prove that a particular person has sent a document electronically and to show that the document has not been changed in transit. On the Internet, which generally lacks face-to-face encounters, it becomes tremendously important to authenticate the sender. The person who receives a document with a digital signature can check the signature with some trusted third party, often called a certificate authority. The trusted third party then confirms that the signature matches the right user.

In the mid 1990s, as people began to realize the importance of digital signatures and trusted third parties, there was a strong effort to adopt harmonized rules. The goal was to create an integrated system for digital signatures so that users all over the world could engage in electronic commerce with each other. In the United States, the state of Utah created a complex regulatory structure in 1995 that proponents hoped would become the model throughout the country.[8] In Europe, Germany adopted a somewhat different regulatory structure, also in hopes that other countries would fall into line.

There has been a growing realization, however, that the complex regulatory schemes are probably standing in the way of the development of digital signatures. As new laws are passed, Stewart Baker observes, "Digital signature technology may be loved to death before it ever gets to really take off."[9] As a practical business matter, the detailed rules in the Utah and German statutes prevent experimentation with new business uses for digital signatures. The up-to-date thinking underlying the statutes can quickly seem out of date. For instance, states in the United States that are now passing digital signature laws are deciding not to include many of the detailed requirements of the Utah approach. Businesses, which once expected digital signatures to provide ironclad assurances, are now finding unexpected uses for "cheap certificates," which provide a more limited assurance of the sender's identity.

In time, after a good deal of experimentation, there may be a helpful role for supranational agreement on digital signature technology. Agreement may be needed on the most essential issues, where harmonization actually ensures interoperability. The history of digital signature statutes, however, illustrates the dangers of codifying law before there has been much practical experience with a technology. The Utah statute in 1995 was the product of well-informed experts, but the experts did not prove adept at guessing the business uses for the technology that would eventually emerge.

Business Models and International Consumer Purchases

The experience with digital signatures suggests the problems created by trying to write legislation before it is even known how a new technology will work. There are steep learning curves for both technology and its regu-

---

8. Utah Digital Signature Act, Utah Code Ann. §§ 46-3-101 to 46-3-504 (1995).

9. Stewart A. Baker, "International Developments Affecting Digital Signatures," *International Lawyer* (forthcoming).

lation. It is especially difficult to regulate before we know the business models that will be used—the ways a transaction can work and who will be responsible when various things go wrong.

Privacy issues will be an important component of the new models for electronic commerce. Many observers are understandably worried that businesses will use personal information in ways people would not like. And, of course, other consumer protection issues will arise. What if the seller takes the money and does not deliver the goods? What if the seller does not live up to promises it has made? What about misleading advertising, or unfounded promises about a good's performance, or failure to warn about its hazards? From the seller's point of view, what if the buyer is using a stolen credit card number or otherwise creates a risk of loss? The privacy debate is a precursor of the sorts of debates we can expect about these other electronic commerce issues.

In business-to-business transactions there are rules and institutions for handling the problems that arise in international trade. Import-export companies become expert at handling the risks of purchasing or selling abroad. Banks use an international network of financial institutions to determine the creditworthiness of distant businesses and to get letters of credit or other guarantees that permit trade to go forward. These practices suggest ways business-to-individual transactions might be handled over the Internet. Buyers' clubs might function the way import-export companies traditionally have. Financial institutions might build dispute resolution into the new payments systems.

In all the hype about electronic commerce, buyers' clubs have received surprisingly little attention. They could prove important, however, in solving legal problems arising from international business-to-individual sales. The largest electronic buyers' club appears to be run by Cendant Corporation, although disclosures beginning in April 1998 cast serious doubt on the accuracy of many of Cendant's figures. When we visited the site in early 1998, its netMarket Web site claimed to offer more than a million products (projected to grow to 3 million) and reported sales of $100 million a

10. Information here is drawn from Evan I. Schwartz, "It's! Not! Retail!," *Wired Magazine*, no. 5.11, November 1997, available at http://www.hotwired.com/wired/5.11/cuc.html and from a visit to http://www.netmarket.com in April 1998. In April 1998 Cendant made the embarrassing revelation that it had materially overstated its revenue. The analysis here of how its buyers' club operates does not appear to be affected, although the volume of its Web business may have been overstated. See Diana B. Henriques, "More Queries in Accounting Drub Cendant," *New York Times*, July 15, 1998, p. D1.

month.[10] The business plan is simple. A visitor to the Web site is offered a three-month membership for only $1.00 a month. Unless the customer cancels, a fee of $69.95 is automatically charged to a credit card at the end of three months, and the same fee is charged annually after that. *Wired* magazine reported that 70 percent of Cendant's members renew every year, although more recent information suggests a figure of only 45 percent.[11] If the customer calls to cancel, the operator offers large discounts and other incentives to keep him.

The netMarket club offers enormous selection and nearly wholesale prices. Customers receive netMarket Cash, with about 5 percent of their purchases credited as bonus points in their account, good for additional purchases. Customers also receive a seemingly unending stream of coupons, rebates, and cross-marketing opportunities. A customer making a hotel reservation, for instance, might be offered $20.00 in gas coupons as an enticement to join an affiliated travel club. And once customers accumulate netMarket Cash and have paid the annual membership fee, they have strong reasons to keep visiting the site.

The buyers' club model can potentially reduce the risks of electronic commerce. The netMarket site already advertises cash back on purchases, a low-price guarantee, and a two-year extended warranty on products.[12] Like the traditional import-export company, the buyers' club can choose the companies, from near or far, with which it wishes to do business. Merchants who misbehave can be banished from the site. The buyers' club can also identify customers who fail to pay or otherwise cause problems, and exclude them. More generally, the buyers' club can act as an insurer against the risks of electronic commerce. Its large volume, overall profitability, and position at the center of the transaction all put it in position to reduce risks and compensate customers or merchants who are the victims of occasional scams. Furthermore, as an "elephant," the buyers' club can expect strict scrutiny from the legal system and the stock market if it engages in fraud or

11. The 70 percent figure apparently applied to members who renewed after fifteen months (the three-month trial period plus the first-year membership). Only about 45 percent of people who take three-month trial memberships pay the full annual fee. Emily Nelson and JoAnn S. Lublin, "How Whistle-Blowers Set Off a Fraud Probe That Crushed Cendant," *Wall Street Journal,* August 13, 1998, pp. A1, A8.

12. The membership agreement also contains a lengthy list of disclaimers by netMarket. The point here is not that this current, still-pioneer site offers the package of legal protections that would be most desirable. The point is that, even at this early stage, the site offers significant consumer protections, even though it is not required to do so by law.

13. Indeed, the market price of the Cendant stock dropped 46 percent in the immediate aftermath

other illegal activity.[13]

Despite these attractive elements, we do not applaud all aspects of Cendant's current operations. One might question, for instance, whether it is fair to have large annual fees charged to customers' credit cards under the current method, when some customers attracted by the $1.00 a month introductory offer might not realize that the charge will be made.[14] Potentially more troubling is the company's use of customers' personal information. A diligent search of the Web site eventually revealed the statement that "individual membership information will be used solely by netMarket and its affiliates on your behalf; we will never sell your individual account information to third parties without your consent." The customer may not know, however, that Cendant has affiliates in a wide range of consumer industries. These affiliates might provide a large part of a household's typical purchases. As *Wired* has written, "the conglomerate will be collecting detailed, intimate data on hundreds of millions of consumers around the world."[15]

A different business model on the Internet would look to the payments system as a way to handle disputes about fraud or other issues arising in business-to-individual transactions. International banks that have long been central in facilitating international trade and international payments mechanisms, including credit card networks, might prove similarly important in making electronic commerce safer for both merchant and consumer.

Credit card and debit card issuers have long protected against unauthorized use of a card. The risk of such use is substantial in ordinary transactions, where a stolen card can be used around town or over the telephone. But the damage from unauthorized use can be even higher over the Internet, for instance if stolen numbers are posted to a bulletin board and used around

---

of the announcement of the accounting irregularities. The company's market capitalization dropped $14.4 billion in two days as the result of a reported accounting misstatement of about $100 million, showing the large market penalties that a publicly traded company may face for fraud or other illegalities. Floyd Norris, "Cendant's Share Price Plunges 46% on 'Accounting Irregularities,'" *New York Times*, April 17, 1998, p. D1. In addition, as of August 1998 dozens of shareholder lawsuits had been filed against Cendant. Nelson and Lublin, "Whistle-Blowers."

14. Cendant does, however, state that upon request a customer can have that year's annual fee refunded.

15. Schwartz, "It's! Not! Retail!"

16. The Internet also offers important possibilities for reducing unauthorized use. For example, credit card companies are working on the SET (secure electronic transactions) protocol, which would prevent the merchant from seeing the user's credit card number. This change would eliminate a major current risk of credit card transactions, that the waiter or store clerk will steal a user's credit card number.

the world by communities of hackers.[16] Under U.S. law, the customer's loss from unauthorized credit card use is typically capped at $50.00.[17] This law was important historically in fostering customer confidence in credit cards and spreading their use. One effect of the law is to make the card's issuer into an insurer, creating an incentive for the company to develop a fraud prevention program.

Credit card companies have also become involved when customers have complained that goods have not been delivered or that the customer should not pay for an amount claimed by a merchant. U.S. law has provided substantial protection for customers in such situations. Under the Truth in Lending Act, for transactions over $50, customers are allowed to assert claims and defenses arising out of the credit card transaction when they have made a good faith attempt to obtain satisfactory resolution of the problem.[18] In practice, customers typically do not need to pay an amount that is in dispute with the merchant. Once again, the issuer's role, at the center of the transaction, has provided a way to create a legal regime that has generally been stable and successful.

It is not yet clear the extent to which those offering credit cards or other payment services wish to facilitate international consumer transactions. U.S. law protects the cardholder only if the place of the initial transaction is in the same state or within one hundred miles of the cardholder. In explaining the geographical limit, one court stated that it "serves to protect banks from consumers who may expose them to unlimited liability through dealings with merchants in faraway states where it is difficult to monitor a merchant's behavior."[19] If it is truly too difficult to monitor merchants' behavior in distant lands, credit card companies may make the business decision not to allow consumers to dispute bills accrued with foreign sellers. But if such protections are not offered, consumers may be understandably reluctant to make important purchases by credit card on the Internet. They may then seek other business models, whether through buyers' clubs or other models that are as yet undiscovered.

Conclusion

Our discussion of buyers' clubs and credit cards illustrates how legal

---

17. 15 U.S.C. § 1643.
18. 15 U.S.C. § 1666.
19. *Israelewitz v. Manufacturers Hanover Trust Co.*, 120 Misc. 2d 125, 465 N.Y.S. 2d 486 (1983).

protections might be built into business-to-individual sales, much as import-export companies and international banks have traditionally reduced the risks of business-to-business international sales. The Internet business models are in the early stages of development. The parties seeking to promote electronic commerce have strong incentives to create models that work for consumers, merchants, and the payments system. Everyone expects Internet commerce to be much greater a decade from now, but there is little consensus about what business models and legal rules are likely to exist by then.

In studying these business models, we believe it would be foolhardy for national or supranational regulators to determine in advance the rules for conducting transactions over the Internet. As with digital signatures, early attempts at regulation might "love the technology to death" and prevent many people from doing mutually beneficial transactions. A great deal of both technological and legal experimentation is needed. With time, buyers' clubs, credit card companies, or other institutions might create business models with unsuspected advantages for consumers and merchants alike.

That said, our discussion has shown the enormous pressure for regulation. Earlier in this chapter we listed the various social harms that countries fear from the Internet. A crucial issue going forward will be the extent to which nations try to ban or regulate the ability of their individual citizens to go on the Internet. A nation might wish to limit its citizens from traveling to so strange a place. If it does so, however, it may also limit its citizens' ability to participate in much of the world's culture and commerce.

With time and experimentation, we can likely learn a good deal from the business models that succeed on the Internet. We will learn what works commercially and where nations agree on the legal rules for handling abuses. In disputes that are relatively technical, the WTO or other international mechanisms can gradually make progress toward harmonization. Other disputes will involve intense social and cultural differences. In such cases, one should not expect supranational harmonization. The WTO and other institutions are ill equipped to handle the complex social conflicts that such harmonization would entail.

Even where harmonization is not possible, there will be pressure for regulation from the nations with the strongest sense of the social harm from a particular practice. Various countries might make a priority of seeking laws to protect privacy, stamp out pornography, or shut down hate speech. They will likely regulate the elephants within their borders, and take other action against those within their jurisdiction. As with the Directive, countries or groups of countries will also use their political and market power to exert pressure on other countries to harmonize their regimes.

The Internet presents new problems about how nations will coexist in an interdependent world. They must seek to separate the relatively strong and weak claims of sovereign nations to create effects outside of their borders. In the context of this book, the European Union has a strong claim that other countries should not systematically seize data on European citizens and set up data havens to intrude on privacy. The United States, which cares intensely about enforcing many of its own laws, should respect European efforts to prevent systematic evasion of the Directive. At the same time, European claims to apply their own rules are weaker in other settings, such as when a Web site in the United States primarily processes data about U.S. citizens. In such circumstances, it is unfair and unrealistic to expect the U.S. Web site to comply with data protection rules drafted an ocean away.

A key effect of the Internet is that it makes it easy for people to conduct transactions across national borders. Regulation then becomes intensely global because the seller or provider of content might be anywhere in the world. This global aspect prompts calls for a unified international regime. At the same time, regulation of the Internet becomes intensely local as the effects of consumer fraud, dissemination of personal information, or other social harms are experienced directly through a family's computer. These local effects prompt calls for rules at the local level, with the toughest enforcement by whichever jurisdiction feels most strongly about a particular social harm.

The challenge is to find a way between the global and the local. Too much of either can stifle the Internet's potential. Too much global harmonization will ignore local values and diversity and prevent needed experimentation. Too much local regulation could lead to governance by the least tolerant as each jurisdiction attempts to impose its social values on outsiders. The answer may be for each nation (or group of nations, such as the European Union) to write its own laws, enforceable on its own territory. In this light, the European Union Directive on Data Protection deserves respect from the world as a set of rules to govern the privacy of people in Europe. People can disagree with provisions in the Directive while upholding the European Union's right to enact it. But if the European Union or individual nation-states attempt to dictate how privacy or other practices must be conducted within other countries, people in those countries might legitimately say "No. *That* is none of your business."

European Union
Directive on Data Protection

Directive 95/46/EC of the European Parliament and of the Council of 24 October 1995 on the protection of individuals with regard to the processing of personal data and on the free movement of such data [for the authoritative text of the directive see *Official Journal of the European Communities*, no. L281, November 23, 1995, p. 31].

Recitals

The European Parliament and the Council of the European Union,

Having regard to the Treaty establishing the European Community, and in particular Article 100a thereof,

Having regard to the proposal from the Commission,[1]

Having regard to the opinion of the Economic and Social Committee,[2]

Acting in accordance with the procedure referred to in Article 189b of the Treaty,[3]

---

1. *Official Journal of the European Communities*, no. C 277, 5. 11. 1990, p. 3; and no. C 311, 27.11.1992, p. 30.

2. *Official Journal of the European Communities*, no. C 159, 17. 6. 1991, p. 38.

3. Opinion of the European Parliament of 11 March 1992 (OJ No C 94, 13. 4. 1992, p. 198), confirmed on 2 December 1993 (*Official Journal of the European Communities* no. C 342, 20. 12. 1993, p. 30); Council common position of 20 February 1995 (no. C 93, 13. 4. 1995, p. 1); and Decision of the European Parliament of 15 June 1995 (no. C 166, 3. 7. 1995).

(1) Whereas the objectives of the Community, as laid down in the Treaty, as amended by the Treaty on European Union, include creating an ever closer union among the peoples of Europe, fostering closer relations between the States belonging to the Community, ensuring economic and social progress by common action to eliminate the barriers which divide Europe, encouraging the constant improvement of the living conditions of its peoples, preserving and strengthening peace and liberty and promoting democracy on the basis of the fundamental rights recognized in the constitution and laws of the Member States and in the European Convention for the Protection of Human Rights and Fundamental Freedoms;

(2) Whereas data-processing systems are designed to serve man; whereas they must, whatever the nationality or residence of natural persons, respect their fundamental rights and freedoms, notably the right to privacy, and contribute to economic and social progress, trade expansion and the well-being of individuals;

(3) Whereas the establishment and functioning of an internal market in which, in accordance with Article 7a of the Treaty, the free movement of goods, persons, services and capital is ensured require not only that personal data should be able to flow freely from one Member State to another, but also that the fundamental rights of individuals should be safeguarded;

(4) Whereas increasingly frequent recourse is being had in the Community to the processing of personal data in the various spheres of economic and social activity; whereas the progress made in information technology is making the processing and exchange of such data considerably easier;

(5) Whereas the economic and social integration resulting from the establishment and functioning of the internal market within the meaning of Article 7a of the Treaty will necessarily lead to a substantial increase in cross-border flows of personal data between all those involved in a private or public capacity in economic and social activity in the Member States; whereas the exchange of personal data between undertakings in different Member States is set to increase; whereas the national authorities in the various Member States are being called upon by virtue of Community law to collaborate and exchange personal data so as to be able to perform their duties or carry out tasks on behalf of an authority in another Member State within the context of the area without internal frontiers as constituted by the internal market;

(6) Whereas, furthermore, the increase in scientific and technical cooperation and the coordinated introduction of new telecommunications

networks in the Community necessitate and facilitate cross-border flows of personal data;

(7) Whereas the difference in levels of protection of the rights and freedoms of individuals, notably the right to privacy, with regard to the processing of personal data afforded in the Member States may prevent the transmission of such data from the territory of one Member State to that of another Member State; whereas this difference may therefore constitute an obstacle to the pursuit of a number of economic activities at Community level, distort competition and impede authorities in the discharge of their responsibilities under Community law; whereas this difference in levels of protection is due to the existence of a wide variety of national laws, regulations and administrative provisions;

(8) Whereas, in order to remove the obstacles to flows of personal data, the level of protection of the rights and freedoms of individuals with regard to the processing of such data must be equivalent in all Member States; whereas this objective is vital to the internal market but cannot be achieved by the Member States alone, especially in view of the scale of the divergences which currently exist between the relevant laws in the Member States and the need to coordinate the laws of the Member States so as to ensure that the cross-border flow of personal data is regulated in a consistent manner that is in keeping with the objective of the internal market as provided for in Article 7a of the Treaty; whereas Community action to approximate those laws is therefore needed;

(9) Whereas, given the equivalent protection resulting from the approximation of national laws, the Member States will no longer be able to inhibit the free movement between them of personal data on grounds relating to protection of the rights and freedoms of individuals, and in particular the right to privacy; whereas Member States will be left a margin for manoeuvre, which may, in the context of implementation of the Directive, also be exercised by the business and social partners; whereas Member States will therefore be able to specify in their national law the general conditions governing the lawfulness of data processing; whereas in doing so the Member States shall strive to improve the protection currently provided by their legislation; whereas, within the limits of this margin for manoeuvre and in accordance with Community law, disparities could arise in the implementation of the Directive, and this could have an effect on the movement of data within a Member State as well as within the Community;

(10) Whereas the object of the national laws on the processing of personal data is to protect fundamental rights and freedoms, notably the right

to privacy, which is recognized both in Article 8 of the European Convention for the Protection of Human Rights and Fundamental Freedoms and in the general principles of Community law; whereas, for that reason, the approximation of those laws must not result in any lessening of the protection they afford but must, on the contrary, seek to ensure a high level of protection in the Community;

(11) Whereas the principles of the protection of the rights and freedoms of individuals, notably the right to privacy, which are contained in this Directive, give substance to and amplify those contained in the Council of Europe Convention of 28 January 1981 for the Protection of Individuals with regard to Automatic Processing of Personal Data;

(12) Whereas the protection principles must apply to all processing of personal data by any person whose activities are governed by Community law; whereas there should be excluded the processing of data carried out by a natural person in the exercise of activities which are exclusively personal or domestic, such as correspondence and the holding of records of addresses;

(13) Whereas the activities referred to in Titles V and VI of the Treaty on European Union regarding public safety, defence, State security or the activities of the State in the area of criminal laws fall outside the scope of Community law, without prejudice to the obligations incumbent upon Member States under Article 56 (2), Article 57 or Article 100a of the Treaty establishing the European Community; whereas the processing of personal data that is necessary to safeguard the economic well-being of the State does not fall within the scope of this Directive where such processing relates to State security matters;

(14) Whereas, given the importance of the developments under way, in the framework of the information society, of the techniques used to capture, transmit, manipulate, record, store or communicate sound and image data relating to natural persons, this Directive should be applicable to processing involving such data;

(15) Whereas the processing of such data is covered by this Directive only if it is automated or if the data processed are contained or are intended to be contained in a filing system structured according to specific criteria relating to individuals, so as to permit easy access to the personal data in question;

(16) Whereas the processing of sound and image data, such as in cases of video surveillance, does not come within the scope of this Directive if it is carried out for the purposes of public security, defence, national security

or in the course of State activities relating to the area of criminal law or of other activities which do not come within the scope of Community law;

(17) Whereas, as far as the processing of sound and image data carried out for purposes of journalism or the purposes of literary or artistic expression is concerned, in particular in the audiovisual field, the principles of the Directive are to apply in a restricted manner according to the provisions laid down in Article 9;

(18) Whereas, in order to ensure that individuals are not deprived of the protection to which they are entitled under this Directive, any processing of personal data in the Community must be carried out in accordance with the law of one of the Member States; whereas, in this connection, processing carried out under the responsibility of a controller who is established in a Member State should be governed by the law of that State;

(19) Whereas establishment on the territory of a Member State implies the effective and real exercise of activity through stable arrangements; whereas the legal form of such an establishment, whether simply 'branch or a subsidiary with a legal personality, is not the determining factor in this respect; whereas, when a single controller is established on the territory of several Member States, particularly by means of subsidiaries, he must ensure, in order to avoid any circumvention of national rules, that each of the establishments fulfils the obligations imposed by the national law applicable to its activities;

(20) Whereas the fact that the processing of data is carried out by a person established in a third country must not stand in the way of the protection of individuals provided for in this Directive; whereas in these cases, the processing should be governed by the law of the Member State in which the means used are located, and there should be guarantees to ensure that the rights and obligations provided for in this Directive are respected in practice;

(21) Whereas this Directive is without prejudice to the rules of territoriality applicable in criminal matters;

(22) Whereas Member States shall more precisely define in the laws they enact or when bringing into force the measures taken under this Directive the general circumstances in which processing is lawful; whereas in particular Article 5, in conjunction with Articles 7 and 8, allows Member States, independently of general rules, to provide for special processing conditions for specific sectors and for the various categories of data covered by Article 8;

(23) Whereas Member States are empowered to ensure the implemen-

tation of the protection of individuals both by means of a general law on the protection of individuals as regards the processing of personal data and by sectorial laws such as those relating, for example, to statistical institutes;

(24) Whereas the legislation concerning the protection of legal persons with regard to the processing data which concerns them is not affected by this Directive;

(25) Whereas the principles of protection must be reflected, on the one hand, in the obligations imposed on persons, public authorities, enterprises, agencies or other bodies responsible for processing, in particular regarding data quality, technical security, notification to the supervisory authority, and the circumstances under which processing can be carried out, and, on the other hand, in the right conferred on individuals, the data on whom are the subject of processing, to be informed that processing is taking place, to consult the data, to request corrections and even to object to processing in certain circumstances;

(26) Whereas the principles of protection must apply to any information concerning an identified or identifiable person; whereas, to determine whether a person is identifiable, account should be taken of all the means likely reasonably to be used either by the controller or by any other person to identify the said person; whereas the' principles of protection shall not apply to data rendered anonymous in such a way that the data subject is no longer identifiable; whereas codes of conduct within the meaning of Article 27 may be a useful instrument for providing guidance as to the ways in which data may be rendered anonymous and retained in a form in which identification of the data subject is no longer possible;

(27) Whereas the protection of individuals must apply as much to automatic processing of data as to manual processing; whereas the scope of this protection must not in effect depend on the techniques used, otherwise this would create a serious risk of circumvention; whereas, nonetheless, as regards manual processing, this Directive covers only filing systems, not unstructured files; whereas, in particular, the content of a filing system must be structured according to specific criteria relating to individuals allowing easy access to the personal data; whereas, in line with the definition in Article 2 (c), the different criteria for determining the constituents of a structured set of personal data, and the different criteria governing access to such a set, may be laid down by each Member State; whereas files or sets of files as well as their cover pages, which are not structured according to specific criteria, shall under no circumstances fall within the scope of this Directive;

(28) Whereas any processing of personal data must be lawful and fair to the individuals concerned; whereas, in particular, the data must be adequate, relevant and not excessive in relation to the purposes for which they are processed; whereas such purposes must be explicit and legitimate and must be determined at the time of collection of the data; whereas the purposes of processing further to collection shall not be incompatible with the purposes as they were originally specified;

(29) Whereas the further processing of personal data for historical, statistical or scientific purposes is not generally to be considered incompatible with the purposes for which the data have previously been collected provided that Member States furnish suitable safeguards; whereas these safeguards must in particular rule out the use of the data in support of measures or decisions regarding any particular individual;

(30) Whereas, in order to be lawful, the processing of personal data must in addition be carried out with the consent of the data subject or be necessary for the conclusion or performance of a contract binding on the data subject, or as a legal requirement, or for the performance of a task carried out in the public interest or in the exercise of official authority, or in the legitimate interests of a natural or legal person, provided that the interests or the rights and freedoms of the data subject are not overriding; whereas, in particular, in order to maintain a balance between the interests involved while guaranteeing effective competition, Member States may determine the circumstances in which personal data may be used or disclosed to a third party in the context of the legitimate ordinary business activities of companies and other bodies; whereas Member States may similarly specify the conditions under which personal data may be disclosed to a third party for the purposes of marketing whether carried out commercially or by a charitable organization or by any other association or foundation, of a political nature for example, subject to the provisions allowing a data subject to object to the processing of data regarding him, at no cost and without having to state his reasons;

(31) Whereas the processing of personal data must equally be regarded as lawful where it is carried out in order to protect an interest which is essential for the data subject's life;

(32) Whereas it is for national legislation to determine whether the controller performing a task carried out in the public interest or in the exercise of official authority should be a public administration or another natural or legal person governed by public law, or by private law such as a professional association;

(33) Whereas data which are capable by their nature of infringing fundamental freedoms or privacy should not be processed unless the data subject gives his explicit consent; whereas, however, derogations from this prohibition must be explicitly provided for in respect of specific needs, in particular where the processing of these data is carried out for certain health-related purposes by persons subject to a legal obligation of professional secrecy or in the course of legitimate activities by certain associations or foundations the purpose of which is to permit the exercise of fundamental freedoms;

(34) Whereas Member States must also be authorized, when justified by grounds of important public interest, to derogate from the prohibition on processing sensitive categories of data where important reasons of public interest so justify in areas such as public health and social protection—especially in order to ensure the quality and cost-effectiveness of the procedures used for settling claims for benefits and services in the health insurance system—scientific research and government statistics; whereas it is incumbent on them, however, to provide specific and suitable safeguards so as to protect the fundamental rights and the privacy of individuals;

(35) Whereas, moreover, the processing of personal data by official authorities for achieving aims, laid down in constitutional law or international public law, of officially recognized religious associations is carried out on important grounds of public' interest;

(36) Whereas where, in the course of electoral activities, the operation of the democratic system requires in certain Member States that political parties compile data on people's political opinion, the processing of such data may be permitted for reasons of important public interest, provided that appropriate safeguards are established;

(37) Whereas the processing of personal data for purposes of journalism or for purposes of literary of artistic expression, in particular in the audiovisual field, should qualify for exemption from the requirements of certain provisions of this Directive in so far as this is necessary to reconcile the fundamental rights of individuals with freedom of information and notably the right to receive and impart information, as guaranteed in particular in Article 10 of the European Convention for the Protection of Human Rights and Fundamental Freedoms; whereas Member States should therefore lay down exemptions and derogations necessary for the purpose of balance between fundamental rights as regards general measures on the legitimacy of data processing, measures on the transfer of data to third countries and the power of the supervisory authority; whereas this should

not, however, lead Member States to lay down exemptions from the measures to ensure security of processing; whereas at least the supervisory authority responsible for this sector should also be provided with certain ex-post powers, e.g. to publish a regular report or to refer matters to the judicial authorities;

(38) Whereas, if the processing of data is to be fair, the data subject must be in a position to learn of the existence of a processing operation and, where data are collected from him, must be given accurate and full information, bearing in mind the circumstances of the collection;

(39) Whereas certain processing operations involve data which the controller has not collected directly from the data subject; whereas, furthermore, data can be legitimately disclosed to a third party, even if the disclosure was not anticipated at the time the data were collected from the data subject; whereas, in all these cases, the data subject should be informed when the data are recorded or at the latest when the data are first disclosed to a third party;

(40) Whereas, however, it is not necessary to impose this obligation of the data subject already has the information; whereas, moreover, there will be no such obligation if the recording or disclosure are expressly provided for by law or if the provision of information to the data subject proves impossible or would involve disproportionate efforts, which could be the case where processing is for historical, statistical or scientific purposes; whereas, in this regard, the number of data subjects, the age of the data, and any compensatory measures adopted may be taken into consideration;

(41) Whereas any person must be able to exercise the right of access to data relating to him which are being processed, in order to verify in particular the accuracy of the data and the lawfulness of the processing; whereas, for .the same reasons, every data subject must also have the right to know the logic involved in the automatic processing of data concerning him, at least in the case of the automated decisions referred to in Article 15 (1); whereas this right must not adversely affect trade secrets or intellectual property and in particular the copyright protecting the software; whereas these considerations must not, however, result in the data subject being refused all information;

(42) Whereas Member States may, in the interest of the data subject or so as to protect the rights and freedoms of others, restrict rights of access and information; whereas they may, for example, specify that access to medical data may be obtained only through a health professional;

(43) Whereas restrictions on the rights of access and information and

on certain obligations of the controller may similarly be imposed by Member States in so far as they are necessary to safeguard, for example, national security, defence, public safety, or important economic or financial interests of a Member State or the Union, as well as criminal investigations and prosecutions and action in respect of breaches of ethics in the regulated professions; whereas the list of exceptions and limitations should include the tasks of monitoring, inspection or regulation necessary in the three last-mentioned areas concerning public security, economic or financial interests and crime prevention; whereas the listing of tasks in these three areas does not affect the legitimacy of exceptions or restrictions for reasons of State security or defence;

(44) Whereas Member States may also be led, by virtue of the provisions of Community law, to derogate from the provisions of this Directive concerning the right of access, the obligation to inform individuals, and the quality of data, in order to secure certain of the purposes referred to above;

(45) Whereas, in cases where data might lawfully be processed on grounds of public interest, official authority or the legitimate interests of a natural or legal person, any data subject should nevertheless be entitled, on legitimate and compelling grounds relating to his particular situation, to object to the processing of any data relating to himself; whereas Member States may nevertheless lay down national provisions to the contrary;

(46) Whereas the protection of the rights and freedoms of data subjects with regard to the processing of personal data requires that appropriate technical and organizational measures be taken, both at the time of the design of the processing system and at the time of the processing itself, particularly in order to maintain security and thereby to prevent any unauthorized processing; whereas it is incumbent on the Member States to ensure that controllers comply with these measures; whereas these measures must ensure an appropriate level of security, taking into account the state of the art and the costs of their implementation in relation to the risks inherent in the processing and the nature of the data to be protected;

(47) Whereas where a message containing personal data is transmitted by means of a telecommunications or electronic mail service, the sole purpose of which is the transmission of such messages, the controller in respect of the personal data contained in the message will normally be considered to be the person from whom the message originates, rather than the person offering the transmission services; whereas, nevertheless, those offering such services will normally be considered controllers in respect of

the processing of the additional personal data necessary for the operation of the service;

(48) Whereas the procedures for notifying the supervisory authority are designed to ensure disclosure of the purposes and main features of any processing operation for the purpose of verification that the operation is in accordance with the national measures taken under this Directive;

(49) Whereas, in order to avoid unsuitable administrative formalities, exemptions from the obligation to notify and simplification of the notification required may be provided for by Member States in cases where processing is unlikely adversely to affect the rights and freedoms of data subjects, provided that it is in accordance with a measure taken by a Member State specifying its limits; whereas exemption or simplification may similarly be provided for by Member States where a person appointed by the controller ensures that the processing carried out is not likely adversely to affect the rights and freedoms of data subjects; whereas such a data protection official, whether or not an employee of the controller, must be in a position to exercise his functions in complete independence;

(50) Whereas exemption or simplification could be provided for in cases of processing operations whose sole purpose is the keeping of a register intended, according to national law, to provide information to the public and open to consultation by the public or by any person demonstrating a legitimate interest;

(51) Whereas, nevertheless, simplification or exemption from the obligation to notify shall not release the controller from any of the other obligations resulting from this Directive;

(52) Whereas, in this context, ex post facto verification by the competent authorities must in general be considered a sufficient measure;

(53) Whereas, however, certain processing operations are likely to pose specific risks to the rights and freedoms of data subjects by virtue of their nature, their scope or their purposes, such as that of excluding individuals from a right, benefit or a contract, or by virtue of the specific use of new technologies; whereas it is for Member States, if they so wish, to specify such risks in their legislation;

(54) Whereas with regard to all the processing undertaken in society, the amount posing such specific risks should be very limited; whereas Member States must provide that the supervisory authority, or the data protection official in cooperation with the authority, check such processing prior to it being carried out; whereas following this prior check, the supervisory authority may, according to its national law, give an opinion or an authori-

zation regarding the processing; whereas such checking may equally take place in the course of the preparation either of a measure of the national parliament or of a measure based on such a legislative measure, which defines the nature of the processing and lays down appropriate safeguards;

(55) Whereas, if the controller fails to respect the rights of data subjects, national legislation must provide for a judicial remedy; whereas any damage which a person may suffer as a result of unlawful processing must be compensated for by the controller, who may be exempted from liability if he proves that he is not responsible for the damage, in particular in cases where he establishes fault on the part of the data subject or in case of force majeure; whereas sanctions must be imposed on any person, whether governed by private of public law, who fails to comply with the national measures taken under this Directive;

(56) Whereas cross-border flows of personal data are necessary to the expansion of international trade; whereas the protection of individuals, guaranteed in the Community by this Directive does not stand in the way of transfers of personal data to third countries which ensure an adequate level of protection; whereas the adequacy of the level of protection afforded by a third country must be assessed in the light of all the circumstances surrounding the transfer operation or set of transfer operations;

(57) Whereas, on the other hand, the transfer of personal data to a third country which does not ensure an adequate level of protection must be prohibited;

(58) Whereas provisions should be made for exemptions from this prohibition in certain circumstances where the data subject has given his consent, where the transfer is necessary in relation to a contract or a legal claim, where protection of an important public interest so requires, for example in cases of international transfers of data between tax or customs administrations or between services competent for social security matters, or where the transfer is made from a register established by law and intended for consultation by the public or persons having a legitimate interest; whereas in this case such a transfer should not involve the entirety of the data or entire categories of the data contained in the register and, when the register is intended for consultation by persons having a legitimate interest, the transfer should be made only at the request of those persons or if they are to be the recipients;

(59) Whereas particular measures may be taken to compensate for the lack of protection in a third country in cases where the controller offers appropriate safeguards; whereas, moreover, provision must be made

for procedures for negotiations between the Community and such third countries;

(60) Whereas, in any event, transfers to third countries may be effected only in full compliance with the provisions adopted by the Member States pursuant to this Directive, and in particular Article 8 thereof;

(61) Whereas Member States and the Commission, in their respective spheres of competence, must encourage the trade associations and other representative organizations concerned to draw up codes of conduct so as to facilitate the application of this Directive, taking account of the specific characteristics of the processing carried out in certain sectors, and respecting the national provisions adopted for its implementation;

(62) Whereas the establishment in Member States of supervisory authorities, exercising their functions with complete independence, is an' essential component of the protection of individuals with regard to the processing of personal data;

(63) Whereas such authorities must have the necessary means to perform their duties, including powers of investigation and intervention, particularly in cases of complaints from individuals, and powers to engage in legal proceedings; whereas such authorities must help to ensure transparency of processing in the Member States within whose jurisdiction they fall;

(64) Whereas the authorities in the different Member States will need to assist one another in performing their duties so as to ensure that the rules of protection are properly respected throughout the European Union;

(65) Whereas, at Community level, a Working Party on the Protection of Individuals with regard to the Processing of Personal Data must be set up and be completely independent in the performance of its functions; whereas, having regard to its specific nature, it must advise the Commission and, in particular, contribute to the uniform application of the national rules adopted pursuant to this Directive;

(66) Whereas, with regard to the transfer of data to third countries, the application of this Directive calls for the conferment of powers of implementation on the Commission and the establishment of a procedure as laid down in Council Decision 87/373/EEC;[4]

(67) Whereas an agreement on a modus vivendi between the European Parliament, the Council and the Commission concerning the implement-

---

4. *Official Journal of the European Communities*, no. L 197, 18. 7. 1987, p. 33.

ing measures for acts adopted in accordance with the procedure laid down in Article 189b of the EC Treaty was reached on 20 December 1994;

(68) Whereas the principles set out in this Directive regarding the protection of the rights and freedoms of individuals, notably their right to privacy, with regard to the processing of personal data may be supplemented or clarified, in particular as far as certain sectors are concerned, by specific rules based on those principles;

(69) Whereas Member States should be allowed a period of not more than three years from the entry into force of the national measures transposing this Directive in which to apply such new national rules progressively to all processing operations already under way; whereas, in order to facilitate their cost-effective implementation, a further period expiring 12 years after the date on which this Directive is adopted will be allowed to Member States to ensure the conformity of existing manual filing systems with certain of the Directive's provisions; whereas, where data contained in such filing systems are manually processed during this extended transition period, those systems must be brought into conformity with these provisions at the time of such processing;

(70) Whereas it is not necessary for the data subject to give his consent again so as to allow the controller to continue to process, after the national provisions taken pursuant to this Directive enter into force, any sensitive data necessary for the performance of a contract concluded on the basis of free and informed consent before the entry into force of these provisions;

(71) Whereas this Directive does not stand in the way of a Member State's regulating marketing activities aimed at consumers residing in territory in so far as such regulation does not concern the protection of individuals with regard to the processing of personal data;

(72) Whereas this Directive allows the principle of public access to official documents to be taken into account when implementing the principles set out in this Directive, have adopted this Directive:

Chapter I   General Provisions

Article 1   Object of the Directive
1. In accordance with this Directive, Member States shall protect the fundamental rights and freedoms of natural persons, and in particular their right to privacy with respect to the processing of personal data.

2. Member States shall neither restrict nor prohibit the free flow of personal data between Member States for reasons connected with the protection afforded under paragraph 1.

Article 2   Definitions
For the purposes of this Directive:

(a) "personal data" shall mean any information relating to an identified or identifiable natural person ("data subject"); an identifiable person is one who can be identified, directly or indirectly, in particular by reference to an identification number or to one or more factors specific to his physical, physiological, mental, economic, cultural or social identity;

(b) "processing of personal data"("processing") shall mean any operation or set of operations which is performed upon personal data, whether or not by automatic means, such as collection, recording, organization, storage, adaptation or alteration, retrieval, consultation, use, disclosure by transmission, dissemination or otherwise making available, alignment or combination, blocking, erasure or destruction;

(c) "personal data filing system" ("filing system") shall mean any structured set of personal data which are accessible according to specific criteria, whether centralized, decentralized or dispersed on a functional or geographical basis;

(d) "controller" shall mean the natural or legal person, public authority, agency or any other body which alone or jointly with others determines the purposes and means of the processing of personal data; where the purposes and means of processing are determined by national or Community laws or regulations, the controller or the specific criteria for his nomination may be designated by national or Community law;

(e) "processor" shall mean a natural or legal person, public authority, agency or any other body which processes personal data on behalf of the controller;

(f) "third party" shall mean any natural or legal person, public authority, agency or any other body other than the data subject, the controller, the processor and the persons who, under the direct authority of the controller or the processor, are authorized to process the data;

(g) "recipient" shall mean a natural or legal person, public authority, agency or any other body to whom data are disclosed, whether a third party or not; however, authorities which may receive data in the framework of a particular inquiry shall not be regarded as recipients;

(h) "the data subject's consent" shall mean any freely given specific and informed indication of his wishes by which the data subject signifies his agreement to personal data relating to him being processed.

Article 3   Scope

1. This Directive shall apply to the processing of personal data wholly or partly by automatic means, and to the processing otherwise than by automatic means of personal data which form part of a filing system or are intended to form part of a filing system.

2. This Directive shall not apply to the processing of personal data:
in the course of an activity which falls outside the scope of Community law, such as those provided for by Titles V and VI of the Treaty on European Union and in any case to processing operations concerning public security, defence, State security (including the economic well-being of the State when the processing operation relates to State security matters) and the activities of the State in areas of criminal law, by a natural person in the course of a purely personal or household activity.

Article 4   National law applicable

1. Each Member State shall apply the national provisions it adopts pursuant to this Directive to the processing of personal data where:

(a) the processing is carried out in the context of the activities of an establishment of the controller on the territory of the Member State; when the same controller is established on the territory of several Member States, he must take the necessary measures to ensure that each of these establishments complies with the obligations laid down by the national law applicable;

(b) the controller is not established on the Member State's territory, but in a place where its national law applies by virtue of international public law;

(c) the controller is not established on Community territory and, for purposes of processing personal data makes use of equipment, automated or otherwise, situated on the territory of the said Member State, unless such equipment is used only for purposes of transit through the territory of the Community.

2. In the circumstances referred to in paragraph 1 (c), the controller must designate a representative established in the territory of that Member State, without prejudice to legal actions which could be initiated against the controller himself.

Chapter II   General Rules on the Lawfulness of the Processing of Personal Data

Article 5

Member States shall, within the limits of the provisions of this Chapter, determine more precisely the conditions under which the processing of personal data is lawful.

Section I   Principles Relating to Data Quality

Article 6

1. Member States shall provide that personal data must be:

(a) processed fairly and lawfully;

(b) collected for specified, explicit and legitimate purposes and not further processed in a way incompatible with those purposes. Further processing of data for historical, statistical or scientific purposes shall not be considered as incompatible provided that Member States provide appropriate safeguards;

(c) adequate, relevant and not excessive in relation to the purposes for which they are collected and/or further processed;

(d) accurate and, where necessary, kept up to date; every reasonable step must be taken to ensure that data which are inaccurate or incomplete, having regard to the purposes for which they were collected or for which they are further processed, are erased or rectified;

(e) kept in a form which permits identification of data subjects for no longer than is necessary for the purposes for which the data were collected or for which they are further processed. Member States shall lay down appropriate safeguards for personal data stored for longer periods for historical, statistical or scientific use.

2. It shall be for the controller to ensure that paragraph 1 is complied with.

Section II   Criteria for Making Data Processing Legitimate

Article 7

Member States shall provide that personal data may be processed only if:

(a) the data subject has unambiguously given his consent; or

(b) processing is necessary for the performance of a contract to which the data subject is party or in order to take steps at the request of the data subject prior to entering into a contract; or

(c) processing is necessary for compliance with a legal obligation to which the controller is subject; or

(d) processing is necessary in order to protect the vital interests of the data subject; or

(e) processing is necessary for the performance of a task carried out in the public interest or in the exercise of official authority vested in the controller or in a third party to whom the data are disclosed; or

(f) processing is necessary for the purposes of the legitimate interests pursued by the controller or by the third party or parties to whom the data are disclosed, except where such interests are overridden by the interests for fundamental rights and freedoms of the data subject which require protection under Article 1 (1).

Section III   Special Categories of Processing

Article 8   The processing of special categories of data

1. Member States shall prohibit the processing of personal data revealing racial or ethnic origin, political opinions, religious or philosophical beliefs, trade-union membership, and the processing of data concerning health or sex life.

2. Paragraph 1 shall not apply where:

(a) the data subject has given his explicit consent to the processing of those data, except where the laws of the Member State provide that the prohibition referred to in paragraph 1 may not be lifted by the data subject's giving his consent; or

(b) processing is necessary for the purposes of carrying out the obligations and specific rights of the controller in the field of employment law in so far as it is authorized by national law providing for adequate safeguards; or

(c) processing is necessary to protect the vital interests of the data subject or of another person where the data subject is physically or legally incapable of giving his consent; or

(d) processing is carried out in the course of its legitimate activities with appropriate guarantees by a foundation, association or any other non-profit-seeking body with a political, philosophical, religious or trade-union aim and on condition that the processing relates solely to the members of the body or to persons who have regular contact with it in connection with its purposes and that' the data are not disclosed to a third party without the consent of the data subjects; or

(e) the processing relates to data which are manifestly made public by the data subject or is necessary for the establishment, exercise or defence of legal claims.

3. Paragraph 1 shall not apply where processing of the data is required for the purposes of preventive medicine, medical diagnosis, the provision of care or treatment or the management of health-care services, and where those data are processed by a health professional subject under national law or rules established by national competent bodies to the obligation of professional secrecy or by another person also subject to an equivalent obligation of secrecy.

4. Subject to the provision of suitable safeguards, Member States may, for reasons of substantial public interest, lay down exemptions in addition to those laid down in paragraph 2 either by national law or by decision of the supervisory authority.

5. Processing of data relating to offences, criminal convictions or security measures may be carried out only under the control of official authority, or if suitable specific safeguards are provided under national law, subject to derogations which may be granted by the Member State under national provisions providing suitable specific safeguards. However, a complete register of criminal convictions may be kept only under the control of official authority.

Member States may provide that data relating to administrative sanctions or judgements in civil cases shall also be processed under the control of official authority.

6. Derogations from paragraph 1 provided for in paragraphs 4 and 5 shall be notified to the Commission

7. Member States shall determine the conditions under which a national identification number or any other identifier of general application may be processed.

Article 9   Processing of personal data and freedom of expression
Member States shall provide for exemptions or derogations from the provisions of this Chapter, Chapter IV and Chapter VI for the processing of personal data carried out solely for journalistic purposes or the purpose of artistic or literary expression only if they are necessary to reconcile the right to privacy with the rules governing freedom of expression.

Section IV   Information to Be Given to the Data Subject

Article 10   Information in cases of collection of data from the data subject

Member States shall provide that the controller or his representative must provide a data subject from whom data relating to himself are collected with at least the following information, except where he already has it:

(a) the identity of the controller and of his representative, if any;

(b) the purposes of the processing for which the data are intended;

(c) any further information such as

—the recipients or categories of recipients of the data,

—whether replies to the questions are obligatory or voluntary, as well as the possible consequences of failure to reply,

—the existence of the right of access to and the right to rectify the data concerning him

in so far as such further information is necessary, having regard to the specific circumstances in which the data are collected, to guarantee fair processing in respect of the data subject.

Article 11   Information where the data have not been obtained from the data subject

1. Where the data have not been obtained from the data subject, Member States shall provide that the controller or his representative must at the time of undertaking the recording of personal data or if a disclosure to a third party is envisaged, no later than the time when the data are first disclosed provide the data subject with at least the following information, except where he already has it:

(a) the identity of the controller and of his representative, if any;

(b) the purposes of the processing;

(c) any further information such as

—the categories of data concerned,

—the recipients or categories of recipients,

—the existence of the right of access to and the right to rectify the data concerning him in so far as such further information is necessary, having regard to the specific circumstances in which the data are processed, to guarantee fair processing in respect of the data subject.

2. Paragraph 1 shall not apply where, in particular for processing for statistical purposes or for the purposes of historical or scientific research, the provision of such information proves impossible or would involve a

disproportionate effort or if recording or disclosure is expressly laid down by law. In these cases Member States shall provide appropriate safeguards.

Section V   The Data Subject's Right of Access to Data

Article 12   Right of access
Member States shall guarantee every data right to obtain from the controller:

(a) without constraint at reasonable intervals and without excessive delay or expense:

—confirmation as to whether or not data relating to him are being processed and information at least as to the purposes of the processing, the categories of data concerned, and the recipients or categories of recipients to whom the data are disclosed,

—communication to him in an intelligible form of the data undergoing processing and of any available information as to their source,

—knowledge of the logic involved in any automatic processing of data concerning him at least in the case of the automated decisions referred .to in Article 15 (1);

(b) as appropriate the rectification, erasure or blocking of data the processing of which does not comply with the provisions of this Directive, in particular because of the incomplete or inaccurate nature of the data;

(c) notification to third parties to whom the data have been disclosed of any rectification, erasure or blocking carried out in compliance with (b), unless this proves impossible or involves a disproportionate effort.

Section VI   Exemptions and Restrictions

Article 13
1. Member States may adopt legislative measures to restrict the scope of the obligations and rights provided for in Articles 6 (1), 10, 11 (1), 12 and 21 when such a restriction constitutes a necessary measures to safeguard:

(a) national security;

(b) defence;

(c) public security;

(d) the prevention, investigation, detection and prosecution of criminal offences, or of breaches of ethics for regulated professions;

(e) an important economic or financial interest of a Member State or of the European Union, including monetary, budgetary and taxation matters;

(f) a monitoring, inspection or regulatory function connected, even occasionally, with the exercise of official authority in cases referred to in (c), (d) and (e);

(g) the protection of the data subject or of the rights and freedoms of others.

2. Subject to adequate legal safeguards, in particular that the data are not used for taking measures or decisions regarding any particular individual, Member States may, where there is clearly no risk of breaching the privacy of the data subject, restrict by a legislative measure the rights provided for in Article 12 when data are processed solely for purposes of scientific research or are kept in personal form for a period which does not exceed the period necessary for the sole purpose of creating statistics.

Section VII   *The Data Subject's Right to Object*

Article 14   *The data subject's right to object*
Member States shall grant the data subject the right:

(a) at least in the cases referred to in Article 7 (e) and (f), to object at any time on compelling legitimate grounds relating to his particular situation to the processing of data relating to him, save where otherwise provided by national legislation. Where there is a justified objection, the processing instigated by the controller may no longer involve those data;

(b) to object, on request and free of charge, to the processing of personal data relating to him which the controller anticipates being processed for the purposes of direct marketing, or to be informed before personal data are disclosed for the first time to third parties or used on their behalf for the purposes of direct marketing, and to be expressly offered the right to object free of charge to such disclosures or uses.

Member States shall take the necessary measures to ensure that data subjects are aware of the existence of the right referred to in the first subparagraph of (b).

Article 15   *Automated individual decisions*
1. Member States shall grant the right to every person not to be subject to a decision which produces legal effects concerning him or significantly affects him and which is based solely on automated processing of data intended to evaluate certain personal aspects relating to him, such as his performance at work, creditworthiness, reliability, conduct, etc.

2. Subject to the other Articles of this Directive, Member States shall provide that a person may be subjected to a decision of the kind referred to in paragraph 1 if that decision:

(a) is taken in the course of the entering into or performance of a contract, provided the request for the entering into or the performance of the contract, lodged by the data subject, has been satisfied or that there are suitable measures to safeguard his legitimate interests, such as arrangements allowing him to put his point of view; or

(b) is authorized by a law which also lays down measures to safeguard the data subject's legitimate interests.

Section VIII   Confidentiality and Security of Processing

Article 16   Confidentiality of processing

Any person acting under the authority of the controller or of the processor, including the processor himself, who has access to personal data must not process them except on instructions from the controller, unless he is required to do so by law.

Article 17   Security of processing

1. Member States shall provide that the controller must implement appropriate technical and organizational measures to protect personal data against accidental or unlawful destruction or accidental loss, alteration, unauthorized disclosure or access, in particular where the processing involves the transmission of data over a network, and against all other unlawful forms of processing.

Having regard to the state of the art and the cost of their implementation, such measures shall ensure a level of security appropriate to the risks represented by the processing and the nature of the data to be protected.

2. The Member States shall provide that the controller must, where processing is carried out on his behalf, choose a processor providing sufficient guarantees in respect of the technical security measures and organizational measures governing the processing to be carried out, and must ensure compliance with those measures.

3. The carrying out of processing by way of a processor must be governed by a contract or legal act binding the processor to the controller and stipulating in particular that:

—the processor shall act only on instructions from the controller,

—the obligations set out in paragraph 1, as defined by the law of the Member State in which the processor is established, shall also be incumbent on the processor.

4. For the purposes of keeping proof, the parts of the contract or the legal act relating to data protection and the requirements relating to the measures referred to in paragraph 1 shall be in writing or in another equivalent form.

Section IX   Notification

Article 18   Obligation to notify the supervisory authority

1. Member States shall provide that the controller or his representative, if any, must notify the supervisory authority referred to in Article 28 before carrying out any wholly or partly automatic processing operation or set of such operations intended to serve a single purpose or several related purposes.

2. Member States may provide for the simplification of or exemption from notification only in the following cases and under the following conditions:

—where, for categories of processing operations which are unlikely, taking account of the data to be processed, to affect adversely the rights and freedoms of data subjects, they specify the purposes of the processing, the data or categories of data undergoing processing, the category or categories of data subject, the recipients or categories of recipient to whom the data are to be disclosed and the length of time the data are to be stored, and/or

—where the controller, in compliance with the national law which governs him, appoints a personal data protection official, responsible in particular:

—for ensuring in an independent manner the internal application of the national provisions taken pursuant to this Directive

—for keeping the register of processing operations carried out by the controller, containing the items of information referred to in Article 21 (2), thereby ensuring that the rights and freedoms of the data subjects are unlikely to be adversely affected by the processing operations.

3. Member States may provide that paragraph 1 does not apply to processing whose sole purpose is the keeping of a register which according to laws or regulations is intended to provide information to the public and which is open to consultation either by the public in general or by any person demonstrating a legitimate interest.

4. Member States may provide for an exemption from the obligation to notify or a simplification of the notification in the case of processing operations referred to in Article 8 (2) (d).

5. Member States may stipulate that certain or all non-automatic processing operations involving personal data shall be notified, or provide for these processing operations to be subject to simplified notification.

Article 19   Contents of notification

1. Member States shall specify the information to be given in the notification. It shall include at least:

(a) the name and address of the controller and of his representative, if any;

(b) the purpose or purposes of the processing;

(c) a description of the category or categories of data subject and of the data or categories of data relating to them;

(d) the recipients or categories of recipient to whom the data might be disclosed;

(e) proposed transfers of data to third countries;

(f) a general description allowing a preliminary assessment to be made of the appropriateness of the measures taken pursuant to Article 17 to ensure security of processing.

2. Member States shall specify the procedures under which any change affecting the information referred to in paragraph 1 must be notified to the supervisory authority.

Article 20   Prior checking

1. Member States shall determine the processing operations likely to present specific risks to the rights and freedoms of data subjects and shall check that these processing operations are examined prior to the start thereof.

2. Such prior checks shall be carried out by the supervisory authority following receipt of a notification from the controller or by the data protection official, who, in cases of doubt, must consult the supervisory authority.

3. Member States may also carry out such checks in the context of preparation either of a measure of the national parliament or of a measure based on such a legislative measure, which define the nature of the processing and lay down appropriate safeguards.

Article 21   Publicizing of processing operations

1. Member States shall take measures to ensure that processing operations are publicized.

2. Member States shall provide that a register of processing operations notified in accordance with Article 18 shall be kept by the supervisory authority. The register shall contain at least the information listed in Article 19 (1) (a) to (e).

The register may be inspected by any person.

3. Member States shall provide, in relation to processing operations not subject to notification, that controllers or another body appointed by the Member States make available at least the information referred to in Article 19 (1) (a) to (e) in an appropriate form to any person on request.

Member States may provide that this provision does not apply to processing whose sole purpose is the keeping of a register which according to laws or regulations is intended to provide information to the public and which is open to consultation either by the public in general or by any person who can provide provide of a legitimate interest.

Chapter III   Judicial Remedies, Liability and Sanctions

Article 22   Remedies

Without prejudice to any administrative remedy for which provision may be made, inter alia before the supervisory authority referred to in Article 28, prior to referral to the judicial authority, Member States shall provide for the right of every person to a judicial remedy for any breach of the rights guaranteed him by the national law applicable to the processing in Question.

Article 23   Liability

1. Member States shall provide that any person who has suffered damage as a result of an unlawful processing operation or of any act incompatible with the national provisions adopted pursuant to this Directive is entitled to receive compensation from the controller for the damage suffered.

2. The controller may be exempted from this liability, in whole or in part, if he proves that he is not responsible for the event giving rise to the damage.

Article 24   Sanctions

The Member States shall adopt suitable measures to ensure the full implementation of the' provisions of this Directive and shall in particular lay down the sanctions to be imposed in case of infringement of the provisions adopted pursuant to this Directive.

Chapter IV   Transfer of Personal Data to Third Countries

Article 25   Principles

1. The Member States shall provide that the transfer to a third country of personal data which are undergoing processing or are intended for processing after transfer may take place only if, without prejudice to compliance with the national provisions adopted pursuant to the other provisions of this Directive, the third country in question ensures an adequate level of protection,

2. The adequacy of the level of protection afforded by a third country shall be assessed in the light of all the circumstances surrounding a data transfer operation or set of data transfer operations; particular consideration shall be given to the nature of the data, the purpose and duration of the proposed processing operation or operations, the country of origin and country of final destination, the rules of law, both general and sectoral, in force in the third country in question and the professional rules and security measures which are complied with in that country.

3. The Member States and the Commission shall inform each other of cases where they consider that a third country does not ensure an adequate level of protection within the meaning of paragraph 2.

4. Where the Commission finds, under the procedure provided for in Article 31 (2), that a third country does not ensure an adequate level of protection within the meaning of paragraph 2 of this Article, Member States shall take the measures necessary to prevent any transfer of data of the same type to the third country in question.

5. At the appropriate time, the Commission shall enter into negotiations with a view to remedying the situation resulting from the finding made pursuant to paragraph 4.

6. The Commission may find, in accordance with the procedure referred to in Article 31 (2), that a third country ensures an adequate level of protection within the meaning of paragraph 2 of this Article, by reason of its domestic law or of the international commitments it has entered into, particularly upon conclusion of the negotiations referred to in paragraph 5, for the protection of the private lives and basic freedoms and rights of individuals.

Member States shall take the measures necessary to comply with the Commission's decision.

Article 26   Derogations

1. By way of derogation from Article 25 and save where otherwise provided by domestic law governing particular cases, Member States shall provide that a transfer or a set of transfers of personal data to a third country which does not ensure an adequate level of protection within the meaning of Article 25 (2) may take place on condition that:

(a) the data subject has given his consent unambiguously to the proposed transfer; or

(b) the transfer is necessary for the performance of a contract between the data subject and the controller or the implementation of precontractual measures taken in response to the data subject's request; or

(c) the transfer is necessary for the conclusion or performance of a contract concluded in the interest of the data subject between the controller and a third party; or

(d) the transfer is necessary or legally required on important public interest grounds, or for the establishment, exercise or defence of legal claims; or

(e) the transfer is necessary in order to protect the vital interests of the data subject; or

(f) the transfer is made from a register which according to laws or regulations is intended to provide information to the public and which is open to consultation either by the public in general or by any person who can demonstrate legitimate interest, to the extent that the conditions laid down in law for consultation" are fulfilled in the particular case.

2. Without prejudice to paragraph 1, a Member State may authorize a transfer or a set of transfers of personal data to a third country which does not ensure an adequate level of protection within the meaning of Article 25 (2), where the controller adduces adequate safeguards with respect to the protection of the privacy and fundamental rights and freedoms of individuals and as regards the exercise of the corresponding rights; such safeguards may in particular result from appropriate contractual clauses.

3. The Member State shall inform the Commission and the other Member States of the authorizations it grants pursuant to paragraph 2.

If a Member State or the Commission objects on justified grounds involving the protection of the privacy and fundamental rights and freedoms of individuals, the Commission shall take appropriate measures in accordance with the procedure laid down in Article 31 (2).

Member States shall take the necessary to comply with the Commission's decision.

4. Where the Commission decides, in accordance with the procedure referred to in Article 31 (2), that certain standard contractual clauses offer sufficient safeguards as required by paragraph 2, Member States shall take the necessary measures to comply with the Commission's decision.

Chapter V   Codes of Conduct

Article 27

1. The Member States and the Commission shall encourage the drawing up of codes of conduct intended to contribute to the proper implementation of the national provisions adopted by the Member States pursuant to this Directive, taking account of the specific features of the various sectors. 2. Member States shall make provision for trade associations and other bodies representing other categories of controllers which have drawn up draft national codes or which have the intention of amending or extending existing national codes to be able to submit them to the opinion of the national authority.

Member States shall make provision for this authority to ascertain, among other things, whether the drafts submitted to it are in accordance with the national provisions adopted pursuant to this Directive. If it sees fit, the authority shall seek the views of data subjects or their representatives.

3. Draft Community codes, and amendments or extensions to existing Community codes, may be submitted to the Working Party referred to in Article 29. This Working Party shall determine, among other things, whether the drafts submitted to it are in accordance with the national provisions adopted pursuant to this Directive. If it sees fit, the authority shall seek the views of data subjects or their representatives. The Commission may ensure appropriate publicity for the codes which have been approved by the Working Party.

Chapter VI   Supervisory Authority and Working Party on the Protection of Individuals with Regard to the Processing of Personal Data

Article 28   Supervisory authority

1. Each Member State shall provide that one or more public authorities are responsible for monitoring the application within its territory of

the provisions adopted by the Member States pursuant to this Directive.

These authorities shall act with complete independence in exercising the functions entrusted to them.

2. Each Member State shall provide that the supervisory authorities are consulted when drawing up administrative measures or regulations relating to the protection of individuals' rights and freedoms with regard to the processing of personal data.

3. Each authority shall in particular be endowed with:

—investigative powers, such as powers of access to data forming the subject-matter of processing operations and powers to collect all the information necessary for the performance of its supervisory duties,

—effective powers of intervention, such as, for example, that of delivering opinions before processing operations are carried out, in accordance with Article 20, and ensuring appropriate publication of such opinions, of ordering the blocking, erasure or destruction of data, of imposing a temporary or definitive ban on processing, of warning or admonishing the controller, or that of referring the matter to national   parliaments or other political Institutions,

—the power to engage in legal proceedings where the national provisions adopted pursuant to this Directive have been violated or to bring these violations to the attention of the judicial authorities.

Decisions by the supervisory authority which give rise to complaints may be appealed against through the courts.

4. Each supervisory authority shall hear claims lodged by any person, or by an association representing that person, concerning the protection of his rights and freedoms in regard to the processing of personal data. The person concerned shall be informed of the outcome of the claim.

Each supervisory authority shall, in particular, hear claims for checks on the lawfulness of data processing lodged by any person when the national provisions adopted pursuant to Article 13 of this Directive apply. The person shall at any rate be informed that a check has taken place.

5. Each supervisory authority shall draw up a report on its activities at regular intervals. The report shall be made public.

6. Each supervisory authority is competent, whatever the national law applicable to the processing in question, to exercise, on the territory of its own Member State, the powers conferred on it in accordance with paragraph 3. Each authority may be requested to exercise its powers by an authority of another Member State.

The supervisory authorities shall cooperate with one another to the extent necessary for the performance of their duties, in particular by exchanging all useful information.

7. Member States shall provide that the members and staff of the supervisory authority, even after their employment has ended, are to be subject to a duty of professional secrecy with regard to confidential information to which they have access.

Article 29   Working Party on the Protection of Individuals with regard to the Processing of Personal Data

1. A Working Party on the Protection of Individuals with regard to the Processing of Personal Data, hereinafter referred to as 'the Working Party', is hereby set up.

It shall have advisory status and act independently.

2. The Working Party shall be composed of a representative of the supervisory authority or authorities designated by each Member State and of a representative of the authority or authorities established for the Community institutions and bodies, and of a representative of the Commission. Each member of the Working Party shall be designated by the institution, authority or authorities which he represents. Where a Member State has designated more than one supervisory authority, they shall nominate a joint representative. The same shall apply to the authorities established for Community institutions and bodies.

3. The Working Party shall take decisions by a simple majority of the representatives of the supervisory authorities.

4. The Working Party shall elect its chairman. The chairman's term of office shall be two years. His appointment shall be renewable.

5. The Working Party's secretariat shall be provided by the Commission.

6. The Working Party shall adopt its own rules of procedure.

7. The Working Party shall consider items placed on its agenda by its chairman, either on his own initiative or at the request of a representative of the supervisory authorities or at the Commission's request.

Article 30

1. The Working Party shall:

(a) examine any question covering the application of the national measures adopted under this Directive in order to contribute to the uniform application of such measures;

(b) give the Commission an opinion on the level of protection in the Community and in third countries;

(c) advise the Commission on any proposed amendment of this Directive, on any additional or specific measures to safeguard the rights and freedoms of natural persons with regard to the processing of personal data and on any other proposed Community measures affecting such rights and freedoms;

(d) give an opinion on codes Community level.

2. If the Working Party finds that divergences likely to affect the equivalence of protection for persons with regard to the processing of personal data in the Community are arising between the laws or practices of Member States, it shall inform the Commission accordingly.

3. The Working Party may, on its own initiative, make recommendations on all matters relating to the protection of persons with regard to the processing of personal data in the Community.

4. The Working Party's opinions and recommendations shall be forwarded to the Commission and to the committee referred to in Article 31.

5. The Commission shall inform the Working Party of the action it has taken in response to its opinions and recommendations. It shall do so in a report which shall also be forwarded to the European Parliament and the Council. The report shall be made public.

6. The Working Party shall draw up an annual report on the situation regarding the protection of natural persons with regard to the processing of personal data in the Community and in third countries, which it shall transmit to the Commission, the European Parliament and the Council. The report shall be made public.

Chapter VII   Community Implementing Measures

Article 31   The Committee

1. The Commission shall be assisted by a committee composed of the representatives of the Member States and chaired by the representative of the Commission.

2. The representative of the Commission shall submit to the committee a draft of the measures to be taken. The committee shall deliver its opinion on the draft within a time limit which the chairman may lay down according to the urgency of the matter.

The opinion shall be delivered by the majority laid down in Article 148 (2) of the Treaty. The votes of the representatives of the Member States within the committee shall be weighted in the manner set out in that Article. The chairman shall not vote.

The Commission shall adopt measures which shall apply immediately.

However, if these measures are not in accordance with the opinion of the committee, they shall be communicated by the Commission to the Council forthwith. In that event:

—the Commission shall defer application of the measures which it has decided for a period of three months from the date of communication,

—the Council, acting by a qualified majority, may take a different decision within the time limit referred to in the first indent.

Final Provisions

Article 32

1. Member States shall bring into force the laws, regulations and administrative provisions necessary to comply with this Directive at the latest at the end of a period of three years from the date of its adoption.

When Member States adopt these measures, they shall contain a reference to this Directive or be accompanied by such reference on the occasion of their official publication. The methods of making such reference shall be laid down by the Member States.

2. Member States shall ensure that processing already under way on the date the national provisions adopted pursuant to this Directive enter into force, is brought into conformity with these provisions within three years of this date.

By way of derogation from the preceding subparagraph, Member States may provide that the processing of data already held in manual filing systems on the date of entry into force of the national provisions adopted in implementation of this Directive shall be brought into conformity with Articles 6, 7 and 8 of this Directive within 12 years of the date on which it is adopted. Member States shall, however, grant the data subject the right to obtain, at his request and in particular at the time of exercising his right of access, the rectification, erasure or blocking of data which are incomplete, inaccurate or stored in a way incompatible with the legitimate purposes pursued by the controller.

3. By way of derogation from paragraph 2, Member States may provide, subject to suitable safeguards, that data kept for the sole purpose of historical research need not be brought into conformity with Articles 6, 7 and 8 of this Directive.

4. Member States shall communicate to the Commission the text of the provisions of domestic law which they adopt in the field covered by

this Directive.

Article 33

The Commission shall report to the Council and the European Parliament at regular intervals, starting not later than three years after the date referred to in Article 32 (1), on the implementation of this Directive, attaching to its report, if necessary, suitable proposals for amendments. The report shall be made public.

The Commission shall examine, in particular, the application of this Directive to the data processing of sound and image data relating to natural persons and shall submit any appropriate proposals which prove to be necessary, taking account of developments in information technology and in the light of the state of progress in the information society.

Article 34

This Directive is addressed to the Member States.

Done at Luxembourg, 24 October 1995.

For the European Parliament   For the Council

The President   The President
K. Hänsch   L. Atienza Serna

Summary of Potential Effects of the EU Directive

Information technologies

Sector or function	Major transborder data flows	Important potential exceptions	Other major means of compliance	Transfers apparently forbidden	Comments
Mainframes	Very large flows for telephone call records, credit card transactions, and so forth	A.26(2) A.26(4)	Self-regulatory measures under A.26(2); A.27. Archiving records within EU. Establishing mainframe in Europe	Potentially large	Large organizations operating mainframes have economies of scale in compliance compared with organizations that use more distributed forms of processing. Contracts and codes of conduct seem especially workable for mainframes
Client-server systems	Used in many applications; data can be processed by the user, not only by centralized processing	A.26(1)(a) A.26(1)(b)		Potentially large	When the server is outside Europe, routine transfers from client to server could be prohibited. A European sales office that needs to send data to the U.S. for bookkeeping or other purposes may be unable to do so. Small and medium-sized enterprises are likely to be disproportionately affected
Intranets	Any data that may be shared within an organization, such as employee skills, customer profiles	A.26(1)(a). Often difficult to fit under any exception	Compliance through new technology (unlikely). Compliance through extensive training in data protection rules. Exclusion of EU operations from organization's intranet	Many transfers between an organization's EU-based operations and U.S. operations	An intranet is defined as a mechanism for sending data within an organization, generally by means of the Internet. "Fire walls" are designed to permit only authorized people to enter the intranet and also to restrict the flow of certain kinds of programs and information into and out of the system

Extranets	Generally any data an organization wishes to share with its suppliers and customers or other strategic partners	A.26(1)(a). Often difficult to fit under any exception	Same as for intranets	Many transfers between an organization's EU-based operations and suppliers or customers outside the EU	Extranet technology permits authorized users and data to jump from inside one organization's fire wall to inside another organization's fire wall. Such an extranet is even more decentralized than an intranet because data flow among organizations. In a global economy, it is increasingly likely that some parts of an extranet will be in both EU and U.S.
E-mail	Millions of people have come to rely on e-mail for many personal and business communications	A.3(2) A.26(1)(a)		Data other than on purely personal or household activity, including data for business and academic purposes	Sending an e-mail (or attaching a file to an e-mail) likely would come within the definition of "processing of personal data" in Article 2. E-mail is just one example of the difficulty in providing a workable way to implement data protection on the Internet
Telecopies	Similar to those for e-mail	A.3(2) A.26(1)(a)		Faxes sent from computer to computer or from a computer to a fax machine if the fax becomes part of a filing system. See A.3(1)	Computer files can typically be searched and sorted in various ways, so telecopies retained as computer files would likely be within the scope of the Directive. A traditional fax printed onto paper would fall within the Directive only if it forms part of a filing system or is intended to form part of one

Sector or function	Major transborder data flows	Important potential exceptions	Other major means of compliance	Transfers apparently forbidden	Comments
World Wide Web	Huge number of users and Web sites makes flows potentially enormous	A.26(1)(a). Often difficult to fit under any exception	Effective enforcement likely to be especially difficult	Any data personally identifying individuals where the Web site is located in U.S.	Unlike a large portion of e-mails and telecopies, for which the provider and receiver of information have consented to the transfer, an ordinary Web user will often not know the identity of the host of the Web site. Jurisdictional issues will arise if EU pursues hosts of Web sites located in U.S. The interaction of Directive and Web seems an ill fit, given jurisdictional issues and the millions of individual "controllers" (often personal computer users) running Web sites who are unlikely to be aware of the Directive's existence
Laptops and personal organizers	Data transported from EU to U.S. by business travelers	A.3(2) A.26(1)(a		Laptops or personal organizers containing personal data carried by business travelers from EU to U.S.	EU officials have been split on whether laptops come within the scope of the Directive

Functions affected by the Directive for many organizations

Human resources records	Employee data of transnational companies	A.26(1)(a)	Retain records in Europe	Data on how best to deploy employees, evaluations of employees, internal employee directories	Many organizations routinely transfer human resource records across borders. These transfers may constitute one of the most widespread and serious compliance problems under the Directive
Auditing and accounting	Auditing and accounting data of transnational companies, including accounts receivable and payroll information	A.26(1)(d)	Hire accounting and auditing teams within EU. Possibly gain EU recognition of codes of practice as sufficient safeguards to permit transfers to U.S.	Personal information to both internal and external auditors to verify overseas operations and track international transactions	The auditing process is governed by a contract between the company and the auditor. Data subjects are rarely aware they are being examined and do not give unambiguous consent. A.26(1)(d) exception hinges on whether auditing procedure serves an important public interest or is necessary to avoid legal claims
Business consulting	Similar to auditing and accounting	A.26(1)(c)	Hire business consultants within EU. Anonymizing names in data provided to consultants	Consulting on personnel and employee issues is especially likely to run into trouble, as is consulting on customer account management for companies selling to the public	Consulting on purely financial issues would generally not require consultants to see personal information. Regarding scrubbing (removing personally identifiable information), consultants within EU would not be similarly affected and thus would have a competitive advantage over non-EU consultants

Sector or function	Major transborder data flows	Important potential exceptions	Other major means of compliance	Transfers apparently forbidden	Comments
Calling centers and other worldwide customer service	Transfers of customer records to persons providing service	A.26(1)(a) A.26(1)(b)	New notice and opportunity to opt out for all customers	Customer service handled outside EU not performed under a contract	As a company offers service to a customer, it may need to transfer customer records to persons providing service. If the customer is within EU and the service provider is in U.S., problems may arise. Servicing customers transnationally is likely to become increasingly common
Financial services sector					
Payment systems	Wire transfers, credit card processing and payment	A.6(1)(a) A.26(1)(b) A.26(1)(c)	For EU-based transactions where a mainframe is outside EU, relocation of mainframe to EU. Contracts approved by EU authorities	Credit card processing done outside EU for European transactions; transactions containing extra personal data for fraud protection, but not necessary to performance of the contract; secondary use of data	Most payment systems transactions fit within an Article 26 exception. If U.S. companies are limited in their permissible secondary uses of data to those allowed in EU, different software and databases for transactions originating in EU would need to be developed

Sale of financial services to individuals	Include purchases of securities, mutual funds, insurance, and taking out loans	Vary by the particular situation. A.26(1)(a) A.26(1)(b) A.26(1)(c)	Contracts approved by EU authorities.	Depends on situation, but analysis often tracks that of direct marketing	When the buyer is within EU and the seller outside, the analysis becomes similar to that of direct marketing over the Internet. Although direct sales may take place over the telephone or by mail, the number of international sales to consumers is likely to rise steeply because of the Internet
Investment banking: market analysis	Analysts outside EU receiving information about people in EU. Analysts in EU and outside EU communicating about a company	A.26(1)(c)		Communications with analysts outside EU about identifiable individuals such as possible successors to company leadership or hiring of key technology or marketing persons	In the course of studying a company, analysts become aware of both corporate and personally identifiable information. By its terms, the Directive governs flows of information to market analysts outside the E.U., and it is not clear that such communications are permitted
Investment banking: hostile takeovers	Analysts outside EU receiving information about people in EU. Analysts in EU and outside EU communicating about a company	A.26(1)(a) A.26(1)(b) A.26(1)(c)	Use investment bank personnel who operate from within EU	Because of hostile nature of the action, A.26(1)(c) exception is not likely to apply, and thus transfer of personal data out of EU is apparently not permitted	Directive appears to ban participation in hostile takeovers by investment bankers outside EU

Sector or function	Major transborder data flows	Important potential exceptions	Other major means of compliance	Transfers apparently forbidden	Comments
Investment banking; due diligence	Data that must be evaluated to comply with U.S. securities laws	A.26(1)(d)		A.26(1)(d) exception should make most transfers of personally identifiable data for due diligence purposes acceptable	Before a security can be publicly issued in the U.S., the company must do extensive research to be sure that the company's statements comply with U.S. securities laws. This research is referred to as "due diligence"
Investment banking: private placements and other sales to Europeans	Data collected by investment banks regarding past customer purchases helpful for matching offerings to customer tastes	A.26(1)(a)		Any transfer of data concerning past transactions and preferences exceeding the currently uncertain level permitted by the Directive to entities outside EU	Investment banks face the familiar question about what information can be transferred to the U.S. regarding customers within EU. If the customer knows the security is being sold in New York, does that constitute "unambiguous consent"?
Mandatory securities and accounting disclosures	Data necessary to comply with various disclosure laws and accounting or stock exchange rules	A.26(1)(d)		Directive might forbid transborder data flow of personal information that goes beyond the strict requirements of legal, accounting, or stock exchange rules	A company might wish to disclose more than required so as to err on the side of caution or to gain public favor ("We have nothing to hide")

Sector	Description	Articles			
Individual credit histories	Any data typically included in a credit history for determining creditworthiness. Credit reports supplied to appropriate parties, such as employers or lenders	A.25(6) A.26(1)(a) A.26(1)(b)	Because of the Fair Credit Reporting Act (FCRA) in the U.S., adequate levels of protection may already exist. In the context of providing credit information, major credit agencies may be parties to contracts approved by EU authorities	If the FCRA meets the concerns of EU authorities, transfers of data in this sector should be comparatively unencumbered	On its face, the Directive poses very significant obstacles to the transfer of credit history information out of EU. This difficulty is not surprising because credit agencies assemble the sort of dossiers on people that are the focus of data protection regimes. But in the U.S. such concerns have been significantly addressed through enactment of the FCRA
Corporate credit histories	Personal data concerning leading individuals in corporations	A.25(6) A.26(1)(a)	Industry codes of conduct satisfactory to EU authorities	Barring applicability of an exception, corporate credit histories containing personally identifiable data may not be transferred from EU to U.S.	FCRA does not apply to corporate credit histories. If a blanket consent in advance from corporate personnel is permissible, much of the difficulty can be avoided. To remove personal data on key personnel from corporate credit histories would severely compromise their usefulness

Other sectors with large transborder activities

Sector	Description	Articles			
Press	Publication, transfers of notes, discussions of a story by e-mail or telephone. Possibilities are nearly endless	A.9		Any transfer of personally identifiable data from EU to U.S. not solely for journalistic purposes and not necessary to reconcile the right of privacy with rules governing freedom of expression	An important role of the press is to publicize personally identifiable information. Generally, the scope of EU country laws protecting freedom of expression is much narrower than in U.S. The language of the Directive seems to favor the privacy right over freedom of expression in close calls

Sector or function	Major transborder data flows	Important potential exceptions	Other major means of compliance	Transfers apparently forbidden	Comments
Nonprofit organizations generally	All the same varieties of data often transferred by for-profit entities. Especially sensitive will be employee and membership records	Depends on context, but the Directive makes no distinction in its treatment of nonprofit organizations	See activity in question as provided in this table	See activity in question as provided in this table	Special difficulties may arise when membership lists of nonprofits are provided to third parties, as often happens when nonprofits hire an outside organization to conduct fund raising. Under Article 14, members may need to be informed before personal data are disclosed for the first time to third parties
International educational institutions	Human resource and student records	A.26(1)(a) A.26(1)(b)	Family Education Right to Privacy Act provides a strong argument that the U.S. has an adequate level of protection for student records	Potentially the transfer of personnel and student records from universities within EU to U.S. universities	Many universities offer courses in both U.S. and EU. All the usual compliance problems for human resource records will be encountered when, for instance, an American professor teaches in EU for a term. New sorts of consent will often be required for students to have information transferred out of Europe
International conferences	Personal information about participants such as names, addresses, phone numbers, and professional affiliations	A.26(1)(a) A.9		Common products of conferences such as lists of the names and addresses of conference participants, or the transfer of such information via laptop or e-mail	Conference hosts might obtain consent in advance for transfer of personal information so as to come under the "unambiguous consent" exception. Journalists could possibly have access to personal information "solely for journalistic purposes" when other conference participants could not

Non-European governments	Personnel and medical records, for instance	A.3(2) A.13	Personnel and medical records concerning government employees and their family members for purposes other than national defense or public security	As of October 1998, the U.S. government may technically be in violation of the Directive when it transfers employment and medical records to Washington, although it is an unlikely target for early enforcement. Suing the U.S. government or other governments would raise difficult legal and political problems
Pharmaceutical and medical device research and marketing	Information for clinical trials for new drugs or medical devices	A.8(3) A.11(2)	Personally identifiable patient data not coming under the preventative medicine or historical-scientific research exceptions contained in A.8(3) and A.11(2), respectively. Scrubbing the names of the patients out of the records. Sectoral legislation for health care privacy in U.S.	The Directive treats "processing of data concerning health" as sensitive, subject to especially strict regulation. "Preventative medicine" exception (A.8(3)) applies only when data are processed by health professionals subject under national laws or codes of conduct "established by competent bodies to the obligation of professional secrecy." Even when names are scrubbed, large amounts of potentially sensitive information taken together may be personally identifying. The blurred line between research and marketing poses thorny problems for transborder transfers

Sector or function	Major transborder data flows	Important potential exceptions	Other major means of compliance	Transfers apparently forbidden	Comments
Business and leisure travel: reservation systems	Travel and leisure reservations involve transborder actions of identifiable individuals. Affected industries include airlines, railroads, cruise lines, charter buses, rental cars, hotels, travel agents	A.26(1)(a) A.26(1)(b)	Contracts approved by EU authorities	Information to assist European travelers when they are in U.S. and information about Americans' travel in Europe may be unavailable for future reference when the traveler returns home	Information on individual travelers is accumulated in reservation systems (often travelers deem that desirable). Some information may even qualify as sensitive under Article 8, and thus be subject to strict regulation. EU authorities have already reached detailed agreements with some European reservation systems about data protection practices
Business and leisure travel: frequent flyer and other affinity programs	Travel sector has a pervasive system of frequent flyer miles and other affinity programs	A.26(1)(a) A.26(1)(b)	Contracts approved by EU authorities	Potentially, transfer of travelers' frequent flyer miles accumulated in Europe back to U.S. Sharing data of partner companies in affinity programs	Whether transfer of frequent flyer miles to U.S. is prohibited depends largely on the notice required to constitute "unambiguous consent." If an airline shares frequent flyer information with a hotel and rental car company, as the information is transferred among these companies, the data controller must provide information to the data subject under Article 11 no later than the time of disclosure. Restrictions on direct marketing in Article 14 may also apply

Internet service providers	Large flows through servers outside Europe for billing, but also for records of e-mail, Web browsing, and other services	A.26(1)(a) A.26(1)(b)	Contracts approved by EU authorities	Except where consent is sufficient or a contract is available, it will be difficult to do many routine transfers	Anonymous browsing might be available on a fee-for-service basis, but it is unlikely to become the dominant way for people to use ISP services. Global nature of the service makes it especially difficult to prevent transfers of personal information out of Europe
Traditional direct marketing	Customer lists, prospect lists, personally identifiable purchase data	A.26(1)(a) A.26(1)(b)	Relocate operations to EU	Transfers of a company's own customer lists for direct marketing for its own use without granting customers the right to object. Transfers of customer lists for direct marketing to third parties, granting the right to object and notifying customers in advance	Traditional direct marketing contrasts with direct marketing over the Internet. Traditional direct marketing has only a small international component except for some sectors such as financial services, travel services, publications, and high-end products. See Articles 11 and 14 for special rules applying to direct marketing. A broad interpretation of "for purposes of direct marketing" will make the Directive more burdensome for direct marketers

Sector or function	Major transborder data flows	Important potential exceptions	Other major means of compliance	Transfers apparently forbidden	Comments
Direct marketing over the Internet	Customer lists, prospect lists, personally identifiable purchase data, highly tailored customer preference data	Unless clear consent is given, often difficult to fit under any exception	Effective enforcement likely to be especially difficult	Transfers of a company's own customer data for direct marketing for its own use without granting customers the right to object. Transfers of customer data for direct marketing to third parties, granting the right to object and notifying customers in advance	Sellers will seek to move from a mass market to a "market of one" because of the exceptional targeting allowed by building profiles of buyers' activity on the Internet. This is a nightmare for EU data protection authorities. International direct marketing over the Internet is easy and inexpensive. Efficiency issues that lead traditional direct marketers to locate within the country they are doing business in are less present in the Internet context; thus marketing over the Internet is likely to grow enormously

Index

Accounting information transfers, 94–97, 149

Adequacy determinations: assessment process, 32, 33, 39–40, 160; data embargoes, 32–33; employee *vs.* business information, 120; importance for privacy regime, 25–26, 31–32, 145, 154; as protectionism, 145–46, 189–93. *See also* Article *25* (adequacy levels); Article *26* (adequacy exceptions)

Affinity programs, compliance difficulties, 135–36

Amadeus reservation system information, 133

American Airlines, 133

America On-Line, 10, 137

Anonymization as compliance strategy, 98, 130–31, 138

Article *2* (data processing): computer applications, 51, 65, 71; overview, 28

Article *3* (data categories): computer processing applications, 65, 67, 71; employee *vs.* business information, 118, 120; exemptions, 26–27, 129; filing system interpretations, 120–21

Article *4*, and Web sites, 68–69

Article *6* (data uses): overview, 28; post-transfer, 105–06

Article *7,* European Union exceptions: compared to non-European exceptions, 99–101

Article *8* (sensitive data): and electronic commerce, 87; employee information transfers, 93; membership information transfers, 125; overview, 30–31, 39; pharmaceutical industry, 129–30, 131; and portable computer systems, 73, 168–69; press information transfers, 124; and reservation system information, 133

Article *9* (freedom of expression): and international conference information, 128; overview, 31; press information transfers, 123–24

Article *10,* controller disclosures, 28–29

Article *11* (controller disclosures): affinity programs, 136; overview, 29; pharmaceutical industry, 130, 131

Article *12,* rights of data subjects, 29–30

Article 13, government exemptions, 27, 129

Article *14* (direct marketing): affinity programs, 136; consent interpretations, 141–42, 144; and extranets, 63–64; and membership records, 125; overview, 30, 140

Article *15,* personal evaluations, 30

Article *22,* noncompliance penalties, 46–47

Article *23,* noncompliance penalties, 46–47

Article *25* (adequacy levels): credit history transfers, 114–15, 117; economic impact, 42–45, 150–51; employee *vs.* business information, 120; importance for privacy regime, 25–26, 31–32, 145, 154; institutional controls, 165, 166; nonprofit organizations, 125; overview, 31–33; pharmaceutical industry, 130; press information transfers, 124

Article *26* (adequacy exceptions): and accounting information, 96; and affinity programs, 135; and business consulting, 97–98; call-in customer service centers, 99; compared to Article *7,* 99–101; direct marketing applicability, 141–42, 144; and distributed computer processing, 59–60, 61, 63; employee information transfers, 91–92, 93; European Commission position, 46; financial services transactions, 107, 108, 109, 110–11, 112; Internet service providers (ISPs), 137–38; and mainframe computer processing, 55–57, 104, 115; nonprofit organizations, 125; overview, 33–37; payment systems, 103; and portable computer systems, 72–73; post-transfer data uses, 104–06; press information transfers, 123–24; and reservation system information, 134; securities and accounting disclosures, 113–14; supervisory authority level, 39–40, 46; Working Party interpretations, 37, 41, 56. *See also* Self-regulatory measures (SRMs)

Article *27* (codes of conduct): Internet service providers (ISPs), 137–38; mainframe computer processing, 57, 104, 115; overview, 37. *See also* Codes of conduct for data protection

Article *28,* supervisory authorities' role, 38–39

Article *29,* Working Party role, 40–41

Article *31,* harmonization process, 39–40

Article *31* Committee, 39–40

Article *33,* technology developments, 174

Audit information transfers, 94–97, 149

Baker, Stewart, 206

Banking regulations as self-regulatory measures (SRMs), 165–66

Bank of Credit and Commerce International (BCCI), 95

Basle Accord, 182

Boston Consulting Group, 80, 83

Brühann, Ulf, 46

Business consulting, information transfers, 97–98, 149

Business principals: consent interpretations, 117; personal information as company information, 110, 111, 118–19, 169

Business Week poll, 80

Buyers' clubs, 207–09

Call-in customer service centers, 98–99, 149

Cate, Fred, 22–23

Cendant Corporation, 207–09

Center for Social and Legal Research, 57–58

Chayes, Abram, 182

Chayes, Antonia, 182

Citicorp, 37

Cividanes, Emilio, 171

Client-server systems: compliance difficulties, 59–60, 147; structure, 58–59

Clinton administration, 181, 184, 185–86, 189, 196

Codes of conduct for data protection:
benefits, 36–37, 157, 158, 170;
described, 157; as exception to
adequacy requirements, 37–38; and
Internet service providers (ISPs), 137–
38; mainframe computer processing,
55, 57–58, 104, 106, 115, 134;
sanctions for violating, 159–61; in
travel industry, 134

Comitology/binding process: to harmonize
national regulations, 39–40

Commerce, U.S. Department of, 181,
185–86, 187, 188

Compliance costs: anonymization, 98; of
business transition activities, 77–78,
155, 174–75; for knowledge of
requirements, 77; measurement
difficulties, 41–45; for non-European
countries, 42–43; variations within
European Union, 42

Compliance strategies: anonymization, 98,
130–31, 138; for client-server systems,
60; education proposal, 177; for
extranets, 63–64; institutional controls,
165–67; for intranets, 61–62; for
mainframe computer processing, 53–
58, 104, 106, 115, 164. *See also* Risks
of noncompliance; Self-regulatory
measures (SRMs)

Confidentiality tradition: as adequacy
determination, 96–97, 172

Consent barriers, 7–8. *See also* Unambiguous consent exception

Contract performance exception:
accounting information transfers, 96;
business consulting, 97–98; call-in
customer service centers, 99; credit
history transfers, 116; direct marketing,
142; educational institutions, 127;
employee information transfers, 93;
financial services transactions, 107,
108, 110–11, 112; nonprofit organiza-

tions, 125; overview, 34–35; payment
systems, 103–04

Contract rules in electronic commerce,
86–87, 198–99

Contracts for data protection: accounting
information transfers, 97; benefits, 36–
37, 157, 158, 170; credit history
transfers, 115; described, 157; as
exception to adequacy requirements,
36–37, 38; and Internet service
providers (ISPs), 137–38; mainframe
computer processing, 55–58, 104, 106,
115, 134; supervisory authority level,
39, 40; in travel industry, 134;
Working Party positions, 37, 41, 163–
64, 172–73

Controller requirements: data uses, 28;
disclosure to data subject, 28–29;
employee information transfers, 92

Council of Europe: data protection
principles, 24

Credit card transactions: Directive
applicability, 103–06; electronic
commerce, 82–83, 209–10

Credit history transfers, 10, 114–17, 118,
149

Customer lists, 141–42

Data embargoes, 32–33

Data havens, limiting, 25–26, 31–32

Data Protection Directive: adoption date,
2; common market purposes, 9, 25;
information technology assumptions,
50–51, 66; overview of requirements,
28–33; as pressure for non-European
privacy legislation, 56, 150–51, 154.
See also specific Articles

Data subjects: and contract performance,
34–35; protection of vital interests, 36;
rights, 29–30, 63–64, 140–42, 144;
sensitive data, 30. *See also* Rights of
data subjects

Denmark, 141

Digital signature regulation, 205–06

Direct marketing: contract performance interpretations, 35; Internet service provider compliance, 138; market of one privacy implications, 143, 150; membership records, 125; and pharmaceutical industry compliance, 131; and rights of data subjects, 29–30, 63–64, 140–42, 144; traditional international methods, 139–40; and travel industry compliance, 132–33, 136. *See also* Electronic commerce

Disclosure requirements: overview, 28–29; in securities and accounting activities, 111–12, 113–14; for unambiguous consent, 34. *See also* Article 14 (direct marketing)

Distributed computer processing: compliance difficulties, 59–60, 61–62, 63–64; structure, 58–59, 60–61, 62–63. *See also* Electronic mail; Fax communications; Portable computer systems; Web sites

Due diligence information, 111–12

Dun & Bradstreet, 117, 172

Educational institutions, compliance difficulties, 126–27

Electronic commerce: business-to-business share, 83–84, 197–98; business-to-consumer share, 84–85; buyers' clubs, 207–09; and consumer confidence, 79–83, 85, 179–80; defined, 76; increasing with regulations, 86–88; market of one implications, 142–44, 150; payment systems for dispute resolution, 209–10; potential social harms, 198–200; privacy regulation as innovation barrier, 77–79, 151; role of OECPP, 184–85; role of World Trade Organization, 196; transnational contracts, 198

Electronic Communications Privacy Act, 171, 172

Electronic mail: Directive applicability, 65–66, 68; in distributed computer processing, 60; enforcement barriers, 66–67; user as controller, 66

Employee information: as business information, 111, 118–21, 169; international transfer barriers, 90–94, 101, 108, 110, 125, 126, 129

Encryption: as adequacy determination, 32; for electronic commerce, 82

Enforcement authority: business and consumer contracts, 198–99; for electronic mail, 66; institutional structure, 38–40, 45–47, 155, 161–63; mainframe computer processing, 54–55, 57–58, 200–02; for portable computer systems, 73; and secondary targets, 202–04; for self-regulatory measures (SRMs), 159–61; for Web sites, 68–69, 70. *See also* Office of Electronic Commerce and Privacy Policy (OECPP)

English Data Protection Registrar, 66–67

Epstein, Richard, 86

Equivalent data protection: for European Union countries, 33, 159

European Coal and Steel Community, 24

European Commission: education for privacy practices, 177; harmonization process, 39–41; privacy divisions, 184; privacy protection development, 44; reservation system information, 133; U.S. privacy protection studies, 117, 170, 171–72

European Court of Justice, 9

European Union: compliance costs, 42, 43; data protection for market unity, 9, 25; data protection trends, 22–24, 44; development, 24; information culture, 36, 152–54, 178; U.S. trade statistics, 3, 44

Exceptions, adequacy. *See* Article 26 (adequacy exceptions)

Executive Office of the President, 186

Exemptions, data, 26–27. *See also* Article 26 (adequacy exceptions)

Experian, 10

Extranets: compliance difficulties, 63–64; structure of, 62–63

Facsimiles. *See* Fax communications

Fair Credit Reporting Act (U.S.): as demonstration of adequacy, 32, 114–16; sanctions for violating, 160

Fair information practices, name lists, 139

Family Education Right to Privacy Act (U.S.), 127

Fax communications, 67–68

Federal Trade Commission, U.S., 115–16, 181, 186, 187

Federal Trade Commission Act (U.S.), 171, 177

Filing system interpretations, 67, 120–21

Financial services transactions: Directive applicability, 106–11, 112, 149; disclosure obligations, 111–12, 113–14

Fire wall technology, 60–61

First Amendment: for information openness, 36, 123; as privacy safeguard, 178

First Orientations on Transfers of Personal Data to Third Countries—Possible Ways Forward in Assessing Adequacy, 37, 41, 163, 172–73

For the Protection of Individuals with Regard to Automatic Processing of Personal Data, 24

Fourth Amendment: as privacy safeguard, 6

France: compliance costs, 42; disclosure requirements, 29; privacy safeguards, 23, 25, 39

Fraud protection programs, compliance strategies, 104

Freedom of expression: Article 9 overview, 31; international conference information transfers, 128; press information transfers, 122–24

Freedom of Information Act (U.S.): for information openness, 36; as privacy safeguard, 7

Free trade rules: adequacy determinations as discrimination, 189–93; data restrictions as protectionism, 145–46; role of World Trade Organization, 190, 194–96

French National Commission on Informatics and Freedoms (CNIL), 23

Frequent flyer mile usage, 135–36

Gellman, Robert, 171

General Agreement on Tariffs and Trade (GATT), 189

General Agreement on Trade in Services (GATS), 189, 190–93

General Electric, 84

Germany: beer purity laws as trade barriers, 9; compliance costs, 42; contracts for data protection, 37; data protection authority, 23, 38; digital signature regulation, 206; employee consents, 93; portable computer systems, 72; privacy legislation, 22, 39

Government operations exemptions, 26–27, 129

Greece, 23, 39, 42

Guidelines on the Protection of Privacy and Transborder Flows of Personal Data, 23–24

Harmonization process: for adequacy determinations, 39–41

Havelange, Bénédicte, 168, 169

Health Insurance Portability and Accountability Act *(1996)* (U.S.), 131

Hostile takeover information transfers, 110–11, 149

Huang, Peter, 86

Institutional controls as compliance
strategy, 165–67
Intellectual property controls, 199,
202–03
International Chamber of Commerce, 170
International conference information,
127–28, 150
International Monetary Fund (IMF), 182
Internet commerce. *See* Electronic
commerce
Internet service providers (ISPs): compliance strategies, 137–38; as regulation targets, 203; services, 136–37,
138
Intranets: compliance difficulties, 61–62,
146, 147–48; structure, 60–61
Investment banking: compliance difficulties, 109–12, 118, 149; and press
information transfers, 123; securities
and accounting disclosures obligations,
111–12, 113–14
Italy, 23, 25, 39, 42

Judging Industry Self-Regulation: on codes
of conduct, 158–59; institutional
dispute resolution, 161–62; sanctions
for code violations, 159–61; verification of compliance, 161

Kang, Jerry, 86

Laptops. *See* Portable computer systems
Legal claims exception: accounting
information transfers, 96; due diligence
information, 112; financial services
transactions, 109; overview, 35–36
Lexis/Nexis services, 10, 149–50
Loan participation, information transfers,
109, 149

McAdams, Richard, 86
Magaziner, Ira, 181, 184, 189

Mainframe computer processing:
compliance difficulties, 52–54;
enforcement visibility, 53, 54–55, 164,
200–02; self-regulatory measures
(SRMs), 55–58, 104, 106, 115, 134,
164; transborder volume, 53
Market analysis, information transfers,
110–11, 118, 149
Market of one, 138, 142–44, 150
Maurici, Danielle, 80
May, Tim, 65
Media reports: compliance difficulties,
122–24, 149–50; as freedom of
expression exception, 123, 128; for
privacy protection, 10–11
Medical information restrictions, 30–31.
See also Pharmaceutical industry
compliance
Membership records, information
transfers, 125–26
Microsoft Network, 137
Model contracts: described, 157; initiatives
for developing, 57, 170
Murphy, Richard, 86

National Association of Securities Dealers,
163
National Telecommunications and
Information Administration, 181, 185
NetMarket Web site, 207–09
Nonprofit organizations: compliance
difficulties, 125–27; sensitive data, 30

Office of Electronic Commerce and
Privacy Policy (OECPP): formation
incentives, 17–18, 179–80, 181;
objections to, 187–88; placement in
governmental structure, 185–86; role,
18, 179, 181–85
Office of Management and Budget
(OMB), 186, 188
Online Privacy Alliance, 12

Organization for Economic Cooperation and Development (OECD): data protection guidelines, 23–24; electronic commerce, 76, 83–85

Overdisclosure, incentives for, 8, 113–14, 131

Payment systems: compliance difficulties, 102–06, 149; contract performance interpretations, 35; for dispute resolution in electronic commerce, 209–10

Personal data, defined, 26

Personal organizers. *See* Portable computer systems

Personal uses of data, exemption, 27

Pharmaceutical industry compliance, 129–31, 150

Platform for Privacy Preferences (P3P), 12–13

Plessar, Ronald, 171

Portable computer systems: compliance difficulties, 70–73, 147; exemption proposal, 73–74; and risk-based privacy protection, 168–69

Posner, Richard, 86

Poullet, Yves, 168, 169

Preliminary Views on the Use of Contractual Provisions in the Context of Transfers of Personal Data to Third Countries, 163–64, 173

Press information transfers, 122–24, 128, 149–50

Privacy Act of *1974* (U.S.): as demonstration of adequacy, 129; as privacy safeguard, 7, 171, 172; regulatory authority, 186, 188

Privacy protection methods: government regulation, 11, 12–13, 82–83; importance, 5–7, 69, 132–33, 143; market failures, 7–9; as marketing tools, 11; media reports, 10–11;

self-regulation, 11–13; technology, 9–10, 12–13, 32, 82. *See also* Self-regulatory measures (SRMs)

Privacy *vs.* security, 81–83

Processing, defined, 26

Property rights in electronic commerce, 86–87

Prospect lists, 141–42

Protectionism effects: role of World Trade Organization, 189–96; types, 145–46

Public interest exception: accounting information transfers, 96; Article *7* compared to Article *26,* 100; business consulting, 97; due diligence information, 112; employee information transfers, 93; financial services transactions, 109; overview, 35–36; securities and accounting disclosures, 113–14

Public opinion: Internet privacy, 1, 64, 80, 179–80; security *vs.* privacy, 83

Public records: and employee information, 120; as exception to adequacy requirements, 36; and press information transfers, 124

Punitive sanctions, 159–61

Reidenberg, Joel, 43, 117, 139, 170, 172

Reinsurance, information transfers, 108, 149

Religious organizations, compliance difficulties, 125

Remedial sanctions, 159–61

Reservation systems, information transfers, 133–35

Rights of data subjects: Article *12* overview, 29–30; in direct marketing, 63–64, 140–42, 144; institutional support for enforcing, 161–63. *See also* Data subjects

Risk-based privacy protection, 167–69

Risks of noncompliance, 46–48, 155–56

SABRE reservation system information,
133
Sanctions for compliance violations,
159–61, 167
Schwartz, Paul: on data protection
commissions, 181; on efficiency of
privacy rules, 86; on name list uses,
139; on U.S. privacy protection, 43,
117, 170, 172
Secondary processing: credit history
transfers, 116; Directive overview, 29;
financial transactions, 103, 104–06;
reservation system information, 134;
security *vs.* privacy, 81–83; U.S.
attitudes, 178. *See also* Direct marketing
Securities and Exchange Commission,
U.S., 113
Security *vs.* privacy, 81–83
Self-regulatory measures (SRMs): benefits,
16–17, 36–37, 38, 157, 158, 170; and
confidentiality tradition, 96–97;
described, 157; dispute resolution,
161–63; institutional controls, 165–
67; Internet service providers (ISPs),
137–38; mainframe computer
processing, 55–58, 104, 106, 115,
134, 164; risk-based approach, 167–
69; role of OECPP, 183; sanctions for
violating, 159–61, 167. *See also*
Contracts for data protection;
Institutional controls as compliance
strategy
Sensitive data: Article 8 restrictions, 30–
31; and electronic commerce, 87; in
employee records, 93; in media reports,
124; in membership records, 125;
pharmaceutical industry, 129–30, 131;
in portable computer systems, 73,
168–69; protection priority, 168–69;
travel industry, 133, 134
Slaughter, Anne-Marie, 182
Social Security Administration, U.S., 10

Spain, 23
Student record transfers, 127
Supervisory authorities: European
Commission divisions, 184; powers,
38–39; for self-regulatory measures
(SRMs), 161–63. *See also* Office of
Electronic Commerce and Privacy
Policy (OECPP)
Supreme Court, U.S., 163
Sweden, 72, 133
Swire, Peter, 86

Trade secret protection, 165
Training as compliance strategy, 61–62, 167
Transgovernmentalism trend, 182
Travel industry compliance, 132–36, 150
Treaty of Rome *(1958),* 24
TRUSTe study, 80, 83
Truth in Lending Act, 210

Unambiguous consent exception:
accounting information transfers, 96;
call-in customer service centers, 99;
and contract performance exception,
34; credit history transfers, 116, 117;
direct marketing applicability, 141–42,
144; employee information transfers,
91–92, 120, 125, 126; financial
services transactions, 106, 108, 110,
112; international conference information, 128; Internet service providers
(ISPs), 137–38; membership records,
125, 126; overview, 34; payment
systems, 103, 104; portable computer
systems, 72–73; reservation system
information, 134; student record transfers, 127; and vital interests of data
subject exception, 36; Web sites, 68
United Nations, 182
United States: compliance costs, 42–44;
credit card regulation, 209–10; credit
history regulation, 32, 114–16, 117,

160; digital signature regulation, 205–06; European Union trade statistics, 3, 44; health care privacy, 131, 170; information culture, 36, 123, 152–54, 178; legislative privacy safeguards, 6–7, 43, 129, 170–71, 172, 177–78; OECD data protection guidelines, 24; privacy protection inadequacies, 44–45, 129, 170, 171–72; student record protections, 127

Utah, digital signature regulation, 206

Verification of compliance, 161

Web sites: as buyers' clubs, 207–09; compliance difficulties, 68–70. *See also* Electronic commerce

Westin, Alan, 57, 80, 170

Wired, 208, 209

Working Party on the Protection of Individuals with Regard to the Processing of Personal Data: on codes of conduct for data protection, 37–38, 158–59; on contractual approaches to data protection, 37, 41, 163–64, 172–73; employee *vs.* business information, 120; role in data protection, 40–41, 174

World Trade Organization (WTO): potential role in data protection disputes, 189–93; suitability for resolving privacy disputes, 194–96, 205, 211

World Wide Web. *See* Web sites